Rules of the Game

Chp 2 - Gender equity
Chp 3 - International Sports & olympic
Chp 5 Governance & Labor issues in Pro sport
Chap 7 - Intellectual property & sports Law
Chp 8 - Privacy, publicity & Defamation
Appendix B Standard Player contract

Rules of the Game

Sports Law

Michael E. Jones

ROWMAN & LITTLEFIELD
Lanham • Boulder • New York • London

Executive Editor: Christen Karniski
Production Editor: Kellie Hagan
Cover Designer: Dustin Watson
Cover Art: Michael E. Jones

Published by Rowman & Littlefield
A wholly owned subsidiary of The Rowman & Littlefield Publishing Group, Inc.
4501 Forbes Boulevard, Suite 200, Lanham, Maryland 20706
www.rowman.com

Unit A, Whitacre Mews, 26-34 Stannary Street, London SE11 4AB

British Library Cataloguing in Publication Information Available

Library of Congress Cataloging-in-Publication Data

Jones, Michael E., author.
Rules of the game : sports law / Michael E. Jones.
pages cm
Includes bibliographical references and index.
ISBN 978-1-4422-5806-8 (pbk. : alk. paper) — ISBN 978-1-4422-5807-5 (ebook)
1. Sports—Law and legislation—United States. I. Title.
KF3989.J655 2016
344.73'099—dc23
2015032719

∞™ The paper used in this publication meets the minimum requirements of American
National Standard for Information Sciences Permanence of Paper for Printed Library
Materials, ANSI/NISO Z39.48-1992.

Printed in the United States of America

Contents

Preface

The purpose of this book is to introduce undergraduate and graduate students to the key legal and ethical concepts arising in the complex regulatory world of intercollegiate, Olympic, and professional sports. The materials are developed and presented for use in a one-semester course. It covers the most topical and current sports law issues in a comprehensive yet highly readable format. The text is not laced with cumbersome footnotes and citations that might bog down non–law school readers.

The textural material presented in chapter form can be covered in any order. After teaching the subject for more than thirty-five years, I designed the chapter flow to be consistent with how I generally present the content. The book begins by providing an introduction to the field of sports law by examining the history, structure, function, and occasional fallacy of the chief college regulatory body, the NCAA. The dynamic area of the impact of the growth of females at all levels of athletic participation follows. Newer concerns of transgender athletes and defining "female" for competitive purposes are addressed in the gender equity material. The relationship between domestic regulatory bodies, international sports federations, and the International Olympic Committee are covered to stimulate discussions on jurisdiction issues. The Lance Armstrong saga weighs strongly in the chapter on performance-enhancing drugs, drug testing, and how to deal with cheaters. The text flows into the impact of antitrust and labor issues on the world of professional sports organizations and teams. The growth of multimillion and even billion-dollar sports franchises requires enhanced professionalism in the arena of negotiating sports and endorsement contracts. The mystery, misery, and majesty of the major players in the sports agency field are covered. One of my favorite topics is intellectual property law, particularly copyrights and trademarks as it concerns licensing of sports broadcasts and sponsorship deals. In the wake of public disclosure of once private affairs, sports figures are crying foul whenever their reputations are damaged. Publicity rights, privacy, and defamation interests are the chief topics covered in the chapter that follows licensing, endorsements, and other rights springing from the right to be left alone, patents, copyrights, and trademarks. A relatively new field of study in the sports world is what to do when players, referees, and spectators are harmed. One of the hottest topics in sports litigation—concussions—is examined in detail. The last topic, which frankly was barely discussed when I first started out in this business, is criminal conduct of athletes both on and off the playing field and how it affects their eligibility to practice and play. Allegations of primarily male college and professional athletes exhibiting a sense of entitlement in sexually harassing and assaulting females on college campuses and private homes are reviewed and analyzed in this closing chapter.

Ultimately, my wish is for this text to stimulate other instructors and students to continue to read, research, analyze, discuss, share, and contribute to growth of this fascinating field of sports law.

Acknowledgments

I owe an enormous debt to my spouse, Christine M. Jones, for her creative spark and enthusiasm in supporting the making of this book. My academic love affair with the field of sports law began at the University of Miami School of Law under the wise tutelage of Professor Robert H. Waters. He and Professor Robert Berry, Boston College Law School, were pioneers in the then-emerging subject of sports law. They graciously mentored and contributed to my growth as an insightful student and scholar in the arena of sports and law. My first sports law text was published more than thirty-five years ago. Since then, I have had the enormous pleasure of teaching the subject to thousands of students. To them I owe gratitude for listening and learning together. One former student and Iraqi war veteran, Michael Hubbard, stands out for his exceptional help in providing research and editorial assistance. A special thank-you is due to Owen Lovely for his assistance in copyediting. This book benefited from the skillful guidance of Christen Karniski, editor, at Rowman & Littlefield.

Chapter One

College Sports and the National Collegiate Athletic Association

"A basic purpose of this Association is to maintain intercollegiate athletics as an integral part of the education program and the athlete as an integral part of the student body and, by doing so, retain a clear line of demarcation between intercollegiate athletics and professional sports."—Article 1, NCAA constitution

A BRIEF HISTORY OF THE NCAA

The headlines from a popular national online newspaper recently asked: "Why Does the NCAA Exist?" It's a fair question. According to the website of the **National Collegiate Athletic Association (NCAA)**, it was "founded in 1906 to protect young people from the dangerous and exploitive athletic practices of the time."

The year before the start of the NCAA, there were 18 deaths and 149 serious injuries reported from the sport of football. In the early days of this sport on the campuses of Yale, Princeton, Cornell, and Michigan, before the dawn of the forward pass, the only "thing" that was thrown were the ball-carrying players, who were frequently picked up and hurtled over the opposing defensive line. The popular "flying wedge" and gang tackling contributed to the horrible number of on-the-field casualties. Helmets were not in use.

In response to public uproar, President Teddy Roosevelt called upon thirteen presidents of the leading colleges and universities to better regulate the sport of football or run the risk of abolishing the sport for danger. Heeding the call of the White House, a football Rules Committee was formed along with the creation of the **Intercollegiate Athletic Association of the United**

1

States (IAAUS). Four years later, in 1910, the IAAUS was renamed the NCAA.

That was then. What about now; why do we still need the NCAA? The answer depends on whom one asks. In the eyes of many, the NCAA went from being a private, voluntary organization interested in promoting safety standards on the athletic field to a tax-exempt, nonprofit, billion-dollar revenue-producing stream for its 1,200-plus members. These critics argue that the NCAA model of organization and operation based on fostering amateurism above all other principles is severely outdated and out of step with the commercial reality of college sports.

A kinder view of the NCAA is that it is an association operating out of Indianapolis dedicated to the sound administration and regulation of intercollegiate athletics played at four-year colleges and universities. It does so by establishing rules for recruitment of high school and transfer students, articulating participation guidelines, imposing minimum academic standards, designing health and safety criteria, entering media contracts and licensing agreements, and hosting national championship events for men and women in more than eighty sports.

REGULATION OF SPORTS

The NCAA is the preeminent rule-making body for intercollegiate athletics. Membership is voluntary. Four-year schools in the United States and Canada that meet its standards may join. Non-upper-division junior and community colleges are not eligible. Many two-year colleges have formed their own regulatory body to create rules for competition and offer championship events. The remaining four-year schools with athletic teams that are not members of the NCAA partner with the **National Association of Intercollegiate Athletics (NAIA)**.

Beyond the college or university walls, there are regulatory bodies for amateur and professional sports. At the high school level, every state has created bodies to oversee the rules of the game and competition requirements for girls and boys. Both public and private high schools are frequently included in state associations. Local school boards and conferences also adopt guidelines in addition to the rules formulated by high schools through their state associations.

While not common, actions taken by state associations, school boards, principals, and athletic directors occasionally are challenged judicially. Historically, courts are reluctant to intervene over administrative decisions on transfer rules, maximum age to compete, eligibility of homeschooled children to participate, validity of online core courses, ban on jewelry when playing, minimum grade point average, and good conduct requirements unless fundamental state or federal rights are at issue. These legal issues can arise at the NCAA level, too. The court's involvement generally depends on whether the associations are viewed as "state" actors or private organizations.

Once a state association is deemed a "state" actor for constitutional law purposes, then it must act in a manner consistent with the fundamental rights guaranteed to all citizens under federal and state constitutions. For associations deemed "state" actors, they must guarantee protection within limits for student conduct when it concerns free speech, expression of religious beliefs, privacy interests, searches and seizures, and due process.

Renowned men's basketball coach Jerry Tarkanian unsuccessfully argued that his state school employer, University of Nevada, Las Vegas (UNLV), delegated its enforcement powers to the private NCAA, thereby making the association a "state" actor. Tarkanian alleged the NCAA instructed UNLV to remove him as coach or suffer harsher penalties for rules' violations. Tarkanian complained he was not afforded *due process* rights before he was suspended. The US Supreme Court (*NCAA v. Tarkanian*, 488 U.S. 179, 1988) held the NCAA was not a "state" actor, therefore the association did not deprive him of property or liberty interests.

There is a significant point in this discussion to remember: *A constitutional right to participate in sports does not exist at any level of competition.* However, once someone is permitted to participate, then a cluster of rights follows. These rights might derive from the basic rules established by the authorized regulatory body, state or federal lawmakers, or the courts in their interpretation of whether any fundamental rights or privileges were violated. Failure to give an aggrieved athlete or coach proper notice and a fair hearing in a dispute involving "life, liberty, or property" is a denial of due process.

STRUCTURE OF THE NCAA

For legislative and competition purposes, the member institutions of the NCAA and their respective conferences are grouped by divisions. Depending on the desired level of competition, colleges and universities are organized into three divisions. Each division maintains its own board of directors comprised of elected school presidents, who are responsible for governance and oversight. These boards and the association's Executive Committee work with the NCAA's permanent professional staff to ensure each division operates in a manner consistent with the organization's policies, purposes, and underlying principles. Administrative rules, policy statements, and operational bylaws for each division are published annually in the NCAA manuals.

Division III schools cannot offer athletic scholarships. Many of the four hundred Division III schools are linked geographically or share common academic standards to form a league or conference. Article 3.3.4.1 of the NCAA's constitution requires conferences regardless of the division to "agree to administer their athletic programs in accordance with the constitution, bylaws and other legislation of the Association (NCAA)." Division III programs are the most student-centered of all the divisions.

Division II institutions may offer athletic scholarships as inducements to attend their schools. They compete at an intermediate level with less emphasis on generating revenue than the larger Division I programs.

The major land-grant state universities and the largest private colleges comprise Division I. Most of the media attention, growth in expenditures on revenue-producing sports (football and basketball), pressure to win from board trustees and alumni, and loss of core academic values occur at this highest level of intercollegiate competition.

In 1978, Division I schools were divided into I-A and I-AA. Schools in the latter category include Towson University, University of New Hampshire, Texas Southern University, North Carolina A&T, Montana, Lamar, and Youngstown State. These programs are among the more than one hundred football teams competing at this lower scholarship level. In 2006, the Division I-AA schools were renamed the **Football Championship Subdivision (FCS)**, with a play-off system managed by the NCAA. Division I-A schools participating in major football play were renamed the **Football Bowl Subdivision (FBS)**. The four-team college football playoff system for Division I FBS schools is the only NCAA-sponsored sport without an official NCAA-organized tournament to determine its national champion. There are 10 conferences and 128 schools in the FBS eligible to compete for a national football championship under a complex and frequently controversial process that selects 4 teams in a single-elimination tournament.

Budgetary anxieties, antitrust lawsuits, low graduation rates and student welfare, the meteoric rise in television and licensing revenue and addressing whether high-profile student-athletes should directly share in profits, and the challenges of maintaining a level playing field have intensified efforts to reorganize the governance system for Division I schools and their conferences. The five highest-resource Division I conferences known as the Power 5—Big Ten, Atlantic Coast Conference (ACC), Pac-12, Big 12, and Southeastern Conference (SEC)—effectively lobbied the Division I board of directors to allow these conferences greater rule-making autonomy on matters affecting the interests of student-athletes.

In particular, pressure has grown to increase financial aid packages for intercollegiate athletes competing in football and basketball so that they include the full cost of attending college, scholarship guarantees beyond traditional year-to-year promises, insurance against loss of future earnings from injury, and enhancements to academic support for at-risk student-athletes. The counterbalancing concern is that, by permitting the five power conferences to confer greater financial and academic support benefits than the other Division I conferences, it continues a schism, or separation, that has widened over time, making it harder for these schools to recruit and compete for postseason championships. The reality is the smaller Division I schools and their conferences cannot afford the changes the major football conferences are seeking.

In 2015, the NCAA acceded to many of the lobbying requests of the five power conferences by permitting schools from these conferences to cover the full cost of attending college (estimated at additional stipends between $2,000 and $5,000 per student-athlete), prohibiting them from pulling scholarships for athletic-only reasons, and granting them the limited right to pass some of their own legislative rules that govern such matters as insurance benefits for players. It is expected that these conferences will loosen current bylaw regulations related to player contacts with agents and benefits for families of student-athletes. Matters related to transfer eligibility rules, scholarship limits, and enforcement remain with all the Division I schools.

CONSTITUTION

The constitution of the NCAA contains six main articles. Collectively these articles refer to the general organizational makeup of the association, the legislative and amendment process, and the principles guiding the conduct of intercollegiate athletics.

The cornerstone of the constitution is the *principles* section. One of the key principles is the requirement that each member school promises to "maintain institutional control over the activities that occur within its athletic-academic community."

In the history of the NCAA, one of the most egregious violations of this principle occurred at Penn State University. There, a culture of "hero worshipping" and an administrative cover-up of child sex abuse by prominent assistant football coach Jerry Sandusky led the NCAA to take unprecedented steps to impose draconian penalties.

Typically, the NCAA *investigates* alleged violations of its constitutional *bylaws* and imposes *penalties* through its *infractions committee*. In Penn State's case, it circumvented its own investigative process by relying on the conclusions reached by former FBI director Louis Freeh, who was retained by Penn State. Under the vocal leadership of the president of the NCAA, the Executive Committee in concert with the Division I board of directors voted to hold the entire university accountable "for the failure of those in power to protect children." It vacated all of the football team's victories from 1998 to 2011, placed the team on probation for five years, levied a $60-million fine, reduced scholarships drastically, and banned the team from postseason competition for four years.

Ultimately, Sandusky was convicted in criminal court on forty-five counts of sexual abuse of ten boys and is now serving a thirty- to sixty-year prison sentence. Legendary Penn State head coach Joe Paterno was fired during the scandal. His 409 victories at the school were reduced to 298. Paterno died during the investigative process. Acting on his behalf, Paterno's family continues to contest these reductions in his win total and presses forward to resurrect his reputation.

The NCAA's bylaws contain a provision to shut down a member's athletic program for repeat major or primary violations over the course of a five-year period. This provision is better known as the **"death penalty"** clause. In 1987, Southern Methodist University (SMU) became the first and only NCAA institution to receive the "death penalty" for flagrant, ongoing alumni booster payments to players. The football program was ineligible to compete for one year by the NCAA. SMU administrators tacked on a second-year ban. The school's football program has never fully recovered from this penalty.

Unlike the SMU case, Penn State was not subject to the "death penalty" because the wrongdoing did not implicate the traditional operational bylaws, and the school received no competitive advantage from the cover-up of Sandusky's criminal conduct.

BYLAWS

The membership of the NCAA annually adopts governing legislation termed **operating bylaws**. These bylaws are meant to promote the constitutional principles (e.g., amateurism and institutional control) and purposes of the members. The NCAA Council and board of directors are responsible for enacting **administrative bylaws** or policies and procedures required to implement the operating bylaws. Administrative bylaws are always subject to review by the full membership.

There are thirteen operating bylaws in the labyrinthine Division I manual, which numbers more than three hundred pages. These bylaws are broken down into the following categories for discussion purposes:

- Recruitment
- Academic Standards
- Fairness, Integrity, and Compliance
- Health and Safety
- Amateurism

Recruitment

The recruiting of athletically gifted students is one of the key building blocks for any successful college sports program. Article 13 of the NCAA bylaws imposes detailed requirements for coaches and athletic administrators recruiting high school students, transfer students from four-year colleges, and junior college students seeking admission into four-year programs of study.

The dizzying array of recruiting rules varies depending on the sport and division. A few years ago, for instance, the NCAA banned all text messaging from coaches to prospective student-athletes even though recruits could text coaches. The ban was largely lifted at the Division I level despite complaints from coaches about disliking text messaging. D-III coaches in all sports are free to text recruits but are prohibited from using Facebook, Instagram, and other forms of social media.

In general, this bylaw permits the recruitment of a student-athlete or a student-athlete's parents or legal guardians only by authorized school members during sport-specific **contact periods**. Contact periods are those times when a college coach may have face-to-face contact with recruits or their parents or legal guardians, watch them compete, visit their high schools, and write or telephone or text message them or their parents or legal guardians.

A contact period is different from an **evaluation period**. Coaches may do everything that is permitted during a contact period except have face-to-face contact with the prospect or the prospect's parents or legal guardians during the evaluation period. Further complicating the recruiting process is the notion of **quiet** and **dead periods**. During quiet periods, coaches may not make any off-campus contacts or evaluations but may make in-person contacts only on the college's campus. This is different from a dead period, when no on-campus or off-campus contact is allowed except for writing, telephoning, or texting.

The NCAA imposed detailed written requirements for recruiting to eliminate the presence of once-common practices used to lure prospects to major universities. A few years ago, a Federal Express driver inadvertently delivered an overnight letter from a Kentucky assistant basketball coach to a person other than the intended male basketball recruit. The letter contained thousands of dollars of cash. Ultimately, the coach was suspended, and the prospect was deemed ineligible to attend Kentucky.

Even after implementing new modifications in communication rules, violations still occur. Iowa State University self-reported to the association fifty-five impermissible telephone calls by noncoaching staff members and twenty-four improper coaches' calls outside the allowable contact periods. Amazingly, Iowa State informed the NCAA that it made 750,000 telephone calls by all coaches in eighteen sports over the three-year investigative period!

The recruiting bylaw makes it illegal to offer *extra benefits* to a recruit or his or her family. For example, extending a job proposal to a recruit's mom or dad, cosigning on a car loan, proposing reduced housing costs for family members, or gifting merchandise and clothing have all been deemed unacceptable recruiting tactics.

The burden for knowing the rules surrounding the recruitment process rests firmly with the prospect. Prospect guidance can be found at http://www.monsterpreps.com, http://www.collegesportsscholarships.com, and the NCAA Eligibility Center at http://www.ncaa.org/student-athletes/future/eligibility-center. Any student who desires to play intercollegiate sports at the D-I and D-II levels must register and be cleared by the NCAA via the **Eligibility Center**.

A highly prized recruit is frequently asked to sign a **national letter of intent (NLI)** to contractually bind that student to a particular D-I or D-II school. Signing an NLI does not guarantee admission. It does effectively end the recruiting process and guarantees a student-athlete at least one year of financial aid. Each sport has a unique NLI signing period. The rules surrounding NLI are governed by a non-NCAA organization called the Collegiate Commissioners Association, although the NCAA through the Eligibility Center administers the program itself.

Academic Standards

On average, every day the NCAA receives thousands of inquires and website log-ons from students, parents, high school administrators, and coaches about initial academic eligibility standards needed to participate in intercollegiate athletics because student-athletes are not permitted to receive financial aid, practice, or play unless minimum academic requirements are satisfied and amateur status is verified. For example, to compete as a college freshman at the Division I level, a student-athlete must meet three initial academic eligibility requirements: sixteen *core high school courses*, a *minimum SAT* (critical reading and math only) or *ACT* (sum of English, math, reading and science) *test score*, and *acceptable grade-point average (GPA)*. A sliding scale matching test scores and GPA is used to determine eligibility to receive financial aid, practice, and compete during the first year of school. The NCAA accepts the GPA calculated from a student's best sixteen core courses off an "approved" list. Any student with a core high school GPA less than 2.00 may not receive athletic-based aid, nor may he or she practice or play in competition.

At the Division II level, prospective student-athletes also need sixteen NCAA-"approved" core courses. Always subject to change, the current minimum SAT score is 820 and ACT sum is 68, along with a minimum core course GPA of 2.00. These are significantly lower academic requirements than D-I schools demand. A sliding scale matching GPA and test scores will soon be implemented by D-II schools.

Assembling these minimum academic standards does not ensure admission into any four-year university or college. Individual schools and conferences are free to establish their own weighted admission criteria of grades, test scores, leadership, community service, character, and fascinating life stories above the NCAA mandates for D-I and D-II prospective student-athletes.

The following outlines the sixteen core courses for both D-I and D-II eligibility:

- four years of English
- three years of mathematics (algebra I or higher)
- two years of natural/physical science (one year of lab if offered by high school)
- one year of additional English, mathematics, or natural/physical science
- two years of social science
- four years of additional courses (from any area above, foreign language, or comparative religion/philosophy)

In the early 1980s, the English teacher–coordinator of the University of Georgia's developmental studies program successfully filed a lawsuit against the school. The teacher, Jan Kemp, had been fired for refusing to change the grades of six failing minority students to keep them academically eligible. In sobering testimony by scores of African American minority student-athletes, it was learned that very few had any actual chance of ever graduating. Once their four years of eligibility to compete was finished, the student-athletes lost their scholarships. The absence of financial aid meant it was even less likely any African American student-athlete at Georgia could complete college with a degree.

On the surface, the Kemp case was about whether the firing was an illegal breach of her contract, which it was. The heart of the case, though, was an indictment of the lack of care, compassion, and obligation to educate by those who were responsible not merely for recruiting African American athletes but also ensuring the opportunity to partake in a meaningful college academic experience.

The aftermath of the multimillion dollar judgment for Professor Kemp, including the firing of key administrators, led the NCAA to raise admission standards to improve graduation rates especially for minorities. By the mid-1990s, the NCAA began requiring minimum standardized test scores as a component of the freshman eligibility package.

These stricter academic standards had the effect of substantially increasing the percentage of minority student-athletes *ineligible* to receive aid, practice, and compete as freshmen. In the late 1990s, the Trial Lawyers for Public Justice filed a federal class-action lawsuit on behalf of African American student-athletes. The complaint alleged the NCAA discriminated against African American students because the standardized examinations are racially and culturally biased. The plaintiffs, or proponents, argued the use of the SAT and ACT violates Title VI of the Civil Rights Act of 1964, which prohibits discrimination by educational institutions receiving federal funds. Under narrow legal grounds, the Third Circuit Court of Appeals dismissed the case because the NCAA is not a "direct" recipient of federal funds (*Cureton v. NCAA*, 198 F. 3d 107, 2001).

The totality of the effects of higher admission standards on recruiting student-athletes and their performance in college is still debated. Nevertheless, a study performed by Joshua Price at Cornell University found that these changes "increased graduation rates significantly for black student-athletes, and had no significant impact on graduation rates for white student-athletes."

In 2003, the association implemented an **Academic Progress Rate (APR)** program as part of a broader academic reform package. It is geared toward helping underperforming athletes who play basketball and football.

These new APR standards apply solely to Division I scholarship student-athletes. Teams are awarded points on the basis of academic eligibility and student-athletes remaining in school. A team score of 1,000 means every student-athlete on that team returned to school or graduated and maintained satisfactory academic progress toward a degree. Points are lost when students drop out of school or transfer or lose eligibility. Teams that fail to meet the minimum APR threshold of 930 are banned from postseason play and may suffer further penalties. Recently, the University of Idaho's football team was denied the opportunity to participate in postseason play and lost practice time because of substandard APR scores over a four-year period.

Article 14 also requires Division I and II student-athletes to remain "in good academic standing and make satisfactory progress toward a degree" to stay eligible. Depending on the division and institution, there are minimum coursework demands; full-time enrollment status; and GPA standards imposed on sophomores, juniors, and seniors. Student-athletes have five years to complete their degrees and receive financial aid, although they may only compete for four years.

Despite these efforts, grievous academic malfeasance continues to plague many institutions of higher learning. In 2011, the *Raleigh News & Observer* first reported incidents of academic fraud at the University of North Carolina (UNC) at Chapel Hill. At the center of the dishonest activities is the African American Studies program, where it is alleged that dozens of football and basketball players enrolled in classes that rarely or never met and still received passing grades.

National Basketball Association (NBA) professional Rashad McCants in an interview with ESPN's "Outside the Line," as reported in print by the *Washington Post* on June 6, 2014, stated during spring 2005 that he didn't attend any of his four African American Studies classes and received straight-A grades. McCants asserts his coaches knew players were steered by academic tutors and advisors to enroll in courses where all they had to do was submit one term paper to receive a grade. Tutors frequently wrote term papers for the top athletes to keep them eligible.

The UNC football team vacated all wins from the 2008 and 2009 seasons and forfeited fifteen scholarships as part of its sanctions from a 2010 NCAA investigation. Meanwhile, the NCAA reopened its investigation of UNC's long-running academic fraud scandal based on new allegations by McCants and others. After an eight-month independent investigation, the NCAA charged the school with five severe violations. The most serious of the allegations includes a charge of failing to "sufficiently monitor" the school's African American Studies program, where many at-risk student-athletes for eighteen years enrolled with the assistance of the school's counselors, who advised them. UNC now faces the real possibility of being the second school to have the death penalty imposed on one or more of its athletic teams.

Fairness, Integrity, and Compliance

The NCAA preaches commitment to enforcing its rules evenly, creating opportunities for fair competition, and holding those responsible for breaking its bylaws accountable. The association's rules apply to member institutions, athletic programs, conferences, coaches, administrators, and student-athletes. Enforcing policies and procedures in a clear, consistent, and credible manner is challenging.

The **Committee on Infractions** is charged with the responsibility of investigating alleged violations. In many instances, the schools conduct their own investigations, self-impose penalties, and report the findings. A **summary disposition** process allows for a cooperative resolution without prolonged in-person hearings. In those situations when schools object to aspects of the investigation after receiving a **notice of allegations**, a full-blown hearing with a right to appeal the findings and penalties before an independent **Infractions Appeals Committee** is available.

A highly publicized infractions case against the University of Miami highlights enforcement issues. The NCAA's case centered on claims made by the convicted Ponzi schemer Nevin Shapiro. He alleged that he paid football and basketball players, furnished access to yachts and cars, and tendered a host of other impermissible benefits.

In the beginning of the investigation, Miami cooperated until it learned the NCAA improperly handled the inquiry. Investigators lied to players and staff by claiming other people made comments they never made. Shapiro's allegations were largely uncorroborated by anyone other than Shapiro. A chief investigator who was later fired paid Shapiro's lawyer to obtain further information against Miami that the NCAA could not lawfully acquire. Eventually, the case was resolved, with Miami losing a handful of football and basketball scholarships after self-imposing a two-year postseason football ban.

The Miami and North Carolina incidents drove home the message that the NCAA must improve its top-to-bottom enforcement process to ensure effective *compliance*. Beginning in 2013, the association implemented a new **Division I infractions model**, designed to hold schools, coaches, and administrators more accountable for issues directly affecting *fairness* and *integrity*. Under the latest NCAA investigations of UNC, the school is subject to the new sanctions structure.

A four-level violation structure ranging from severe to incidental violations replaces the prior two-tier, major or secondary violation standard.

Level I: Severe Breach of Conduct, which threatens the integrity of the NCAA model, includes any violation providing competitive advantage, substantial or impermissible benefit, or excessive recruiting:

- Academic fraud
- Unethical or dishonest conduct
- Failure to cooperate in an NCAA enforcement investigation
- Lack of institutional control

Level II: Significant Breach of Conduct provides more than a minimal but less that a substantial or extensive recruiting, competitive, or other advantage:

- Failure to monitor
- Systematic or multiple recruiting, financial aid, or eligibility violations not amounting to lack of institutional control
- Collective Level III violations

Level III: Breach of Conduct provides more than minimal recruiting, competitive, or other advantage yet is isolated or limited in nature:

- Multiple Level IV violations
- Exceeding the permissible number of contacts with a prospective student-athlete
- Providing team gear to a prospective student-athlete
- In-person, off-campus visits during a dead recruiting period

Level IV Incidental Issues are incidental or inadvertent and technical in nature, result in negligible or no competitive advantage, and will not affect eligibility.

Under this new bylaw violation structure, head coaches can be suspended for an entire season even when the egregious violations are conducted by staff. Additional penalties include placing a team on probation, limiting off-campus recruiting, reducing financial aid awards, banning postseason or bowl competition, and requiring institutional recertification of compliance with all NCAA regulations.

The purpose behind the rule changes is to impose a sense of personal, not solely institutional, responsibility and integrity for following the bylaws by creating a tone and culture of compliance. The tiered violations and penalties are intended to ensure a sense of fairness and flexibility especially for unintentional or incidental violations.

Health and Safety

President Barack Obama waded into the debate over the safety of playing sports when he was asked whether he would permit his sons to play football, if he had any. He responded, "I'd have to think long and hard." Highlighting the troubling concern of parents, coaches, players, leagues, and medical professionals over concussions at all levels of sport, the president called for conducting more research on how to improve safety for those participants most at risk.

In response, the National Football League (NFL), after agreeing to pay $765 million to settle concussion claims for thousands of former players, committed $25 million to promote youth sports safety. The NCAA through its Sports Science Institute partnered with the Department of Defense to earmark $30 million to conduct research, promote policies, and develop health and safety education materials.

All sport activities come with inherent risks. The NCAA is pledged to create a safe and healthy college environment and experience. Concussions are not the sole college campus safety issue. Hazing, bullying, harassment, and sexual assault are all forms of preventable violence.

The Benedict/Crosset study reveals that one in three college sexual assaults are committed by athletes. The decision by the Florida state attorney's office not to file sexual assault charges against Heisman Trophy winner Jameis Winston demonstrates the difficult and intrusive process women can face when they report a sexual assault to authorities, especially when the serious allegation involves a star athlete.

In a related college abuse matter, the filing of a civil suit for emotional distress heaped on a former Rutgers basketball player by ex–head coach Mike Rice demonstrates the lack of personal and institutional responsibility

Coach who threw balls at Play ers

for player safety occurring on some college campuses. In an all-too-familiar video first broadcast on ESPN, viewers observe Coach Rice physically and psychologically targeting and berating players. According to the civil lawsuit, Rutgers ignored repeated complaints about the coach's behavior "undoubtedly to protect Rutgers' multi-million dollar athletics program and its impending entry into the Big Ten conference with the millions of dollars of revenue that opportunity presented."

The growing concern by athletic administrators over the use of performance-enhancing drugs at all levels of sport was addressed from a constitutional law perspective in an early case that is still relevant. In *Brennan v. Board of Trustees for University of Louisiana Systems* (691 So. 2d 324, La. App. 1997), the court supported the NCAA's drug-testing program for student-athletes against a charge that it is a *right-to-privacy* violation. In legal terms, the NCAA mandates that it is a "condition precedent" for practicing and playing intercollegiate sports that all student-athletes are required to sign a written consent form to random drug testing for prohibited substances.

The NCAA imposes its drug-testing policy to protect the health of student-athletes and to preserve the sense of a level competitive playing field. The list of banned substances is found in *bylaw 31*. It includes the following classes of drugs and any drugs related to these classes of drugs:

- Stimulants (examples: Adderall, guarana or caffeine, Ritalin, cocaine)
- Anabolic agents (example: testosterone)
- Alcohol and beta-blockers (banned for rifle only)
- Diuretics and other masking agents
- Street drugs (examples: marijuana, heroin)
- Peptides
- Hormones and analogues (examples: human growth hormones, EPO)
- Anti-estrogens
- Beta-2 agonists

The association's bylaw warns student-athletes to be careful of ingesting over-the-counter dietary and nutritional substances because they may contain traces of banned substances. Any product containing a supplement is taken at the student-athlete's risk.

Amateurism

In 1916, the NCAA defined *amateurism* for the first time in its bylaws: "An amateur athlete is one who participates in competitive physical sports only for the pleasure and the physical, mental, moral and social benefits directly derived therefrom." The "amateur" concern in the association's early days was whether college football players should be allowed to play summer baseball for pay. The rule was in place barring the practice. Policing the rule was left to individual schools, which did not always happen.

The NCAA began allowing student-athletes to compete as a professional in one sport while retaining amateur status in other sports in 1974. Twenty years later, a controversial book by former NCAA executive director Walter Byers, *Unsportsmanlike Conduct: Exploiting Student-Athletes*, asserted that control over student-athletes' amateurism amounted to "economic tyranny." Annual salaries for college coaches can exceed $5 million. Athletic administrators can earn more than a million dollars a year. NCAA-imposed amateur eligibility status largely limits student-athletes' benefits to covering the cost of tuition, room, board, and a few incidentals.

Student-athletes who contract with professional teams, play sports for money, accept prize money above actual and necessary expenses, try out or practice or play with professionals, sign or accept benefits from an agent, in general, are not deemed amateur athletes. All incoming NCAA student-athletes must be certified as amateurs to practice or play.

The NCAA believes maintaining amateur status is crucial for preserving an environment where education is its first priority and athletics are subordinate. The conduct of many major D-I institutions and their conferences while playing football and basketball belies this principle. Data from the Equity in Athletics website reveals, in the most recent reported year, that the University of Texas football team generated significantly more than $100 million in revenue, while net profits exceeded $80 million. Each school in the SEC shares in excess of $30 million per year from television rights' deals with the SEC television network for football and basketball.

In a landmark class-action lawsuit filed by former University of California, Los Angeles (UCLA), basketball player Ed O'Bannon, he and other former intercollegiate athletes on antitrust grounds challenged the NCAA's right to define *amateurism*. O'Bannon's lawsuit successfully claimed that the association is "illegally restraining competition for services of players" by not allowing player compensation beyond the "amateur" minimums. In ruling for the players, US district court judge Claudia Wilken determined the association cannot prevent players from marketing the rights to their names, images, and likenesses for compensation. The decision was not a complete victory for college athletes. The lower court capped the amount of money Football Bowl Subdivision players and Division I basketball players could receive at a maximum of $5,000 per player for each year of eligibility. However, upon appeal to the Ninth Circuit Court of Appeals, a three-judge panel ruled that the NCAA may restrict colleges from compensating student-athletes beyond the cost of attending school. School revenue generated by television contracts from using a player's publicity rights are to be placed in a trust fund for payment upon leaving college. The ruling takes effect for the class of 2020.

In a somewhat similar legal action involving publicity rights, an out-of-court settlement was reached by a group of ex–college athletes led by former Arizona and Nebraska football quarterback Sam Keller. The NCAA agreed to pay $20 million to current and former athletes who sued over their unauthorized likenesses in basketball and football video games. In response to this decision, which serves as an example of how the NCAA can redefine *amateurism* to suit its needs, the association stated that moving forward a "blanket eligibility" waiver would be granted for current student-athletes so they would not be sanctioned for receiving licensing payments.

Finally in what was originally perceived as a blockbuster, potentially "game-changing" ruling, a Chicago-based regional National Labor Relations Board in 2014 held that college football players at Northwestern University, a private school, are "employees" for labor law purposes. The NCAA immediately appealed the decision to the full five-member National Labor Relations Board. In 2015, the board dismissed the players' petition to seek a union and engage in collective bargaining with their college. The board failed to address the issue of whether scholarship athletes are employees. It did address concern over the instability an affirmative-action ruling might have on college sports.

SUMMARY

The NCAA was founded to protect college athletes from physical dangers and exploitive practices. Today it is a billion-dollar, tax-exempt, private organization as concerned with building brand value and generating revenue as preserving the antiquated notion of amateurism.

The NCAA is the primary rule-making body for four-year colleges and universities that voluntarily choose to join. The member schools are divided into divisions centered on the desired level of competition, each with their own operating and administrative bylaws. The operating bylaws establish rules related to recruitment, academic standards, eligibility, fairness, integrity, compliance, health and safety, and amateurism. The five power conferences recently gained some legislative autonomy from the NCAA's rule-making process in the area of improving benefits for student-athletes.

The NCAA is still responsible for independently investigating a member school's failure to comply with its bylaws and retains the power to sanction schools for breaches under a new four-level standard for severe violations and two-level standard for minor violations. The alleged academic fraud charges leveled by the NCAA and former student-athletes against the University of North Carolina point to serious institutional governance failures. Different forms of litigation have occurred from current and former student-athletes over economic benefits and concern for players' well-being that challenge the NCAA's longstanding principle of amateurism.

KEY WORDS

Academic Progress Rate (APR). A program implemented in 2003 as part of a broader academic reform package. It is geared toward helping underperforming student-athletes who play basketball and football.

Administrative Bylaws. Policies and procedures required to implement the operating bylaws. Administrative bylaws are always subject to review by the full membership.

Amateurism. An *amateur* is defined by the NCAA as "one who participates in competitive physical sports only for the pleasure and the physical, mental, moral and social benefits directly derived therefrom."

Committee on Infractions. Charged with the responsibility of investigating alleged violations by NCAA schools.

Contact Periods. Times when a college coach may have face-to-face contact with recruits or their parents or legal guardians, watch them compete, visit their high schools, and write or telephone or text message them or their parents or legal guardians.

Dead Periods. No on-campus or off-campus contact is allowed, except for writing, telephoning, or texting.

Death Penalty. The NCAA's bylaws contain a provision to shut down a member's athletic program for repeat major or primary violations over the course of a five-year period.

Division I Infractions Model. In 2013, the NCAA implemented this model designed to hold schools, coaches, and administrators more accountable for issues directly affecting fairness and integrity. A four-level violation structure ranging from severe to incidental violations replaces the prior two-tier, major-or-secondary-violation standard.

Eligibility Center. Any student who desires to play intercollegiate sports at the D-I and D-II levels must register and be cleared by the NCAA via this center.

Evaluation Periods. Coaches may do everything that is permitted during a contact period, except have face-to-face contact with the prospect or the prospect's parents or legal guardians during the evaluation period.

Football Bowl Subdivision (FBS). In 2006, the Division I-A schools participating in major football play was renamed the Football Bowl Subdivision (FBS).

Football Championship Subdivision (FCS). In 2006, the Division I-AA schools were renamed the Football Championship Subdivision (FCS).

Infractions Appeals Committee. An independent committee convened when schools object to aspects of the investigation after a notice of allegations. It is a full-blown hearing with a right to appeal the findings and penalties.

Intercollegiate Athletic Association of the United States (IAAUS). After President Teddy Roosevelt's request for college presidents to make football safer on their campuses for participants, a football Rules Committee was formed along with the creation of the Intercollegiate Athletic Association of the United States (IAAUS). Four years later, in 1910, the IAAUS was renamed the NCAA.

Kemp, Jan. The English teacher–coordinator of the University of Georgia's developmental studies program who successfully filed a lawsuit against the school and was fired for refusing to change the grades of six failing minority students to keep them academically eligible.

National Association of Intercollegiate Athletics (NAIA). Non–upper division junior and community colleges do not belong to the NCAA. Many two-year colleges have formed their own regulatory body to create rules for competition and offer championship events. The balance of the four-year schools sponsoring athletic teams that are not members of the NCAA partner with the NAIA.

National Collegiate Athletic Association (NCAA). Organization that was founded in 1906 to protect young people from the dangerous and exploitive athletic practices of the time. The NCAA, or association, is the preeminent rule-making body for intercollegiate athletics. Membership is voluntary. Four-year schools in the United States and Canada that meet its standards may join.

National Letter of Intent (NLI). A highly prized recruit is frequently asked to sign an NLI to contractually bind that student to a particular D-I or D-II school. Signing an NLI does not guarantee admission. It does effectively end the recruiting process and guarantees a student-athlete at least one year of financial aid. Each sport has a unique NLI signing period. The rules surrounding NLI are governed by a non-NCAA organization called the Collegiate Commissioners Association, although the NCAA through the Eligibility Center administers the program itself.

NCAA Manuals. Manuals in which administrative rules, policy statements, and operational bylaws for each division are published annually.

Notice of Allegations. NCAA's notification to a school of alleged infractions.

Operating Bylaws. These bylaws are meant to promote constitutional principles (e.g., amateurism and institutional control) and purposes of the members. There are thirteen operating bylaws in the Division I manual, which numbers more than three hundred pages.

Quiet Periods. Periods during which coaches may not make any off-campus contacts or evaluations but may make in-person contacts only on college campuses.

Summary Disposition. Process that allows for a cooperative resolution without prolonged in-person hearings.

DISCUSSION QUESTIONS

1. Q: What rights does an individual have to participate in sports in the United States?

A: A constitutional right to participate in sports does *not* exist at any level of competition. However, once someone is permitted to participate, then a cluster of rights follows. These rights might derive from the basic rules established by the authorized regulatory body, state or federal lawmakers, or the courts in their interpretation of whether any fundamental rights or privileges were violated.

2. Q: Which NCAA programs are the most student centered?

A: Division III programs are the most student centered of all the divisions.

3. Q: What are the five highest-resource Division I conferences?

A: The five highest-resource Division I conferences are the Big Ten, ACC, Pac-12, Big 12, and SEC.

4. Q: What are the categories of the operating bylaws of the Division I manual as broken down in this book?

A: The bylaws are broken down into the following categories for discussion purposes:

• Recruitment
• Academic Standards
• Fairness, Integrity, and Compliance
• Health and Safety
• Amateurism

5. Q: What are some examples of complicated recruiting rules?

A: A few years ago, the NCAA banned all text messaging from coaches to prospective student-athletes even though recruits could text coaches. The ban was largely lifted at the Division I level despite complaints from coaches about disliking text messaging. D-III coaches in all sports are free to text recruits but are prohibited from using Facebook, Instagram, and other forms of social media.

6. Q: What are some unacceptable recruiting tactics?

A: Extending a job proposal to a recruit's mom or dad, cosigning on a car loan, proposing reduced housing costs for family members, or gifting merchandise and clothing have all been deemed unacceptable recruiting tactics.

7. Q: Who governs the rules surrounding the national letters of intent (NLI)?

A: The rules surrounding NLI are governed by a non-NCAA organization called the Collegiate Commissioners Association, although the NCAA through the Eligibility Center administers the program itself.

8. Q: What must a student-athlete accomplish if they wish to compete as a college freshman at the Division I level?

A: To compete as a college freshman at the Division I level, a student-athlete must meet three initial academic eligibility requirements: sixteen core high school courses, minimum SAT (critical reading and math only) or ACT (sum of English, math, reading, and science) test scores, and acceptable grade-point average (GPA).

9. Q: What APR threshold must teams meet in order to not be penalized?

A: Teams that fail to meet the minimum APR threshold of 930 are banned from postseason play and may suffer further penalties.

10. Q: What occurred at UNC Chapel Hill in 2011 involving their football and basketball programs that has led to new charges of academic fraud?

A: In 2011, the *Raleigh News & Observer* first reported incidents of academic fraud at UNC, Chapel Hill. At the center of the dishonest activities is the African American Studies program, where it is alleged that dozens of football and basketball players enrolled in classes that rarely or never met and still received passing grades. The NCAA reopened its investigation against the school, which led to five new severe violations charges, including lack of institutional control.

11. Q: What types of student-athletes are not deemed amateur?

A: Student-athletes who contract with professional teams, play sports for money, accept prize money above actual and necessary expenses, try out or practice or play with professionals, sign or accept benefits from an agent, in general, are not deemed amateur athletes.

12. Q: Why does the NCAA believe that maintaining amateur status for student-athletes is important?

A: The NCAA believes maintaining amateur status is crucial for preserving an environment where education is its first priority and athletics are subordinate.

13: **Q: What is unique about the student-athletes at Northwestern University in 2014?**

A: In 2014, a Chicago-based National Labor Relations Board originally ruled that college football players at Northwestern University, a private school, are "employees" for labor law purposes. Players thought they could decide whether to form a union and negotiate "wages, hours, and other terms and conditions of employment" with their employer, the university. This decision could have opened the door for players to receive additional benefits and compensation for practicing and playing their sport. However, the full National Labor Relations Board dismissed the players' petition on the grounds it might bring instability to college sports.

Chapter Two

Gender Equity in Sports

"When I was a little girl, I wanted to be a boy because I thought that was the only way I could play professional basketball."—Former UConn and WNBA star player Rebecca Lobo

HISTORY OF WOMEN AND SPORTS

In 1900, women were permitted to participate in the Olympic Games for the first time. Initially, they were limited to playing croquet, golf, and tennis. The United States Olympic Committee (USOC) was slow to culturally accept women as competitive athletes. Swimmers became the first US female athletes to compete in the Olympics in 1920. In the 1930s, some countries required female athletes to be accompanied by male chaperones to participate in Olympic events. By the 1980s and '90s, the Olympic movement took affirmative steps to open more sports for women, although men still had nearly twice as many Olympic sporting events available than women. At the 2012 summer Olympics, female athletes outnumbered their male counterparts for the first time.

It was not until the early 1960s at the intercollegiate level that women were allowed to compete for their own national championships in sports like basketball, gymnastics, and softball. Just before the passage of the landmark **Title IX** federal legislation in 1972, which prevented nonprofessional athlete discrimination on the basis of gender, only 30,000 women across all colleges and universities participated in recreation or competitive sporting activities. Today nearly 190,000 women participate in NCAA-sponsored athletics.

Sex discrimination is one of many gender and sports issues facing women, but there are others. For instance, the International Olympic Committee (IOC) report on women and sports highlights the role of sports in preventing

23

violence against women worldwide. Addressing religious and cultural differences in many Muslim countries that forbid or discourage female athletes
from performing in public remains a pressing concern. Increasing the number
of women working in sports administration at all professional levels remains
a goal of the **Women Sports Foundation**, an advocacy organization. In
another glaring statistic pointing to disparate treatment, according to the US
Department of Education, the pay gap between male and female college
coaches is widening.

The difficulty of deciding objectively where to draw the line between a
male and a female athlete presents a quandary in a sporting world where
competitors participate based on gender classification. The young South
African runner Caster Semenya, who won the 800 meters world championships a few years ago, was accused of winning unfairly. Competitor athletes
alleged she raced with an unfair competitive advantage. According to reports
at the time, it was alleged that she exhibited "manly" characteristics. The
International Association of Athletics Federation (IAAF), the organization
that oversees all international competitions outside the Olympics, conducted
an investigation into her gender that led to a determination that she could
compete in international races as a woman. According to leaked reports,
Semenya's body has both male and female characteristics.

The controversy surrounding the verification of Semenya's gender status,
which also included charges of racism, ultimately led the IOC to address an
issue it has struggled with for many years. As early as 1960, any doubt about
an athlete's gender during the Olympics was resolved by having the athlete
pull her shorts down. If she looked female, then she was deemed a female.
Later on, the IOC came to realize that the outside appearance might not
match what is inside. Therefore, it shifted to a chromosome test and, when
that proved inadequate, an SRY (male) gene detection test. After the Sydney
Olympics in 2000, this test was also abandoned.

In response to the Semenya case, which began initially in 2009, the IOC
put together a medical commission of leading experts in the field to determine the best method of deciding gender for Olympic competition purposes.
The findings concluded that the source of a natural competitive edge in
sports rests largely with testosterone levels. Based on this medical guidance,
the IOC elected to determine on a case-by-case basis whether a person must
compete as a man or woman based on testosterone levels. Therefore, a person that self-identifies as a woman but has a high level of male testosterone
must compete as a male, not as a female. The debate in this complex gender
classification arena has only just begun, especially in light of the possibility
of surgical interventions or hormone therapy for transgender athletes.

The public decision by former male Olympic decathlete gold medal
champion Bruce Jenner to transition to female serves as a wake-up call for
sports-governing bodies at all levels to develop policies on how to include

transgender persons in athletic participation. A few years ago, the IOC took the lead on this issue when it voted to permit a transgender athlete to compete in the Olympics subject to certain conditions: The athlete must have had gender reassignment surgery, his or her gender reassignment is recognized in his or her home country, and at least two years of the appropriate hormone therapy must have been completed. Balancing a nondiscriminatory transgender participation policy with the need for fair competition remains a unique challenge for many sports organizations and teams.

These are merely some of the examples of the leading gender equity in athletics issues facing society.

GENDER EQUITY: TITLE IX

Sexual Discrimination

Richard Nixon was president when Title IX was signed into law in 1972. The statute itself is an amendment to the 1964 Civil Rights Act. Surprising to many, the word *sports* isn't even mentioned in the act, nor are sports part of the bill's legislative history. In remarkably simple terms, Title IX (20 U.S.C. section 1681 [a]) states, "No person in the United States shall, on the basis of sex, be excluded from participation in, be denied the benefits of, or be subjected to discrimination under any education program or activity receiving Federal financial assistance." By federal statute, the Department of Education is charged with implementing this congressional mandate. The *administrative regulations* that accompany Title IX make it *illegal* to *deny athletic opportunities*, *treatment*, and *benefits on the basis of sex or gender*, subject to some exceptions. The term *athletic opportunities* means varsity sports participation and club and intramural activities.

To assist schools receiving federal funds with compliance of Title IX, the **Office of Civil Rights (OCR)**, which is the administrative body charged with enforcing the law, established a three-prong test:

1. Are opportunities for female and male athletes proportionate to their enrollment?
2. Does the school have a history of expanding athletic opportunities for the underrepresented sex?
3. Has the school demonstrated success in meeting the needs of those students?

The first major legal challenge to Title IX occurred in 1984. Grove City College, a small religious-based school in Pennsylvania, successfully argued before the US Supreme Court that the law applied only to specific programs or activities that receive federal financial assistance. When the OCR failed to demonstrate that the college's athletic department directly received federal funds, the court held that the sports programs did not have to comply with the mandates (*Grove City College v. Bell*, 465 U.S. 555, 1984).

This decision seriously limited the reach of Title IX and the OCR's jurisdiction over athletic programs at schools. Over the president's veto, Congress amended the act in 1987. The **Civil Rights Restoration Act** broadened the definition of *program* to include all activities in any school, including athletic departments that accept federal financial assistance. Today, Title IX covers nearly all secondary and higher education institutions because, so long as any program or department receives federal funding, the entire school is obliged to follow Title IX.

A few years after this statutory amendment, the OCR issued new policy interpretations to assist investigators in determining whether academic institutions are in compliance. The following program factors in abbreviated form are part of the review process:

1. The selection of sports and level of competition to effectively accommodate the interests and abilities of members of both sexes.
2. The provision of equipment and supplies.
3. Scheduling of games and practice times.
4. Travel and per-diem allowance.
5. Opportunity to receive coaching and academic tutoring.
6. Assignment and compensation of coaches and tutors.
7. Provision of locker rooms and practice and competitive facilities.
8. Provision of medical and training facilities and services.
9. Provision of housing and dining facilities and services.
10. Publicity.

For each of these factors, any differences between the male and female sports programs must be negligible. For instance, in the area of financial assistance, the money spent on the respective programs do not have to be precisely equal. However, the *benefits* provided from funding must be equal. In general, financial aid in the form of scholarships must be **substantially proportional** for its male and female student-athletes. The Department of Education has the authority to withhold federal funding for noncompliant schools, although it has never taken this severe action.

Since the passage of Title IX, there have been a number of significant lawsuits beyond the Grove City College decision challenging the commitment of schools to equalize athletic opportunities for women. A handful of landmark cases stand out.

The First Circuit Court of Appeals (*Cohen v. Brown University*, 991 F.2d 888, 1st Cir. 1993) found that Brown University was in violation of Title IX and its regulations when it eliminated school funding for women's gymnastics and volleyball. Both sports retained varsity status but became donor funded. Men's water polo and golf lost school funding, too. Before reaching the appeals court, a lower court held the university failed to comply with any part of the three-prong OCR compliance factors, which was affirmed by the appeals court. It is worth noting that at that time Brown had one of the largest and most equitable women's athletic programs in the country. The US Supreme Court let stand the appeals court verdict without review (*Brown University v. Cohen*, 520 U.S. 1186, 1997).

In response to this class-action lawsuit, Brown added school-funded sports for women. The university agreed to increase the number of athletic opportunities available to mirror the ratio of women to men in the school's undergraduate student body.

Meeting Title IX standards through the *substantial proportionality* test, as Brown did under its settlement terms with the women who brought the civil complaint, is the surest way for schools to ensure compliance. The OCR refers to this test as the only **safe harbor** to avoid liability.

Despite the initial euphoria surrounding the *Brown* decision, overall compliance with Title IX as applied to athletics across the United States has proven difficult. Division I programs that offer the full NCAA compliment of eighty-five football scholarships plus nonscholarship walk-ons can rarely meet the substantial proportionality test as the sole condition of compliance. No women's sport provides anywhere near the 100 to 120 participation spots that football offers, complicating the task of matching statistical equity.

Assume, for example, that women comprise 60 percent of a school's undergraduate student body. Following the substantial proportionality test requires that 60 percent of the participants in a school's entire intercollegiate sports program are women. Cutting non-revenue-producing sports for men (e.g., wrestling, swimming, and track and field) and severely limiting the number of male participants in sports like baseball and soccer are two ways major universities with varsity football programs have sought to comply using this test. This addition-by-subtraction technique alone doesn't add female athletic opportunities. It merely reduces opportunities for men, which is not discriminatory so long as men's participation opportunities on the whole is substantially proportionate to their presence in the school's student body, but it is unfair. Table 2.1 identifies the total number of allowable NCAA sports scholarships by gender for Division I schools.

Astute students might ask why the revenue-producing sports of football and basketball aren't exempt from Title IX's requirements. After all, according to the NCAA, the average Division I men's basketball team generates more than $10 million in revenue per year. The top twenty income-producing college football programs easily generate revenue that exceeds $50 million annually. There are only four women's college sports teams that reported earning in excess of $4 million, with none recognizing a profit more than

Table 2.1.

Division I Sports	Men's Scholarships	Women's Scholarships
Baseball/Softball	11.7	12
Basketball	13	15
Football	85	0
Golf	4.5	6
Gymnastics	6.3	12
Field Hockey	0	12
Ice Hockey	18	18
Lacrosse	12.6	12
Rowing	0	20
Soccer	9.9	12
Swimming/Diving	9.9	8.1
Tennis	4.5	8
Track and Field	12.6	18
Volleyball	4.5	12
Water Polo	4.5	8
Wrestling	9.9	0

$500,000, as per the Department of Education. The answer is that Congress has *blocked* legislative attempts to limit Title IX compliance to non-revenue-producing sports, in large part because the American public across political lines believes sports participation is as important for women as for men.

Education institutions that can demonstrate a *history and continued practice of expanding* sports programs and athletic participation opportunities for women may still comply with the gender equity demands of Title IX. Besides this second prong of compliance, schools may comply by showing the disproportionality is not due to discriminatory practices but rather reflects an *accommodation* of the interests and abilities of female students. This is the third, and legally the fuzziest, of the tests because it relies on student surveys, online inquiries, e-mail correspondence, and on-campus interviews.

Around the same time as the *Brown* sex discrimination case was resolved, a different appeals court interpreted Title IX regulations in two telling ways. A high school or college may lawfully deny a woman the opportunity to participate in a contact sport against men because of differences in size, strength, and skill. However, once a school permits a woman to try out for a single-sex contact sport, such as football, then she is afforded protection against discriminatory treatment from players, coaches, and administrators.

[handwritten marginalia: allowed; Girls hey; Girls]

[handwritten note at bottom: Girls Participation in Contact sports ↑]

For Title IX purposes, at the high school and college levels, contact sports include boxing, wrestling, ice hockey, football, rugby, basketball, and other sports where the major activity involves **body contact**.

In a well-documented case dealing with gender equity and contact sports, Heather Sue Mercer, an all-star high school kicker, was allowed to practice and work out with Duke University's football team. After she hit the winning field goal during the team's spring intrasquad football game, Duke's head coach, Fred Goldsmith, informed her that she had made the team. During the next football season, she claimed that she was treated in a discriminatory manner because she was not permitted to attend summer training camp, denied equal chances to kick during practices, and was told to sit in the stands with her boyfriend rather than on the sideline with other players during games. Coach Goldsmith then told her she was dismissed from the team.

Mercer filed suit against Duke, claiming she was cut from the team because she was a woman and she was treated differently than the male football players, all in violation of Title IX. In a back-and-forth decision, a lower trial court ultimately agreed with her discriminatory treatment arguments and discounted Goldsmith's opinion that she was cut from the team because she lacked the speed, size, and leg strength to play. She was awarded compensatory and punitive damages. Duke then appealed that decision. The appeals court concurred with the lower court's finding that Duke discriminated against her based on her gender. However, the appeals court did vacate the $2 million award of punitive damages on the grounds that Title IX does not allow for punitive damages in private actions. The court kept the ludicrously low $1 compensatory damage award and substantial attorney fees in place (*Mercer v. Duke University*, 19 F.3d 643, 4th Cir. 1999).

In the prior chapter on the NCAA as a regulatory body, a judicial ruling was cited that held that the NCAA was not a "state" actor for due process purposes involving the discipline of a college coach. The issue of when the NCAA may be sued occurred again when the NCAA denied a female college volleyball player, Renee Smith, an athletic waiver to compete as a graduate student. Smith claimed that the association discriminatorily granted more waivers for male athletes than female athletes, in violation of Title IX. In a narrowly decided opinion, the US Supreme Court in *NCAA v. Smith* (525 U.S. 459, 1999) unanimously determined that the receipt of dues money by the association from its member schools who do receive federal funds does not make the NCAA subject to lawsuits under Title IX.

In 1994, Congress mandated that coeducational institutions of higher education that participate in any federal student financial aid program and has an intercollegiate athletic program must disclose gender and sport information to the public on an annual basis. The **Equity in Athletics Disclosure Act** report requires schools to calculate the number of male and female undergraduate students; varsity sports and participation levels based on gender;

operating expenses by team; revenue generated by team; expenditures by team, including scholarships and recruiting; and average coaching salaries for male and female teams.

The documentation submitted by schools provides a treasure trove of data ripe for individual review and school-by-school comparison. By and large, women at the Division I level are still substantially underrepresented in intercollegiate sporting opportunities and funding, the first prong of the OCR regulations. The government web page "The Equity in Athletics Data Analysis Cutting Tool" (http://ope.ed.gov/athletics) is the starting web-based source for retrieving and fully analyzing the data collected. By law, schools must make their annual reports available to the public at their admissions offices, libraries, and athletic departments.

Sexual Harassment and Assault

Undeniably, Title IX has yielded dramatic gains in female participation in recreational and competitive sports. Since its passage into law, high school athletic participation for young women has increased by nearly 1,000 percent, while increasing nearly 600 percent for college women. However, reports that nearly two-thirds of college students and 80 percent of secondary students have experienced sexual harassment have refocused the national debate on how to prevent unwanted physical and nonphysical behavior. *Sexual harassment is a form of sexual discrimination.* Title IX protects students from unlawful sexual harassment in all of a school's activities or programs.

As early as 1992, the US Supreme Court held that a high school student who was sexually harassed by her physical education teacher may sue the school for monetary damages (*Franklin v. Gwinnet County Public Schools*, 503 U.S. 60, 1992). Later court rulings have refined this decision to require a showing that a school has actual knowledge of the harassment or sexual relations between a high school student and her coach or teacher and failed to take appropriate action to stop it before holding a school liable. Peer-to-peer harassment at a school may also be actionable under Title IX.

The OCR defines sexual harassment as conduct that:

- Is sexual in nature;
- Is unwelcome; and
- Denies or limits a student's ability to participate in or benefit from a school's education program.

In a major wake-up call for all universities, the University of Colorado, Boulder, reached a multimillion-dollar out-of-court settlement with a woman who alleged she was gang-raped by football players and high school recruits at an off-campus party. Her Title IX lawsuit claimed that school and athletic officials knew women were at risk of sexual harassment or assault by football players and recruits and did nothing to prevent it.

In telling language before the parties reached a resolution, the Tenth Circuit Court of Appeals unanimously concluded Colorado's athletic department had an "official policy of showing high-school football recruits a 'good time' on their visits to the CU campus." The university's lack of supervision over the football players who served as hosts for the recruits was deemed the result of "deliberate indifference." Colorado agreed to hire a full-time Title IX coordinator who reports directly to the chancellor in the aftermath of this sorrowful incident. The coordinator's hiring is expected to serve as a model for other postsecondary schools that want to take affirmative steps to prevent and respond to sexual assault on campus and to comply with OCR's legal requirements (*Simpson v. University of Colorado, Boulder*, 500 F.3rd 1170, 10th Cir. 2007).   *Gang raped student by players recruits*

The perception that schools will protect student-athletes over the alleged victim or even more than other students is pervasive. Accusations of Oklahoma State, Florida State, and Vanderbilt officials botching their respective investigations and reports of alleged assaults on women by football players highlight this claim.

Sexual harassment does not have to be perpetrated by someone of the opposite sex to state a cause of action. For example, hazing rituals by teammates against underclass student-athletes or bullying by coaches, as discussed in chapter 1 involving the Rutgers men's basketball coach, that deny a student's ability to participate in or benefit from a school's athletic program may constitute an unlawful form of sexual harassment.

Title IX's reach prohibits sexual harassment by any employee, including coaches and teachers or agents of a school. In 2012, the NCAA *recommended* to its member schools that they institute an unambiguous policy that prohibits sexual relationships between coaches and student-athletes. The policy cites the possibility of conflicts of interest, including favoritism or punishment, depending on the status of the relationship and the differences in power between college-aged athletes and adult coaches.

Based on a 2013 settlement between the OCR and the University of Montana, a clarification on the definition of sexual harassment was issued that applies to all schools. The OCR recognizes a *distinction between sexual harassment* and a *hostile work environment* under Title IX. Sexual harassment may occur when there is "unwelcome conduct of a sexual nature." Federal law recognizes two types of sexual harassment: quid pro quo (Latin for "this for that") and hostile work environment. An example of a quid pro quo form of harassment is when a coach offers preferential treatment to a player in exchange for a date. When the sexual harassment at an educational institution is sufficiently severe or pervasive as to disrupt a person's ability to participate in an education program, this form of discrimination creates a hostile work environment.

A free online e-book available for public reading titled *A Victim's Guide to Sexual Harassment* (www.sexualharassmentlawyersanjose.com/online-e-book) provides helpful examples of hostile work environment and quid pro quo sexual harassment cases for those who want to investigate this area of the law further.

EQUAL PROTECTION

The **Equal Protection Clause** of the Fourteenth Amendment to the US Constitution serves as another legal tool to protect women from gender-based discrimination. Specifically, the Fourteenth Amendment states, "No State shall make or enforce any law which shall . . . deny to any person . . . the equal protection of the laws." In brief, this means all people similarly situated must be treated the same.

This post–Civil War amendment to the Constitution initially applied to male African Americans who had just gained equal status under the law as citizens. Nowadays, other protected groups or individuals besides African Americans may use the Fourteenth Amendment to seek comparably equal treatment and dismantle vestiges of discrimination. Keep in mind that the Equal Protection Clause only forbids federal, state, and local governments from discriminating, not private actors.

Federal and state courts apply different standards of equal protection review depending on the group or class of individuals claiming illegal discrimination and the interest affected by the classification. The US Supreme Court ruled that all government *classifications* for equal protection purposes based on *race*, *alienage*, and *national origin* are "*suspect*" categories that require *strict scrutiny* or review. For schools, this means that a high school or college must demonstrate a "*compelling government purpose*" for trying to separate sports teams based on race, alienage, or national origin distinctions—a highly unlikely situation. The strict scrutiny test might also apply whenever a *fundamental right* is at stake. Judges have *not* deemed participating in a sport or recreation activity as a fundamental right.

Sports teams separated on the basis of gender or sex are *not* reviewed under the strict scrutiny standard for their fairness. Instead, *gender classifications* are subject to *heightened scrutiny*. A school must demonstrate an *exceedingly pervasive justification* for separating teams on the basis of sex or not permitting one gender to participate in the traditional sport of another gender. The source for this legal standard occurred when the US Supreme Court determined that Virginia Military Institute (VMI), the last male-only public-funded college in the United States, unlawfully discriminated against women by denying admission. The high court was unmoved by VMI's offer to create a similar military training institute solely for women. The proposal failed to pass constitutional muster because it would not create similar education opportunities for women, thereby failing the Equal Protection Clause test. Instead, because VMI could not demonstrate "exceedingly persuasive justification" for its single-sex admission policy, it became a state-funded military college for men and women beginning in 2001 (*United States v. Virginia*, 518 U.S. 515, 1996). *Girl wanting to join VMT being denied*

In another frequently cited Fourteenth Amendment case, a federal court rejected a Colorado state high school association's ban on allowing girls to try out for the boys' soccer team on the basis that it was unsafe because of the gender differences in strength and speed. At the time, soccer was a boys-only sport at the high school level in the state of Colorado. Had the high school created a separate soccer team of boys and girls, as many schools throughout the country now do, and the programs were supported equally, then it might have been permissive. The court determined that female athletes were unfairly burdened and denied the opportunity to fully participate in the sport of soccer by the regulation (*Hoover v. Meiklejohn*, 430 F.Supp. 164, 1997).

Both Title IX and the Equal Protection Clause permit **"separate but equal"** teams in the same sport for both genders. The key point in assessing whether separate teams in the same sport for men and women meet constitutional muster is that schools demonstrate that funding, coaching expertise, locker room facilities, means of transportation to games, times of play, seasons of play, equipment, uniforms, officiating, a school's commitment to competitive teams, and playing fields or arenas are comparably equal. This position is personified in *O'Connor v. Board of Education of School District No. 23* (449 U.S. 1301, 1980), which held that gender-based basketball teams are constitutionally permissive and complied with Title IX by having a team for each gender. Factually, the US Supreme Court refused to issue a preliminary injunction to allow a talented sixth-grade girl to play on the boys' basketball team even though she was too good for the girls' team. The school district was justified in their reasoning in separating contact teams on the basis of gender because of the potential physical harm.

Historically, as the *O'Connor* case demonstrates, should a school wish to classify a sport as a *contact sport* for men only, then it must show that this heightened scrutiny classification serves an important government objective. On the whole, society has recognized that among *some age groups* there are physical differences between boys and girls and men and women. Related to this variance in physical strength, height, weight, speed, and quickness is the potential for harm. This overly broad distinction is frequently cited in the court literature.

When a sport involves *body contact*, Title IX regulations also permit schools to exclude or discriminate against women. The traditional **contact**

sports exceptions are boxing, wrestling, rugby, ice hockey, basketball, and football. Remember, though, based on the *Mercer* decision, once a woman is permitted to compete in a contact sport, then she must be afforded treatment equal to men.

Under the intermediate level of constitutional scrutiny for gender-based discrimination, other arguments besides the *physical differences* between the sexes are frequently articulated as justification. These reasons include the following: Maintaining separate teams *ensures more athletic participation opportunities* for women, and—the corollary argument—were men allowed to compete on teams designated for women, then they might *dominate*.

Numerous judicial opinions make it clear that the purpose of the Equal Protection Clause is to *eliminate* artificial gender discrimination. In those situations, such as little league major division baseball, where exclusions were made solely on the paternalistic basis of sex or gender without considering skill levels and lack of physical gender differences between the ages of nine and twelve years, the discriminatory treatment does not hold.

One court allowed a girl to try out for the traditional noncontact high school boys' sport of baseball even though her school had a softball team. In detailed analysis, the court concluded that softball was a strikingly different sport than baseball. The dissimilarities included distances between the bases, lack of mound elevation in softball, ball and bat sizes, and underhand versus overhand pitching. In essence, the court found the two sports were not substantially equivalent. The school had to permit the young woman to try out for the baseball team and then let her competitive skill level determine whether she was a talented enough ballplayer to play with the boys.

The various options or variations in team sports may be summarized as follows: *Variations in team sport*

- Men's team but no substantially equivalent women's team
- Women's team but no substantially equivalent men's team
- Men's team with a substantially equivalent women's team
- Women's team with a substantially equivalent men's team
- Contact sports team
- Mixed-gender team

Naturally, the next intriguing issue is whether it is a discriminatory practice to deny a man the chance to play on a team designated for women.

An Arizona court dismissed a lawsuit filed by a group of boys when they were barred from playing on the girls-only high school volleyball team. The court in *Clark v. Interscholastic Association* (695 F.2d 1126, 9th Cir. 1982) found that the public school's interest in redressing past discrimination against girls in athletics was a "legitimate and substantial" government interest. On the matter of whether the exclusion of boys is "substantially related"

Guy wanting to play women's volleyball

to this concern, the court reasoned that, because of the "average physiological differences, males would displace females to a substantial extent."

This logic is still the prevailing view for schools that have a women's team without a substantially equivalent men's sport. In time, the need to redress past gender discrimination by preserving athletic spots solely for women may dissolve. Depending on the ages and skill levels of the participants, the physiological differences argument may carry less weight in affecting the classification outcome.

In situations where male and female sports are considered substantially equivalent, such as the contact sport of basketball, then separating the teams on gender is viewed as nondiscriminatory. (See the above *O'Connor v. Board of Education of School District* 23, 449 U.S. 1301, 1980, where a lower court ruling permitted separate but substantially equal men and women teams in contact sports.) For noncontact separate but equal sports, the concerns for the health and safety of women are not as compelling. Several schools, especially at the high school level, are electing to compete in some sports with mixed-gender teams.

Many states have enacted **equal rights amendments** to their state constitutions that may support state-based gender equity petitions for relief. Pennsylvania and Washington, for instance, have held that relegating a woman to the female squad solely because of her sex might be a denial of equality under state law.

Federal discrimination lawsuits by women who lost their athletic scholarships or were denied an extra year of eligibility because of their pregnancies led the NCAA to enact a bylaw granting them a hardship waiver to compete an extra year. There is no substantially equivalent paternal waiver for a male athlete who wants to take time off to spend time with a newborn baby.

In 2014, the Seventh Circuit Court of Appeals in *Hayden v. Greensburg Community School Corporation* (no. 13-1757) ruled that an unwritten high school policy regulating hair length for members of the young men's basketball team violated the Equal Protection Clause and Title IX. The court noted that, while there was no fundamental legal right in the length of an athlete's hair, there was a cognizable *liberty* interest. The Indiana public school's policy was *prima facie* discriminatory, meaning unambiguously discriminatory, and there was no evidence that female athletes were subject to comparable hair-grooming restrictions.

EQUAL PAY

Gender equity pay issues apply to school employment. Increasingly, female athletic administrators, academic coordinators, trainers, and coaches are suing schools for sex discrimination. A federal statute, the **Equal Pay Act,** requires equal pay for equal work subject to exceptions. In the case of women employed in sports, the *exceptions are the rule.*

The leading case on this subject came about when the women's basketball coach, **Marianne Stanley**, at the University of Southern California (USC), a private university, sued because her base pay and perks were lower than the men's head basketball coach, George Raveling. In denying her claim, the federal appeals court determined the pay discrepancy was based on factors other than gender.

Permissible exceptions to equal pay for equal work under the Equal Pay Act occur when the jobs are not the same based on seniority, accomplishments, and merit. In the USC case, Raveling had more than thirty years of coaching experience, twice was named national and conference coach of the year, authored books on coaching, spoke extensively at booster events, performed as a university goodwill ambassador, and served as an Olympic coach. In contrast, Stanley had spent seven years coaching, never coached an Olympic team, and never authored a book (*Stanley v. USC*, 178 F3d 1069, 9th Cir. 1999).

It is well documented that coaches of women's teams earn less than coaches of men's teams, especially in the revenue-producing and media-attentive comparable sport of basketball. At the Division I level, head coaches for women's teams receive on average less than half the salaries of the head coaches of men's teams. The source of the pay differentials frequently is generated from third-party endorsement deals with shoe and apparel companies, summer coaching clinics, and appearance fees not always available to women coaches.

A somewhat fascinating and counterintuitive fact is that, while the number of college women athletic teams has double over the past twenty years, the percentage of women serving as head basketball college coaches has slipped from nearly 80 percent to under 60 percent.

Gender pay inequity extends to professional sports. The total prize earnings for the Professional Golfers Association (PGA) golfers are more than five times the Ladies Professional Golf Association (LPGA) golfers' earnings. The victorious 2015 women's World Cup soccer championship team received four times less than the 2014 men's World Cup team that lost in the round of 16. The average salary in the NBA tops out around $4.5 million. The maximum salary in the women's counterpart to the NBA—the Women's National Basketball Association (WNBA)—is approximately $100,000. The exorbitant salary differentials are directly related to fan interest and revenue garnered from attending games and watching teams on television, which is permissible under the law. None of these activities are regulated by Title IX prescriptions.

Not all professional sports distribute compensation unevenly. Female Team USA swimmers who medal at the Olympics receive the same financial perks as male medal winners. Beginning in 2007, Wimbledon has awarded women single tennis players the same prize money as the men single winners, even though the men play best of five set matches to determine a winner, while women play best of three set matches. The top fifteen men and women receive the same prize money at the Boston Marathon.

Media exposure in major print and online newspapers varies dramatically based on gender. The latest statistics indicate that less than 8 percent of the total media coverage related to sports focuses on women's sports. To date there is no female professional sporting event that captures fan appeal and media-crazed attention like the NFL's Super Bowl, baseball's World Series, Fédération International de Football Association's (FIFA) World Cup soccer matches, or an NBA Final featuring tweeting male celebrity–star athletes.

SUMMARY

There is little dispute that Title IX has dramatically enhanced the opportunities for women to participate and compete in school-sponsored sports and recreation activities. The three principal tests to determine whether a federally funded school is in compliance with Title IX are: substantial proportionality, history of enhancing opportunities, and accommodating the interest of women. These tests are used for verifying compliance in addition to the OCR program factors.

The Equal Protection Clause is used less frequently to remedy complaints of gender discrimination. In the context of sports, it exists to ensure comparable nondiscriminatory program and participation opportunities for women. Substantially equal but separate teams for men and women is the permissible norm.

Increasingly, the issue of bullying and sexual harassment in schools has drawn public attention and scrutiny. A school that fails to effectively institute appropriate policies and police its athletes, coaches, and staff may run afoul of laws prohibiting sexual discrimination.

KEY WORDS

Body Contact. A sport that involves body contact may be used to exclude or discriminate against women under Title IX.

Civil Rights Restoration Act. An amendment to Title IX in 1987 by the US Congress to include all activities in any school, including athletic departments that accept federal financial assistance.

Contact Sports Exceptions. Sports that traditionally exclude women, including boxing, wrestling, rugby, ice hockey, basketball, and football.

Equal Pay Act. A federal statute that requires equal pay for equal work subject to exceptions.

Equal Protection Clause. Clause of the Fourteenth Amendment to the US Constitution that serves as another legal tool to protect women from gender-based discrimination. Specifically, the Fourteenth Amendment states, "No State shall make or enforce any law which shall . . . deny to any person . . . the equal protection of the laws." In brief, this means all people similarly situated must be treated the same.

Equal Rights Amendments. Amendments enacted by states on their constitutions that may support state-based gender-equity petitions for relief.

Equity in Athletics Disclosure Act. Report that requires schools to calculate the number of male and female undergraduate students; varsity sports and participation levels based on gender; operating expenses by team; revenue generated by team; expenditures by team, including scholarships and recruiting; and average coaching salaries for male and female teams.

Office of Civil Rights (OCR). The administrative body charged with enforcing law and assisting schools receiving federal funds in complying with Title IX.

Safe Harbor. Test utilized by the OCR to determine compliance of Title IX standards by schools employing the substantial proportionality test.

Separate but Equal. Used by both Title IX and the Equal Protection Clause. The key point in assessing whether separate teams in the same sport for men and women meet constitutional muster is for schools to demonstrate funding, coaching, locker rooms, transportation, times of play, seasons of play, equipment, uniforms, and playing fields or arenas are comparably equal.

Stanley, Marianne. University of Southern California women's basketball coach who sued because her base pay and perks were lower than the men's head basketball coach, George Raveling. In denying her claim, the federal appeals court determined the pay discrepancy was based on factors other than gender.

Substantially Proportional. Term used to describe the obligation that any differences between the men's and women's athletics programs must be negligible. In the area of financial assistance, the money spent on the respective programs do not have to be precisely equal. However, the benefits provided from funding must be equal.

Title IX. An amendment to the 1964 Civil Rights Act that was signed into law by President Nixon in 1972. The title states, "No person in the United States shall, on the basis of sex, be excluded from participation in, be denied the benefits of, or be subjected to discrimination under any education program or activity receiving Federal financial assistance."

Women Sports Foundation. An advocacy organization that works to increase the number of women working in sports administration.

DISCUSSION QUESTIONS

1. **Q: Which athletes were the first US female athletes to compete in the Olympics?**
A: Swimmers became the first US female athletes to compete in the Olympics in 1920.

2. **Q: Who is tasked with implementing Title IX?**
A: The Department of Education is charged with implementing this congressional mandate.

3. **Q: What is the three-prong test used by the OCR to determine compliance with Title IX?**
A: The three-prong test used by the OCR to determine compliance with Title IX includes the following:

1. Are opportunities for female and male athletes proportionate to their enrollment?
2. Does the school have a history of expanding athletic opportunities for the underrepresented sex?
3. Has the school demonstrated success in meeting the needs of those students?

4. **Q: What caused the US Congress to amend Title IX in 1987?**
A: The first major legal challenge to Title IX occurred in 1984. Grove City College successfully argued before the US Supreme Court that the law applied only to specific programs or activities that receive federal financial assistance. When the OCR failed to demonstrate that the college's athletic department directly received federal funds, the court held that the sports programs did not have to comply with the mandates (*Grove City College v. Bell*, 465 U.S. 555, 1984).

5. **Q: Why did the First Circuit Court of Appeals find that Brown University was in violation of Title IX in *Cohen v. Brown University*, 991 F.2d 888 (1st Cir. 1993)?**
A: The First Circuit Court of Appeals (*Cohen v. Brown University*, 991 F.2d 888, 1st Cir. 1993) found that Brown University was in violation of Title IX and its regulations when it eliminated school funding for women's gymnastics and volleyball. Both sports retained varsity status but became

donor funded. Men's water polo and golf lost school funding, too. Before reaching the appeals court, a lower court held that the university failed to comply with any part of the three-prong OCR compliance factors, which was affirmed by the appeals court.

6. Q: What is considered the full NCAA Division I compliment for football, and why is it a problem for schools?

A: Division I programs that offer the full NCAA complement of eighty-five football scholarships plus nonscholarship walk-ons can rarely meet the substantial proportionality test as the sole condition of compliance. No female sport provides anywhere near the 100 to 120 participation spots that football offers, complicating the task of matching statistical equity. In many jurisdictions, though, schools are free to choose any one of the three-prongs available under OCR regulations.

7. Q: Describe *Mercer v. Duke University*, 19 F.3d 643 (4th Cir. 1999).

A: Mercer was a female kicker who was allowed to practice and work out with Duke University's football team. After being told she had made the team, she was dismissed the following season. She blamed her dismissal on her gender. The lower court agreed and awarded her damages. The appeals court concurred but vacated the award of punitive damages, finding them unavailable to impose under Title IX, and kept the $1 compensatory verdict.

8. Q: How does the OCR define *sexual harassment*?

A: The OCR defines sexual harassment as conduct that:

1. Is sexual in nature;
2. Is unwelcome; and
3. Denies or limits a student's ability to participate in or benefit from a school's education program.

9. Q: What did the University of Colorado, Boulder, do to prevent and respond to sexual harassment on campus, and how does it affect other athletic programs?

A: Colorado agreed to hire a full-time Title IX coordinator who reports directly to the chancellor. Her hiring may serve as a model for other postsecondary schools that want to take affirmative steps to prevent and respond to sexual assault on campus and to comply with OCR's legal requirements.

10. Q: What must schools do in order to separate teams on the basis of sex?

A: A school must demonstrate an exceedingly pervasive justification for separating teams on the basis of sex or not permitting one gender to participate in the traditional sport of another gender.

Chapter Three

International Sports and the Olympics

"Many of life's disappointments, even major ones [like not having the oppor-
tunity to participate in the Olympics], do not enjoy constitutional protection.
This is one such instance."—Judge David Pratt, *DeFrantz v. USOC*, 492 F.
Supp. 1181

INTRODUCTION TO INTERNATIONAL SPORTS AND THE OLYMPICS

The summer and winter Olympic Games bring together athletes in individual
and team events from different countries for intense international competition. Until 1986, the summer and winter Olympic Games were held in the
same year every four years. Now they are scheduled in different, even years,
two years apart.

In between these years, thousands of local, regional, national, and global
championships in every sporting activity imaginable take place. These
events, like the Olympics, are governed and sanctioned by various national
and international athletic associations, governing bodies, and federations.
Some of these championship contests serve as qualifiers for individual athletes seeking to be named to their Olympic teams.

Sporting competition is not limited to so-called able-bodied athletes. The
[firs]t organized international competition for wheelchair athletes took place
[dur]ing the day of the opening ceremony for the 1948 London Olympic
[Ga]mes. By 1960, the Olympic movement embraced four hundred athletes
[fro]m twenty-three countries at the first official Paralympic Games held in
[R]ome. The winter Paralympic Games began in 1976 and were staged in
[S]weden.

While there is little disagreement about the Olympic Games playing a significant role in the globalization of sports, it does not stand alone as the only major international athletic movement. The World Cup soccer (or football as it is known outside the United States) finals involve thirty-two countries competing as national teams in various cities within a host country every four years. Television viewership for the World Cup finals exceeds that for the summer Olympic Games. World Cup soccer championships are held for both men and women national teams.

In 1978, forty-eight years after the first World Cup finals for men, fifteen swimmers, runners, and cyclists gathered on the shores of Waikiki Beach in Hawaii for the launch of the initial IRONMAN triathlon. Today, across the world, more than a million athletes participate in the sport of triathlon annually.

The sports of soccer and triathlon are among the fifty-six official sports in the modern Olympics. French nobleman **Baron Pierre de Coubertin** spearheaded the international movement to revive the Olympics. According to historical records, the initial Olympic Games began in 776 BC on the ancient plains of Olympia. The early Olympic Games began with twenty sports open only to men, who prepared rigorously, and not always ethically, for the chance for victory and immortality through poems and statues. The Roman emperor Theodosius banned the games in 393 AD, cursing them as pagan cults.

Coubertin's reason for creating the modern Olympic Games was to promote physical education for men by positioning the sport as a model for peace and harmony. In 1896, 13 nations sent 280 male athletes, who competed in 43 events at the first modern Olympics. By 1924, the popularity of the games exploded: 44 nations, 3,000 athletes (100-plus women), and a closing ceremony, for the first time. The summer Olympic Games today draw more than 11,000 professional and amateur, male and female competitors from 200 countries. Any new sport added to the Olympics must provide for female competition.

As part of the new Olympic movement, Coubertin needed to invent an organization to draft rules, policies, and procedures. In 1894, the French Union des Sports Athletiques created the **International Olympic Committee (IOC)**, which became the official governing body for this modern international sports competition and movement.

The IOC has found itself in the thicket of contentious legal, cultural, and political controversies. Beyond discussions centered on whether women could participate, the evolution of athletes performing for the joy of a sport to full-time, twelve-months-a-year professionals raised the issue of whether to permit paid athletes to compete. A politically inspired boycott of the Olympic Games in 1980 by Eastern Bloc communist countries, and the US boycott in 1984, occurred despite the fact the that IOC and the Olympic Games are nonpolitical entities. IOC Charter Rule 40, which prevents athletes from promoting or advertising, including via Facebook, blog, Instagram, or Twitter, non-official-sponsor product brands during the games, is under attack by current Olympians.

Disturbing or controversial issues involving performance-enhancing drugs, gender variance, homophobic policies, cheating among judges, bribing referees, corruption within sports-governing bodies, politics of host-city selection, coaches sexually abusing prodigy athletes, eligibility, and due process rights for athletes are serious and sometimes grievous, not fully resolved, global sports issues. Deciding these cases when they implicate governing bodies and federations from different nations with diverse and conflicting laws and customs remains a challenge.

MISSION AND STRUCTURE OF THE IOC AND RELATED GOVERNING BODIES

According to the *IOC charter*, the mission of the IOC is to serve as the supreme authority of the *Olympic movement*. The IOC is a private, nonprofit society registered under the laws of Switzerland. The official headquarters of the IOC is located in Lausanne, Switzerland. The charter governs the IOC's overall operations and organization.

By definition, the Olympic movement includes the following: **international federations (IFs)**; **national Olympic committees (NOCs)**; organizing committees of the Olympic Games (OCOGs); **national associations or national governing bodies (NGBs)**; and, most particularly, the athletes themselves. Collectively, these assorted federations, organizations, and governing bodies, along with the athletes, coaches, judges, media, broadcast partners, numerous United Nations agencies, and sponsors, comprise the operational Olympic movement responsible for promoting the values and success of the games. The IOC charter forms the basis of Olympic international sport law.

To fully appreciate the reach and context of the Olympic movement and Olympic competition, one must comprehend how the regulatory governing bodies structurally relate. Using the sport of swimming as an example, figure 3.1 illustrates their interconnectedness. Every sport within the Olympic movement is served by an IF, which must act in accordance with the Olympic charter. The IF establishes and enforces the global technical rules for that particular sport. It also administers a sport's world championships by establishing the minimum requirements for participation, lists the events contested, ascertains rules for each athletic activity, chooses a host site, and names officials and referees. All IFs are nongovernmental agencies.

You may remember the controversy surrounding competitive swimmers wearing a patented high-tech full-body bathing suit known as the LZR Racer Suit at the 2008 summer Olympics in Beijing. Marketed by Speedo as the "world's fastest suit," it was worn by Michael Phelps, who impressively and majestically won a record-setting eight gold medals. World records were broken in twenty-three of the twenty-five contested swimming events at the Beijing Olympics. Swimmers wearing the acclaimed Speedo drag-efficient suit set all the records.

Originally, the international federation governing the sport of swimming, known as the **International Swimming Federation (FINA)**, or Fédération Internationale de Natation, approved the LZR Racer Suit and other neck-to-ankles bathing suits constructed with similar fabric. World and national records continued to fall at swimming events after the 2008 Olympics. Critics charged that wearing the impermeable suit was a form of "technology doping." Concerns were raised that only swimmers from wealthy nations could afford these expensive suits, putting athletes from lesser-developed or less financially well-off countries at a distinct competitive disadvantage.

At the 2009 World Aquatic Championships, FINA reversed course and banned all full-body suits for men. Effective 2010, the new regulations forbade the wearing of any bathing suit not made from a woven material or fabric for men and women in FINA-authorized international swim races,

Banning of full Bod Suits for Swimming

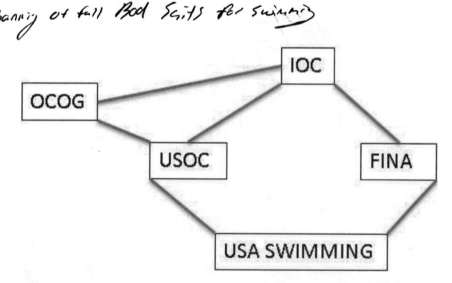

Figure 3.1.   IOC: International Olympic Committee; FINA: Fédération Internationale de Natation (International Swimming Federation); USOC: US Olympic Committee (a national Olympic committee); USA Swimming: the national governing body for swimming in the United States; OCOG: local community organizing committee for the Olympic Games.

including the Olympics. Not long thereafter, USA Swimming, the NGB for the sport of swimming in the United States, voted to ban the high-technology suits in domestic competition.

The **US Olympic Committee (USOC)**, a private nonprofit organization, serves as the official NOC body for the Olympic movement in the United States. It is legally bound to the principles and rules enunciated in the IOC charter. The USOC assists athletes, coaches, and administrators through its NGBs. Support includes providing altitude-training facilities in Colorado Springs (CO); financial aid for national team members; and elite performance services comprising sports medicine, sports psychology, nutrition guidance, conditioning, and performance-enhancing technology.

In addition to promoting the development of US athletes and coaches, as part of its Olympic responsibilities, it nominates host cities for selection by the IOC. In conjunction with the NGBs, the USOC decides the athletes who will participate in the Olympic Games as members of Team USA. The USOC is one of 205 NOCs.

Returning to a competitive swimming example, USA Swimming, acting in accordance with the substantive and procedural requirements of the **Ted Stevens Olympic and Amateur Sports Act**, chooses the swimmers to compete at the Olympics from a winner-take-all Olympic trials. The swimming trials are conducted a few months before the games. The names of the top two performers who are US citizens at the trials for each of the twenty-six individual swimming events for men and women who meet FINA's qualifying time standards are forwarded to the USOC. FINA also permits one relay entry per country for each of the six relay events—three relays for men and three relays for women.

Usually the USOC accepts the outcome of the NGB process and procedure for deciding which athletes represent the United States at the Olympic Games. There are exceptions. In 2008, Jessica Hardy, after earning two coveted individual Olympic swimming spots, learned from the **US Anti-Doping Agency (USADA)** she tested positive for a low level of a banned substance at the trials. Hardy was automatically subject to a two-year ban from swimming unless she successfully appealed her positive drug test. Ultimately, she withdrew her name from the team, which allowed USA Swimming and the USOC to designate a substitute swimmer.

Hardy's decision to withdraw saved the USOC from publicly declining her. A more complex matrix occurred four years earlier. Tammy Cox, a synchronized swimmer, earned a spot on the Olympic Team based on her performance. A year before the trials, she was operating a motor vehicle apparently under the influence of some level of alcohol when it crashed, killing her two passengers.

After the trials' competition but *before* the Olympic Games in Athens, she elected not to contest two misdemeanor counts of vehicular homicide at trial.

The state judge found her guilty. Her ninety-day sentence was delayed until about a month after the games were concluded. The USOC, which has the legal right to reflectively review and reject a qualifier, named her to the US Olympic Team roster over vociferous objections that her conduct was inconsistent with the *core* Olympic movement values of *respect, friendship,* and *excellence.* Unfortunately for other members of the US synchronized swimming team at the Olympics, the controversy surrounding Cox's selection became a distraction during the games because of media attention on the incident.

It is not always achievable for governing bodies to swiftly and accurately resolve disputes and disagreements. For instance, at the 2014 World Cup finals in Brazil, the international governing body for the sport of soccer suffered criticism for failing to quickly act when Mexican and Brazilian fans chanted an alleged homophobic slur, "puto," during an opposing team's goal kicks. Soccer's worldwide governing body, the **Fédération Internationale de Football Association (FIFA)**, was prompted to investigate the national soccer federations of Brazil and Mexico after an antidiscrimination group monitoring abusive fan behavior reported the chants.

FIFA's statutes bar discriminatory conduct against any person playing or fans watching soccer on account of race; skin color; ethnic, national, or social origin; gender; language; religion; political opinion or any other opinion; wealth; birth or any other status; sexual orientation; or any other reason. Offending fans are subject to expulsion. Teams are exposed to point reductions.

Mexican soccer officials claimed that the chants were not offensive and popular at national professional soccer matches. Policing and preventing overt acts of racism directed at players of color at European and World Cup soccer matches remains a longstanding test. The failure to condemn and stop offensive and illegal practices may serve as an invitation for the behavior to continue.

Perhaps no professional athlete has suffered the indignities of disgusting and disturbing racist and sexist remarks more than Serena Williams and her sister, Venus. In the words of sociologist Della Douglas, sports commentators and social media users frequently attribute their tennis athleticism simply to their ethnicity (Sociology of Sport Online). In particular, inappropriate public scrutiny and sexualization of Serena's body size and shape continues even as she closes in on Steffi Graf's record of twenty-two Grand Slam tennis wins. Recently, the president of the Russian Tennis Federation referred to the Williams sisters as "brothers." Besides being publicly condemned for his comments, the World Tennis Association (WTA) banned the official from the women's tennis tour for a year and fined him $25,000.

Meanwhile, on a different front, FIFA for a number of years has had to deal with a string of embarrassing and purportedly illegal incidents of bribery

[handwritten: sisters being called out & scrutinized in tennis globally b/c they are Black]

related to voting members allegedly offering to sell or trade their votes for past and present World Cup bids, extending to the selection of Qatar as the host site for the 2022 World Cup. In the wake of these initial bribery accusations, which were largely addressed internally by FIFA, the players' union for professional soccer players asked the organizers to grant players a greater voice in World Cup host country selection. However, in 2015, the scandal took a completely different turn and reerupted globally when the US Department of Justice accused FIFA of "rampant, systematic and deep-rooted corruption" and indicted several leading soccer officials and sports marketing representatives tied to FIFA. A handful of prominent soccer figures entered guilty pleas. Separate criminal probes by Swiss, Brazilian, and other FIFA countries' officials have led to further indictments and arrests for misconduct amid charges of money laundering as well. The longstanding president of FIFA, Joseph "Sepp" Blatter, who has denied any wrongdoing, was forced to resign.

TED STEVENS OLYMPIC AND AMATEUR SPORTS ACT

Sports controversies occur not solely at the global leadership level. For example, in the United States, athletes have complained for years about the limited participation rights and lack of legal protection for individual competitors. The leading case that deals with the exclusive authority of the USOC to regulate Olympic sports, and the athletes that compete within this framework, is *DeFrantz v. USOC* (492 F.Supp. 1181, D.D.C. 1980).

In 1979, the former Soviet Union invaded Afghanistan. President Jimmy Carter organized an international boycott of the 1980 Olympic Games in Moscow as a means of protesting the military incursion by the Soviets. Neither the president nor Congress had the legal authority to decide whether to send US Olympic athletes to the Moscow summer Olympic Games. The US State Department, though, informed the USOC that any athletes who traveled to Moscow to compete would be stripped of their passports. In response, twenty-five athletes sued the USOC to stop it from carrying out a decision not to send an Olympic team to participate in the 1980 summer Olympics in Moscow. The **Amateur Sports Act of 1978**, later amended and renamed the Ted Stevens Olympic and Amateur Sports Act, assigned to the USOC complete responsibility of all matters related to the United States competing in the Olympic Games (and Paralympics and Pan American Games). The court found that the USOC did not exceed its congressional-mandated statutory powers when it succumbed to unprecedented political pressure from Vice President Mondale on behalf of President Carter and the State Department to withhold participation.

Less than a decade later, the US Supreme Court affirmed the reach of the USOC's powers when it acknowledged that this same act granted it exclusive property rights in the word *Olympic* and the associated symbol of five inter-locking rings. The case began when a San Francisco–based organization began promoting the "Gay Olympic Games" over the USOC's objection to the use of the word *Olympics*. The USOC and its affiliated NGBs are non-government actors, so all discrimination and equal protection arguments were summarily dismissed (*San Francisco Arts & Athletics v. USOC*, 483 U.S. 522, 1987).

In contrast, the USOC approved the right to use the word *Olympics* to the Special Olympics organization, a global sports-empowering organization for people with intellectual disabilities pioneered by Eunice Kennedy Shriver.

In 1992, President Clinton signed the Ted Stevens Olympic and Amateur Sports Act into law. Key components of the revised statute are the extensive expansion of due process rights for athletes, especially in resolving disputes, by establishing grievance procedures, including a hearing before impartial fact-finders with the right to ask questions, present evidence, and appeal an adverse finding, and granting athletes 20-percent voting rights on any board or committee within their NGBs. These legal rights are significant because the nongovernmental nature of the NGBs and the USOC means athletes otherwise lack meaningful constitutional protections from arbitrary and potentially unfair decisions.

Truly one of the most bizarre disputes dealing with an athlete's right to a hearing regarding eligibility arose when figure skater Tanya Harding alleged-ly helped "mastermind" a violent clubbing on a fellow skater, Nancy Kerri-gan. Harding's bodyguard attacked Kerrigan at the 1994 national skating championships, which served as a component of the selection process for determining members of the Olympic Team. Kerrigan's injury prevented her from competing, leaving an opening for Harding to win the title and seal a berth on the Olympic Team.

US Figure Skating Association (USFSA), the sport's US national gov-erning body, convened an ethics violation hearing against Harding a month after the incident but before it officially placed her name before the USOC. The panel, without hearing from Harding, found reasonable grounds for a violation. Under the Ted Stevens Olympic and Amateur Sports Act, she was entitled to a hearing with the assistance of legal counsel *no sooner* than thirty days from the panel's findings.

The *earliest* appeals hearing date was to assemble *after* the start of the winter Olympic figure-skating events in Lillehammer, Norway. Fearing a civil lawsuit claiming loss of endorsements and performance should USFSA withhold Harding's name, the national governing body elected to submit her name as an Olympic figure-skating team member, along with Kerrigan's.

Meanwhile, the USOC decided to commence its own disciplinary hearing, apart from both the USFSA's actions and a state criminal investigation. This hearing was slated to begin a week before the start of the Olympic skating competition. Harding filed for immediate injunctive relief in her home state of Oregon to halt the proceedings. The presiding judge indicated that the USOC's disciplinary rules applied to conduct while a person was a member of the US Olympic Team, not prior to being named to the team.

The USOC dropped its pending hearing. Harding was permitted to compete and placed eighth. Kerrigan captured a silver medal before a global television audience of millions. Harding later pled guilty to criminal charges. Her misconduct violations led to a lifetime ban from figure skating by the USFSA. Kerrigan has refused to speak to Harding.

ARBITRATION OF DISPUTES

A 1990s jurisdiction and discipline controversy regarding a world-record-setting US sprinter led to major procedural improvements over handling Olympic-related disputes. In an all-too-familiar fact pattern, the runner "Butch" Reynolds tested positive for the banned steroid nandrolone at a track meet in Monte Carlo. Track's international federation, the **International Amateur Athletic Federation (IAAF)**, immediately imposed a two-year ban. In addition, it threatened to bar from Olympic competition any athlete who might compete in an event Reynolds enters, which was not an uncommon practice at that time.

Reynolds initially sought relief in a federal district court. He then reversed course after realizing an athlete must first exhaust administrative remedies before seeking judicial intervention. He submitted his case before an arbitrator, who found strong evidence that the urine tested was not his. The IAAF refused to acknowledge the arbitrator's findings because it was not conducted under the auspices of its rules and procedures.

Meanwhile, following the protocol of the Amateur Sports Act, Reynolds appealed to his US national track-governing body. After a further hearing, it, too, raised "substantial doubt of the validity of (Reynolds's) drug test." Once more, the IAAF failed to accept these findings. Instead, it conducted its own hearing and determined the initial drug test was valid. Reynolds's two-year ban was upheld, which theoretically prevented him from competing in the 1992 Olympics in Barcelona.

Reynolds filed a federal lawsuit against both his national and international track federations, seeking the right to compete in the Olympics and damages for defamation or harm to reputation and loss of business opportunities. The case worked its way to the US Supreme Court. In a favorable judgment, he was permitted to participate in the Olympic trials. He failed in his bid to finish among the top qualifiers.

Reynolds's complicated administrative and judicial steps to seek a fair and impartial hearing that all Olympic bodies recognize, alongside the Harding case, demonstrated the need for an alternative adjudication process.

In 1983, prior to these two cases, the IOC established the **Court of Arbitration for Sport (CAS)** as an arm of the IOC to resolve Olympic-related controversies. Its close association with the IOC led to charges of political influence, lack of fairness, and conflicts of interest. In response to this criticism, the CAS became part of the **International Council of Arbitration for Sport (ICAS)** eleven years later.

Despite the word *court* in its name, the CAS is closer to an arbitration tribunal. Its three hundred arbitrators are geographically and culturally diverse and trained experts in international sports law. The CAS's forum serves as the final arbitrator in Olympic and international sports disputes. All international sports federations, except one, and the IOC have agreed to the CAS's jurisdiction. By rule the NGBs for each IF, and their athletes, must submit all disputes with their IFs to the CAS for resolution. There is no appeal from the CAS's findings. The typical CAS dispute is resolved in four to five months.

Substantive international sports conflicts that the CAS frequently is asked to resolve either through arbitration or mediation involve such matters as sponsorship disputes, questions about an athlete's eligibility or selection, and disagreements concerning competition results. During the 2004 Athens Olympics, US gymnast Paul Hamm won the all-around gold medal. Later, it was discovered judges incorrectly reduced the score of South Korea's Yang Tae Young. This inadvertent error led to Tae Young receiving the bronze medal instead of the gold.

On behalf of the South Korean gymnast, the Korean Olympic Committee unsuccessfully appealed to the USOC to voluntarily correct the scoring mistake and ask Hamm to return his gold medal to Tae Young as a demonstration of "fair play" to the world. The Korean Olympic Committee, upon learning of the USOC's rejection of its proposal, turned to the CAS. The arbitration panel as a matter of policy elected to dismiss the appeal. It ruled the court might interfere with an error only when it is "tainted by fraud or arbitrariness or corruption" (*Yang Tae Young v. International Gymnastics Federation*, Arbitration CAS 2004/A/704, Award of October 21, 2004).

In response to timely controversies occurring on the brink of the start of the games that need immediate resolution, the CAS created a special **ad hoc division** to hear urgent cases for each Olympic summer and winter games that arise during or ten days before the start of the Opening Ceremony.

At the recent 2014 Sochi Olympics, the CAS ad hoc division heard four cases. In perhaps the most intriguing of the controversies, the CAS was asked to decide a novel question. The issue arose when a skier received an e-mail from her NGB that suggested she might be named to Austria's Winter Olympic Team. She argued the correspondence raised a "legitimate expectation" of participating. Ultimately, the Austrian ski governing body selected a younger skier after it was determined she lacked the requisite technical skill to compete in the half-pipe freestyle event. The CAS determined the decision was not "arbitrary, unfair or unreasonable."

The CAS cases that draw the most attention involve matters related to the transfer of soccer players' contracts and doping or performance-enhancing-drug issues. The latter subject is more fully discussed in the next chapter. The Brazilian soccer player Matuzalem allegedly violated the terms of his contract when he unilaterally breached it by signing with another soccer club. FIFA rules on the status and transfer of players require a breaching player to pay financial compensation to the club he left without permission. The CAS determined that, in the interest of contract stability, or what lawyers call the sanctity of a contract, FIFA rules regarding transfer of players are necessary and not unreasonable in this instance. The amount of damages due is determined on a case-by-case basis. Matuzalem, the athlete, together with the club that illegally signed him to the contract, was ordered to pay more than $13 million.

The Matuzalem case is distinguishable from a European Court of Justice (ECJ) decision holding that FIFA's transfer fee rules in some instances violate the freedom of movement guaranteed by the Treaty of Rome. Unless the professional soccer clubs demonstrate that the transfer fees one club must pay another club when a player moves from team to team have a legitimate objective, such as compensation for expenses related to training young soccer players, then the fees are illegal (*Union Royale Belge des Societes de Football Association, Royal Club Liegois, and Union des Associations Europeennes de Football [UEFA] v. Jean-Marc Bosman*, Case C-415/93, European Court of Justice, December 15, 1995). Both rulings carry immense significance in the contract world of international professional soccer.

MEDIA AND BROADCAST RIGHTS

The magazine *Bloomberg Businessweek* likes to refer to cable broadcaster ESPN as the "Everywhere Sports Profit Network." Emerging from a small investment from Getty Oil built around broadcasting Australian Rules Football, ESPN has become among the most profitable television networks in history.

ESPN's business strategy begins by paying top dollar for the rights to big-ticket sporting events that attract a mass global audience. Incorporating a variety of media platforms—television, broadband Internet, radio, and mobile telephony—it effectively packages, promotes, and influences the way audiences consume sports as entertainment.

More than one-half of all the live sports watched in the United States are seen on ESPN. It owns some aspect of the broadcast rights to Major League Soccer, all four Grand Slam tennis championships, golf's British Open, the MLB, the NFL, and the NBA. One hundred million dollars was spent for the limited broadcast rights in English in the United States for the last two FIFA World Cups. The Connecticut-based broadcaster eked out a small profit on its $1.28 billion investment in the 2012 London Olympic Games.

ESPN or any broadcaster acquires the broadcast licensing rights from the *copyright* owner of the "sport." Under the terms of a 1961 international law, the **International Convention for the Protection of Performers, Producers of Phonograms, and Broadcasting Organizations (Rome Convention)**, licensed broadcasters have exclusive right to rebroadcast original programming for twenty years.

The IOC owns the global media rights for the Olympic Games. The IOC sold the Japanese radio, Internet, mobile, and television rights for two winter and two summer Olympic Games through 2014 for $1 billion. South Korea hosts the 2018 winter Olympics, and Tokyo hosts the 2020 summer Olympics. NBC paid a record $7.75 billion to the IOC to extend its US broadcasting rights through 2032.

Sponsorship arrangements can follow broadcasting deals. The Japanese tire manufacturer Bridgestone became a global Olympic sponsor through 2024 after agreeing to pay $344 million to the IOC. Panasonic is another major Japanese-based company that signed up as an international sponsor.

Beyond the Olympics, STAR Sports, an Asian media company, acquired the rights from the International Hockey Federation (IHF) to broadcast international hockey from 2015 until the end of 2022 in more than two hundred countries. National Football League (NFL) fans in Europe can watch selected US football games on FOX International Channels. The global sports-governing body for triathlon, the **International Triathlon Union (ITU)**, reached a multiyear, multiplatform arrangement to broadcast international triathlon events in the United States with Universal Sports Network. During the four-year cycle leading up to and including the 2014 World Cup final, FIFA earned more than $5.7 billion. FIFA's major television sponsors, known as "partners," are Coke, Adidas, Hyundai, Emirates, Visa, and Sony. The effect the criminal indictments of former and current soccer officials and sports-marketing executives might have on future sponsorships of World Cup events is unclear. In the future, advertisers might seek to insert a "morals" clause in their contracts as leverage to pull out of a sponsoring arrangement should their brand reputations suffer at the hands of criminal behavior by sports-governing officials.

According to the World Intellectual Property Organization (WIPO), the sale of broadcasting and media rights is the largest source of revenue for most sports organizations. In the case of the Olympics, broadcast funds are split among the host organizing committee, the IOC, international federations, and national Olympic committees.

Revenue generated from licensed live coverage of sporting events is threatened by signal privacy. The various global sports organizations working with the WIPO aim to design international legal frameworks that protect against theft of digital broadcast signals. A long-awaited opinion from the US Supreme Court held that an innovative cloud technology firm violated copyright laws by delivering network broadcasting, including sports shows over the public airways, to its paid subscribers over the Internet. It was the Internet start-up firm Aereo that failed to pay transmission fees to the major network broadcasters as required by federal law.

Overall Issues

SUMMARY

The global popularity growth in competing, hosting, and watching sports has given rise to challenging domestic and international legal issues. The legal relationship between an athlete and the assorted governing bodies having jurisdiction over matters ranging from eligibility, rules of the sport, and dispute resolution is ever evolving. Due process rights of US athletes are favorably recognized under the Ted Stevens Olympic and Amateur Sports Act. At the Olympic level of competition, the CAS is the final arbitrator of Olympic controversies.

While the leading international and national sports-governing bodies are all private entities, they are still subject to the rules, customs, and laws of where they conduct events and engage in business activity. The behavior of some FIFA officials, past and present, related to allegations of accepting bribes to determine World Cup host city sites and laundering money via US banks has led to unprecedented criminal indictments and pleas. The criminal charges' effect on sponsorship and broadcast rights of future World Cup soccer games is undetermined at this time.

KEY WORDS

Ad Hoc Division. A special division of the CAS created to hear urgent cases for each summer and winter Olympic Games that arise during the ten days before the start of the Opening Ceremony.

Amateur Sports Act of 1978. Now known as the Ted Stevens Olympic and Amateur Sports Act.

Coubertin, Baron Pierre de. A French nobleman who spearheaded the international movement to revive the modern Olympics.

Court of Arbitration for Sport (CAS). Organization set up as an alternative adjudication process for the IOC. Its close association with the IOC led to charges of political influence, lack of fairness, and conflicts of interest. Eleven years after its inception, the CAS became a part of ICAS.

Fédération Internationale de Football Association (International Association of Federation Football; FIFA). The governing body of all international football- and soccer-related events, including the World Cup.

International Amateur Athletic Federation (IAAF). International federation for track-and-field and running events.

International Council for Arbitration for Sport (ICAS). ICAS is closer to an arbitration tribunal. Its three hundred arbitrators are geographically and culturally diverse and trained experts in international sports law. The ICAS's forum serves as the final arbitrator in Olympic and international sports disputes.

International Federation (IF). Each Olympic sport has an IF specifically governing its rules.

International Olympic Committee (IOC). The international governing body of the Olympics.

International Swimming Federation (FINA). Fédération Internationale de Natation; internationally recognized governing body of aquatic events.

International Triathlon Union (ITU). The global sports-governing body for triathlon.

National Governing Body (NGB). Each nation's individual governing body for a sport.

National Olympic Committee (NOC). Each nation's individual governing body for the Olympics.

Rome Convention for the Protection of Performers, Producers of Phonograms, and Broadcasting Organizations. This convention licensed broadcasters to have exclusive rights to rebroadcast original programming for twenty years.

Ted Stevens Olympic and Amateur Sports Act. Assigned to the USOC complete responsibility of all matters related to the United States competing in the Olympic Games (and Paralympics and Pan American Games).

United States Anti-Doping Agency (USADA). Created in 2000 as an independent anti-doping agency for Olympic sports in the United States. It is charged with testing, educating, researching, and adjudicating doping-related issues for US Olympic, Paralympic, and Pan American athletes.

US Figure Skating Association (USFSA). The sport of skating's US national governing body.

US Olympic Committee (USOC). US governing body of the Olympics.

World Intellectual Property Organization (WIPO). An agency within the United Nations that specializes in the protection of international intellectual property.

DISCUSSION QUESTIONS

1. Q: What is the mission of the IOC?
A: According to the IOC charter, the mission of the IOC is to serve as the supreme authority of the Olympic movement.

2. Q: Who is credited with reviving the modern Olympic Games?
A: French nobleman Baron Pierre de Coubertin spearheaded the international movement to revive the Olympics.

3. Q: The ancient Olympics began and ended when?
A: According to historical records, the initial Olympic Games began in 776 BC on the ancient plains of Olympia. The Roman emperor Theodosius banned the games in 393 AD, cursing them as pagan cults.

4. Q: How many sports were originally played in the ancient Olympics?
A: The early Olympic Games began with twenty sports open only to men.

5. Q: How many official sports are in the modern Olympics?
A: There are fifty-six official sports in the modern Olympics.

6. Q: What was the ultimate decision in regards to swimmers' use of full-body suits?
A: At the 2009 World Aquatic Championships, FINA reversed course and banned all full-body suits for men. Effective 2010, the new regulations forbade the wearing of any bathing suit not made from a woven material or fabric for men and women in FINA-authorized international swim races, including the Olympics. Not long thereafter, USA Swimming, the NGB for the sport of swimming in the United States, voted to ban the high-technology suits in domestic competition.

7. Q: What are the key components of the Ted Stevens Olympic and Amateur Sports Act?
A: Key components of the revised statute are the extensive expansion of due process rights for athletes, especially in resolving disputes, by establishing grievance procedures, including a hearing before impartial fact-finders

with the right to ask questions, present evidence, and appeal an adverse finding, and granting athletes 20-percent voting rights on any board or committee within their NGBs.

8. Q: How long does it take for a typical CAS dispute to be resolved?
   A: The typical CAS dispute is resolved in four to five months.

9. Q: Which CAS cases draw the most attention?
   A: The CAS cases drawing the most attention involve matters related to the transfer of soccer players' contracts and doping or performance-enhancing-drug issues.

10. Q: For international and US athletes, which act handles due process rights, and which organization is the final arbitrator of Olympic controversies?
   A: Due process rights of US athletes are favorably recognized under the Ted Stevens Olympic and Amateur Sports Act. At the Olympic level of competition, the CAS is the final arbitrator of Olympic controversies.

11. Q: How are broadcast funds split in the case of the Olympics?
   A: In the case of the Olympics, broadcast funds are split among the host organizing committee, the IOC, international federations, and national Olympic committees.

Chapter Four

Performance-Enhancing Drugs and Testing

"If people think I cheated to win the Tour de France, they're f——ing dumb. All two hundred guys that started the race broke the rules. We all would have lied. You would have lied."—Lance Armstrong in *Cycle of Lies*

The subject of *testing* athletes for performance-improving drugs is fairly new to amateur and professional sports. The *use* of magic hallucinogens, stimulants, animal potions, and other medications to improve athletic performance is not new.

The Greeks who participated in the ancient Olympic Games (776 BC–393 AD) were among the first documented athletes to experiment with herbal medications, drink wine potions, and ingest other substances to gain a competitive advantage. In what may be a surprise to some, the early Olympians and the organizers of the games did not discourage the use of supplemental herbs and ergogenic substances to help the athletes run faster, throw farther, fight off fatigue, and enhance the ferocity of their athletic battles.

Concerns over the availability and acceptability of consuming external ingredients to gain a competitive edge in sports began to rise dramatically in the mid-1980s. It was at that time that physicians began to speak publicly about the prevalence of steroids, stimulants, diuretics, and peptide hormones in sport and their potential harmful side effects. Elite athletes from Western countries observed extraordinary feats of speed and strength, especially by female Olympic athletes from the Iron Curtain countries of East Germany, Romania, and others, and questioned the legitimacy of many of their astounding results. The playing field did not appear to be level anymore. Unfortunately, at the time, testing methods limited the capacity of officials to detect serious drug abuse beyond alcohol and tranquilizers in most cases.

The language of drug abuse practices started to become part of the vernacular of sports officials and athletes. One of the first popular terms was *doping*. It refers to using a substance (e.g., anabolic steroid) or technique (e.g., blood doping) during training or competition to gain a physical or mental advantage over an opponent. *Doping*, now with negative connotations, became part of the lexicon of sports.

In 1928, the first rules prohibiting doping in sports were enacted by the sport of track and field. The IAAF, forerunner organization to the current international federation for track and field, banned a practice that is now called doping forty years before the IOC established the first testing require-ic Games. It is reported that a popular soft drink during the middle of the twentieth century to oca leaf (cocaine) and coffee beans (caffeine) mixed with alcohol. After a prominent cyclist died from a drug overdose of alcohol and amphetamines during the Tour de France in 1967, the IOC created the Medical Commission to investigate and recommend steps to prevent doping at the Olympics. In 1968, the IOC instituted mandatory drug testing for alcohol and stimulants. Advancements in testing protocol led to the inclusion of anabolic steroids to the list of banned substances years later. In 1988, Canadian sprinter **Ben Johnson** became the most famous Olympic athlete to lose a gold medal for racing with illegal anabolic steroids in his system.

Meanwhile, a 1969 investigative journalism story in *Sports Illustrated* discovered that there was "not a single major U.S. sporting organization, amateur or professional" with explicit anti-doping policies and enforcement apparatus. The NCAA initiated a modest drug-testing program in 1986. The National Football League (NFL) reluctantly instituted its own testing initiative for selective drugs, excluding steroids, a few years earlier. The failure of Major League Baseball (MLB) to test for performance-enhancing drugs until 2003 led to the scandalous "**steroid era**," which resulted in unprecedented increases in offensive output and widespread charges of duplicitous conduct as attendance at games soared.

Nowadays, taking illicit drugs that range from tranquilizers ingested by modern pentathlon athletes to human growth hormones (HGH) consumed by high school football players to gain a competitive advantage is universally viewed as a form of cheating. The modern-day poster child for a once-inspiring athlete who misled sponsors, foundations, fans, and race organizers about his illegal use of erythropoietin (EPO), blood transfusions, and testosterone to win seven Tour de France titles is Lance Armstrong. His devastating legal-induced fall from grace is told in detail later in the chapter.

REGULATORY ENVIRONMENT

Schools

The use of substances, whether injected or consumed, to augment an athlete's ability to perform during training or elite competition is now universally disapproved on ethical, health, and fair-play grounds. All sports organizations at the amateur and professional levels have the legal authority to some degree to discipline and penalize wrongdoers.

The most prevalent method for determining whether an athlete is using artificial means to gain a physical or mental advantage is by requiring mandatory drug testing both in and out of competition. However, telling an athlete to submit a blood sample or "pee" in a bottle raises questions of the constitutional right to privacy, illegal search and seizure, and due process.

In analyzing drug-testing protocols, it is important to distinguish between assessments conducted by a state organization versus a private body. The legality of various testing schemes may vary depending on whether the state actor is a middle school, high school, or college as opposed to a private school, private governing body, or private professional sports league.

For instance, in a landmark opinion involving an Oklahoma public high school's drug-testing policy, the US Supreme Court ruled that high school athletes have a *lower expectation of privacy* than other students. Therefore, even without having to demonstrate a Fourth Amendment *probable cause* of illegal drug use by an athlete before testing, the mandatory testing policy was a legitimate condition for participating in school sports (*Vernonia School District v. Acton*, 515 U.S. 646, 1995).

A few years later, in another case involving a middle and high school in Tecumseh, Oklahoma, Justice Thomas writing for the majority tempered *Vernonia* by holding:

> Within the limits of the Fourth Amendment, local school boards must assess the desirability of drug testing schoolchildren. In upholding the constitutionality of the Policy, we express no opinion as to its wisdom. Rather, we hold only that Tecumseh's Policy is a reasonable means of furthering the School District's important interest in preventing and deterring drug use among its schoolchildren.

Together these cases stand for the proposition that a public school's interest in detecting and discouraging harmful and illegal drug use is a valid public policy purpose (*Board of Education v. Earls*, 536 U.S. 822, 2002).

Previously reviewed cases, including Coach Tarkanian's unsuccessful lawsuit against the NCAA for due process violations, have concluded that courts refuse to classify the NCAA as a state actor because it is registered as a private, nonprofit organization.

Coach Tarkanian! (lawsuit

A lawsuit by students at Stanford University, a private college, challenged the imposition of mandatory drug testing regardless of a lack of finding of probable cause after the NCAA mandated its requirement for all of its member schools. The case was brought under California's state constitution, which includes a specific inalienable right to privacy provision, unlike the federal constitution. The state Supreme Court first found that California's right-to-privacy clause applies to nongovernment entities, including the NCAA. Next it determined that the manner of gathering urine and other private medical information was not a serious intrusion on privacy. Further, the court ruled that the NCAA has a recognized interest in protecting the health of its student-athletes and in preserving the integrity of intercollegiate sports. Finally, in what some pundits viewed as an unrealistic alternative, the court stated that the student-athletes could always withdraw from competing in college sports and then not face a drug test (*Hill v. NCAA*, 865 P. 2d 633, Cal. 1994).

The NCAA continues to require student-athletes to sign an annual consent form before participating in intercollegiate sports as a condition for eligibility. Appendix A contains a copy of an NCAA drug testing consent form.

Olympics

In 1961, the communist country of East Germany erected a wall separating East Berlin from the democratic West Berlin. Twenty-eight years later, that physical and symbolic barrier was destroyed in a wave of euphoria as the former East Germany collapsed, leading to the reunification of West and East Germany.

Two years thereafter, many members of the Olympic community claimed that they were stunned to learn from former East German swimming coaches that the remarkable international achievements of their female swimmers was the result of a state-supported system of anabolic-steroid doping. No East German swimmer had ever tested positive for a banned substance, even though swimmers and swimming coaches from around the world always suspected that they were not playing fair. Years later, hundreds of East German athletes, especially women, reported serious medical side effects and lasting psychological and physiological injuries.

In light of these events, plus baseball superstar Mark McGwire's admission of ingesting a steroid precursor the year he smashed seventy homeruns, Tour de France blood-doping scandals, public comments by legendary runner and coach Alberto Salazar that it is difficult to finish among the top five in any distance event without consuming EPO or HGH, and a record number of Chinese athletes failing drug tests, a global conference on doping in sports was held in Lausanne, Switzerland, the home of the IOC.

The IOC was forced to address increasing public mistrust in the international sport community's ability and even desire to fight against what was perceived as rampant doping to enhance performance that was free from consequences. In 1999, the conference led to the creation of an international anti-doping agency, the **World Anti-Doping Agency (WADA)**. The purpose of WADA is to internationally promote and coordinate efforts against doping in sports. From its inception, it has had pretty much unqualified support from international sport federations, national governing bodies, the IOC, and national governments. By the start of the summer Athens Olympic Games in 2004, the IOC had transferred complete control over its banned list of drugs to WADA, which now included EPO but not HGH for lack of suitable detection methods.

In 2000, the United States responded to a domestic outcry over lack of credibility, accountability, and transparency in drug protocols by creating its own independent anti-doping agency for Olympic sports, the **US Anti-Doping Agency (USADA)**. Its mandate is to test, educate, research, and adjudicate doping-related issues for US Olympic, Paralympic, and Pan American athletes. Its mission is significantly broader than that of WADA but excludes control over professional sports leagues and teams. The United States has formally incorporated the list of banned substances by WADA to its catalog of prohibited drugs. Every October, WADA, and by correlation the USADA, updates its list of banned substances. *New list every October*

In the United States, the USADA and various international federations perform the actual athletic drug testing for the sports over which they have jurisdiction. Unlike WADA, which does *not* actually test athletes for banned substances, the IOC conducts testing at the Olympics. The private sports organizations that make up the global sports-governance community are compliant of the **World Anti-Doping Code**. The code is the governing document that lists all prohibited substances, articulates the prevailing anti-doping–testing procedures, and identifies the appropriate manner of processing and maintaining the integrity of samples collected.

Professional Sports

A 2002 *Sports Illustrated* article rocked the professional sporting establishment when it reported a claim by 1996 National League MVP **Ken Caminiti** that about half the players in the MLB use steroids. Caminiti admitted to taking cocaine and steroids while playing. Two years after the story was published, Caminiti died at the age of forty-one; drugs were a contributing factor according to the medical examiner.

The task of identifying a list of prohibited substances, designing a sound drug-testing protocol, and creating meaningful rehabilitative and disciplinary policies while preserving a modicum of confidentiality in the world of professional team sports is a dramatically different enterprise than for the Olympics or school athletic events. In professional sports, doping policies and procedures must come about through collective bargaining. The athletes for major professional team sports are employees and members of a union or players' association. Under US federal labor law, the owners or managers of professional teams must *negotiate players' consent by negotiating drug-testing contract terms* and not by unilaterally imposing a consent form. Of course, Congress could always legislatively mandate drug-testing requirements and penalties for professional sport violators.

Professional sports leagues and the unions representing players were slow to the point of being delinquent in their joint failure to responsibly address the escalating drug problem. By drawing public attention to the issue, leagues were fearful of damaging their images and losing their fan bases. On the other hand, the players were worried about loss of privacy, damage to their public reputations, and forfeiture of earnings from suspensions.

Finding a common ground over issues, like which players to test and how often, who conducts the tests, which are banned substances and whether to include so-called recreational drugs, when treatment is preferred over punishment, and if there is a right to challenge a positive finding and subsequent discipline, all proved difficult.

Meanwhile, a number of significant external events were happening outside the collective-bargaining framework. In 2002, Senator John McCain and Senator Byron Dorgan told the commissioner of baseball, Bud Selig, and baseball's union head, Donald Fehr, at a Senate Commerce Committee hearing that they must negotiate a strict drug-testing program in their next collective-bargaining agreement. At the time, the big leagues tested for illicit drugs only upon a prior determination of probable cause to inquire. The MLB players' union and owners, in response, agreed to conduct anonymous pilot random drug testing during the 2003 season without any penalties for positive findings. In a strange quirk, the results of the tests were accidently made public. Not surprisingly, the findings revealed that a large number of major league baseball players were deceitfully using performance-enhancing drugs, which also was adversely affecting the integrity of the game. Meanwhile, according to the *New York Times*, prominent players whose names appeared on the "anonymous" list included David Ortiz and Manny Ramirez of the Boston Red Sox and Alex Rodriguez of the New York Yankees. By 2005, Congress became increasingly worried over baseball's failure to halt the endemic use of steroids and other performance-improving drugs. In addition, members of Congress publicly stated their concerns about the effect steroid abuse in baseball was having on impressionable young athletes in high school and college. As one Congressman related, "Kids aren't just talking about their favorite teams' chances in the pennant race." Today they are just as likely to talk about "which players are on the juice." A Center for Disease

Control's report submitted to Congress supported this public health view. It revealed that 500,000 high school teens had taken steroids, in part, to emulate the performance of their sports heroes.

In 2003, federal investigators raided a California-based laboratory, **Bay Area Laboratory Co-operative (BALCO)**, suspected of providing "designer"—and therefore literally undetectable—steroids for scores of prominent athletes, including Barry Bonds (baseball), Marion Jones (track), and Bill Romanowski (football). The chief executive of BALCO, Victor Conte, and its lead trainer, Greg Anderson, both pleaded guilty to unlawful steroid distribution and money laundering a year later.

Another somber incident that not only went to the heart of reinforcing claims of lax drug protocols by sporting officials in the United States but also supported allegations that positive test results for prohibited drugs were covered up by the USOC was exposed in the **Wade Exum Report**. Exum was a former anti-doping chief for the USOC. The report disclosed the names of more than one hundred US Olympic athletes who had tested positive for banned substances between 1988 and 2000 but were cleared internally by the USOC. Standout track-and-field athlete Carl Lewis, who was awarded the gold medal in the 100-meter Olympic dash after Ben Johnson was disqualified for steroid abuse, was one of the premiere athletes whose name was on the cleared-to-compete list.

In 2004, President George W. Bush signed into law the **Anabolic Steroid Control Act**. This federal statute included testosterone-related substances and steroid-based drugs and precursors, such as the drug Mark McGwire admitted to consuming during his banner hitting season, in the list of substances that are banned from over-the-counter sale without a prescription. Two years later, in 2006, President Bush added gene doping to the list of banned substances. In 2014, the Anabolic Steroid Control Act was amended further to make it illegal to falsely market anabolic steroids as nutritional or dietary supplements.

In response to growing public pressure, in 2006, the commissioner of MLB retained former US senator George Mitchell to independently investigate the use of performance-enhancing drugs in baseball. Baseball's players' union refused to cooperate with Mitchell. After a lengthy investigation, which failed to review the role baseball's team management had in any player abuse of stimulants and steroids, the **Mitchell Report** was released. His scathing 409-page report chronicled the history of performance-enhancing abuse by players; identified 89 doping offenders, such as Barry Bonds, Jason Giambi and Roger Clemens; and outlined preventative practice recommendations.

Collectively, concern mounted to the point where all the major US professional leagues and their players' unions began to seriously improve their identification of substances to test and frequency, methodology, punishment

Chapter 4

for different levels of offenders, due process, and appellate rights through collective-bargaining negotiations. Frankly, part of their fear was that Congress would legislatively impose even stricter standards unless they acted.

For the first time in 2008, the National Association for Stock Car Auto Racing (NASCAR) joined the list of professional sport activities to enact a sweeping anti-doping policy. Crewmembers and racecar drivers were subject to random testing for banned substances and abuse of prescription medications. Four years later, Sprint Cup driver A. J. Allmendinger tested positive for amphetamines and was suspended from competing until he completed NASCAR's Road to Recovery treatment program.

BANNED SUBSTANCES AND METHODS

By definition, the term **prohibited substances** is the list of all drugs, supplements, and other substances and methods that are banned from use in sports. Depending on the sport, and the governing body regulating that sport, there may be different classes of substances or methods of doping that are unacceptable because they artificially and unfairly have the purpose and effect of improving performance. Not all drugs and methods are always illegal. Some drugs are permitted out of competition but not during competition.

There are special situations where use of a banned substance does not constitute a violation. The typical situation occurs when an athlete suffers from a legitimate preexisting medical condition, consults with a medical doctor, and receives a **therapeutic use exemption (TUE)** from his or her governing body. The USADA, for instance, can grant a Team USA Pan American athlete a TUE in compliance with WADA's standards for issuing a TUE.

However, there are growing concerns regarding athletes misusing TUEs to gain an unfair "exempt" competitive advantage. According to the book *Blood Sport: Alex Rodriguez, Biogenesis and the Quest to End Baseball's Steroid Era*, during the 2007 and 2008 seasons, Rodriguez received a TUE to use testosterone, an otherwise prohibited substance under the doping rules of MLB. In 2007, he was named league MVP and led the league in homeruns. Rodriguez then opted out of his contract and signed a new ten-year, $275-million contract with the New York Yankees.

Athletes from the sport of baseball apparently are not alone in seeking exemptions to use erstwhile-banned substances. Based on the latest data from the International Tennis Federation, as reported at http://tennishasasteroidproblem.blogspot.com, about one-half of all the ranked male and female professional tennis players are playing with a TUE.

Increasingly, the blurred boundary between therapeutic drugs and ergogenic or performance-enhancing doping raises concerns about the effective-

ness and costs related to administering and policing anti-doping policies. A minority of medical experts argues that a medically supervised doping policy offers a more sensible, realistic, and less expensive approach to this complex subject. Opponents counter that, by allowing athletes to dope, even under medical supervision, society is altering the traditional values of fair play, sacrifice, and hard work and might set in motion a public health nightmare.

For those athletes who are caught violating doping rules, the typical punishments handed out by a sports body range from loss of medals and world titles to lifetime suspensions from competition for repeat offenders. At the Olympic level, a two-year ban and loss of any medals is the norm. *Two year Ban*

Special circumstances, such as what happened to swimmer Jessica Hardy when it was determined that she accidently ingested a substance containing a banned substance, causing her to fail a drug test, may lead to a reduction in the suspension period. Sadly, in Hardy's case, the banned substance was found in a nutritional supplement supplied by one of her sponsors.

WADA rules on banned substances cover coaches and trainers who supply or support athletes who dope. They, too, are subject to a lifetime ban from coaching in their sports.

The detected presence of a banned substance raises a prima facie case of illegal doping. The burden of disproving or refuting this presumption rests with the athlete. It is not an easy task for an athlete to prove the negative.

Drawing urine is the most common method for testing for a prohibited substance. When urine is collected, it is divided into two samples: A and B. A positive result from the A sample then leads to notification to the athlete before the B sample is tested. This notice allows the athlete the opportunity to be present at the unsealing and second round of testing. Should both samples prove positive, then the relevant sports organization is informed to determine the nature and length of penalties to impose. The results during the testing process are confidential and not publicly disclosed.

A similar procedure of drawing two samples is carried out when blood testing is used to detect such drugs as artificial oxygen carriers and the popular EPO used by endurance athletes. As with the urine-testing protocol, the results remain private until they are disclosed to the appropriate governing body and any discipline is imposed.

A controversial development to the traditional drug testing is the growing use of a **biological passport**, approved in 2011 by WADA. The new passport centers on using long-term blood and steroid profiles of biological drug markers resulting from testing athletes over time. The **"whereabouts" component** of the program, which requires athletes to provide their location on a daily basis and submit to testing anywhere from one hour to twenty-four hours in advance, depending on the regulatory body, is viewed by many athletes as a major invasion to their privacy, especially among older elite athletes with families.

At the international sports level, more than six hundred sports organizations, including the IOC and USOC, have adopted WADA's list of banned substances and methods. The professional sports leagues discussed earlier, including the NFL, MLB, NBA, WNBA, and NHL, along with the NCAA, do not adhere to WADA's list of nearly two hundred banned performance-enhancing substances and methods. Annually, as mentioned earlier, WADA updates the prohibited list in its World Anti-Doping Code.

Instead of identifying prohibited substances by name, WADA lists entire classes of drugs while providing some common names as examples. According to anti-doping experts, the list is provided in this manner to prevent pharmacologists and chemists, as occurred in the BALCO scandal, from creating a hard-to-detect designer drug for an athlete and then having that athlete claim as an affirmative defense when caught that the new, discrete drug was not on the banned list.

Not all substances or methods listed by WADA or various other sports-governing bodies enhance an athlete's ability to focus or perform. There are drugs on the list that may have the potential for being dangerous to an athlete's physical or mental well-being or violate the spirit of the sport. Michael Phelps's three-month suspension from competition by USA Swimming, the national governing body for swimming in the United States, after admitting to smoking marijuana while out of competition is an example of this rule at work.

Here is a list of the major prohibited classes of drugs or substances from WADA; some are prohibited at all times, whereas others are prohibited only during competition. The NCAA's list of prohibited substances provided in an earlier chapter is similar. A complete list can be found at http://list.wada-ama.org:

1. Stimulants (amphetamines, ephedra, cocaine)
2. Narcotics
3. Anabolic agents (steroids)
4. Diuretics and masking agents
5. Human growth hormones (HGH)
6. Erythropoietin (EPO), peptide and glycoprotein hormones, and analogues
7. Cannabinoids

The list of prohibited methods banned at all times include:

1. Blood doping
2. Artificial oxygen carriers
3. Tampering with samples and intravenous infusion
4. Gene doping

At one point, caffeine was banned as an artificial stimulant during competition. Its consumption is now permitted. Depending on the sport, alcohol and beta-blockers are prohibited.

THE LANCE ARMSTRONG SAGA

On August 23, 2012, triathlete-turned-cyclist **Lance Armstrong** was stripped of all seven of his Tour de France cycling titles. The USADA and the international federation governing cycling, Union Cycliste International (UCI), waged an epic legal battle over who had jurisdiction to investigate and punish him for taking banned drugs and using illegal doping methods. Ultimately, UCI conceded and joined USADA's decision to strip the most decorated cyclist in Tour history of his finishes. Armstrong was banned for life from competing in any elite competitive sport, including any sport at the Olympics. He chose not to contest the results before the CAS.

Based on evidence uncovered by USADA, led by its CEO **Travis Tygart**, and supported by Armstrong's own statements, cycling's international federation shares blame for this shame by allegedly assisting Armstrong in "covering up" his doping activities. Some critics claim the UCI, not unlike what occurred in baseball during the steroid era, ignored its own anti-doping rules to protect the sport's superstar and to guard cycling's reputation.

Doping allegations against Armstrong and other cyclists on the famed US Postal Service (USPS) team began in the late 1990s. **Greg LeMond**, the first American to win the Tour de France, publicly raised questions about his doping. Meanwhile, dogged investigative journalists, like David Walsh, wrote that the incredible bike-riding performances were tainted and hollow victories.

Armstrong and his cadre of cycling supporters, including his now-disgraced coach **Johan Bruyneel** and members of his medical staff and fellow riders, for years emphatically professed his innocence. Not infrequently, he sued members of the media who published reports of his use of EPO, testosterone, or blood transfusions.

The riveting story of Armstrong surviving a 50-50 chance of testicular cancer, creating a foundation that has raised more than $500 million for cancer research, and cuddling with singer Sheryl Crow after Tour stage wins came to a crushing end after eleven of his former teammates admitted to the USADA that they, and he, systematically cheated by benefiting from banned substances.

Former teammate **Floyd Landis**, in an interview with ESPN, revealed he won the Tour in 2006 by consuming EPO, HGH, and testosterone and from blood transfusions. He specifically accused Armstrong of orchestrating the team's use of performance-enhancing drugs. Landis was subsequently stripped of his Tour win.

Landis filed a federal whistleblower lawsuit against Armstrong. The federal government joined the lawsuit that claimed the Texas-born cyclist defrauded taxpayers by accepting USPS sponsorship money while engaging in doping and other wrongful conduct.

According to Juliet Macur, award-winning journalist for the *New York Times*, as reported in her book, *Cycle of Lies*, Armstrong stands to lose as much as $135 million from the fraud-related lawsuits brought by insurance companies, sponsors, Landis, and the federal government.

Armstrong's first public admission to having violated the anti-doping rules of professional cycling occurred during his 2013 two-part television interview with Oprah Winfrey. Shortly after Armstrong's calculated mea culpa, he was forced to step aside from his foundation LIVESTRONG. After the USADA report, Nike and other sponsors terminated their contracts.

Veteran sportswriter Rick Reilly may have summed up the public's reaction to Armstrong's years of twisted, deceitful, and harmful lying when he posted the following remark on Twitter: "After years of lying to my face, Lance Armstrong apologizes in an email. He can keep it." The faith of all those who wanted to believe his on- and off-the-bike narrative is now permanently scarred.

Unfortunately, Armstrong was not alone in his doping. The top three finishers in each of his seven Tour de France wins from 1995 to 2005 were all implicated or suspended for using banned substances or methods. Armstrong's sophisticated doping system was merely better than what was in place for his cycling competitors.

SUMMARY

The permissibility of mandatory drug testing for athletes attending state schools or governed by state sports associations as a condition of participation is strongly supported by courts on public health and safety grounds. This constitutionally permissive legal logic extends to the NCAA and its member schools. The lack of privacy occurring during the process of collecting blood or urine is generally viewed as benign.

The long history of undetected doping by Olympic and professional athletes and the win-at-all-costs ethics of such performers as Lance Armstrong and Alex Rodriguez have tainted the victories of honored athletes and brought shame to organizers and managers of numerous teams and sports organizations. Despite the reforms that occurred after IOC investigations, BALCO, and the Mitchell Report, the taking of illegal performance-enhancing drugs continues to plague professional and amateur sports. The growing use of TUEs by athletes raises concerns about a new form of "legalized" banned substance abuse.

At the Olympic level, testing has become more sophisticated through the advent of the biological passports, although the unpopular "whereabouts" contact requirement continues to raise privacy concerns. Professional sport teams in the United States have elected not to embrace the banned-substance list established by WADA and followed by the USADA. Instead, MLB, NFL, NHL, NBA, and WNBA as obligated under federal labor laws have negotiated their own drug-testing rules and punishment schemes.

KEY WORDS

Anabolic Steroid Control Act. Federal statute signed into law by President George W. Bush that included testosterone-related substances and steroid-based drugs and precursors in the list of substances that are banned from over-the-counter sale without a prescription.

Armstrong, Lance. Professional cyclist who was stripped of all seven of his Tour de France wins for use of banned drugs and illegal doping methods.

Bay Area Laboratory Co-operative (BALCO). California-based laboratory suspected of providing designer steroids for scores of prominent athletes.

Biological Passport. The passport centers on using long-term blood and steroid profiles of biological drug markers resulting from testing athletes over time.

Bruyneel, Johan. Lance Armstrong's now-disgraced coach.

Caminiti, Ken. The 1996 National League MVP who claimed in a 2002 *Sports Illustrated* article that half of the players in Major League Baseball have used steroids.

Doping. Refers to the use of a substance or technique during training or competition to gain a physical or mental advantage over an opponent.

Johnson, Ben. Canadian Olympic sprinter who became the most famous Olympic athlete to lose a gold medal for racing with illegal steroids in his system in 1988.

Landis, Floyd. Winner of the 2006 Tour de France who publicly revealed his use of illegal substances and Lance Armstrong's orchestration of the distribution of performance-enhancing drugs. Landis was stripped of his Tour win.

LeMond, Greg. The first American to win the Tour de France; publicly raised questions about doping in cycling.

Mitchell Report. Report issued in 2007 by former Senate leader George Mitchell on the widespread use of performance-enhancing drugs by ballplayers. Eighty-nine players were identified in the report as having used banned substances.

Prohibited Substances. The list of all drugs, supplements, and other substances and methods that are banned from use in sports.

Steroid Era. MLB's failure to test for performance-enhancing drugs until 2003 led to rampant use among players over a lengthy period of time.

Therapeutic Use Exemption (TUE). Situation where an athlete who suffers from a legitimate preexisting medical condition may use a banned substance after consulting with his or her medical doctor and has the exemption approved by the sport's governing body.

Tygart, Travis. CEO of USADA who spearheaded the investigative doping campaign against Lance Armstrong.

United States Anti-Doping Agency (USADA). Created in 2000 as an independent anti-doping agency for Olympic sports in the United States. It is charged with testing, educating, researching, and adjudicating doping-related issues for US Olympic, Paralympic, and Pan American athletes.

Wade Exum Report. Report named after the former anti-doping chief for the USOC that revealed the names of more than one hundred US Olympic athletes who had tested positive for banned substances between 1988 and 2000 but were cleared internationally by the USOC.

" Whereabouts" Component. Requires athletes to provide their location on a daily basis and submit to testing anywhere from one hour to twenty-four hours in advance, depending on the regulatory body.

World Anti-Doping Agency (WADA). The international anti-doping agency whose purpose is to internationally promote and coordinate efforts against doping in sports.

World Anti-Doping Code. Document created by WADA to standardize anti-doping testing procedures, processing, and maintaining the integrity of samples collected.

DISCUSSION QUESTIONS

1. **Q: Who were the first documented athletes to use drugs and other substances to gain a competitive advantage?**

   A: The Greeks who participated in the ancient Olympic Games (776 BC–393 AD) were among the first documented athletes to use drugs and other substances to gain a competitive advantage.

2. **Q: The first rules prohibiting doping in sports occurred when and by whom?**

   A: The IAAF, forerunner to the current international federation for track and field, banned doping forty years before the IOC established the first testing of athletes at the Olympic Games.

3. **Q: Who became the most famous Olympic athlete to lose a gold medal for racing with illegal steroids in his system, and from which nation did he come?**

A: In 1988, Canadian sprinter Ben Johnson lost his gold medal for racing with illegal steroids in his system.

4. Q: What is the best way for determining whether an athlete has used artificial means to gain a physical or mental advantage?

A: The most prevalent method for determining whether an athlete is using artificial means to gain a physical or mental advantage is by requiring mandatory drug testing, both in and out of competition.

5. Q: What was determined in *Vernonia School District v. Acton* , 515 U.S. 646 (1995), and why was it important?

A: *Vernonia School District v. Acton*, 515 U.S. 646 (1995), was a landmark opinion involving an Oklahoma public high school's drug-testing policy. The decision was important because the US Supreme Court ruled that high school athletes have a lower expectation of privacy than other students. Therefore, even without having to demonstrate Fourth Amendment probable cause of illegal drug use by an athlete before testing, the mandatory testing policy was a legitimate condition for participating in school sports.

6. Q: The NCAA's drug-testing consent form requires student-athletes to do what?

A: The NCAA continues to require student-athletes to sign an annual consent form before participating in intercollegiate sports as a condition for eligibility.

7. Q: Which organization conducts testing at the Olympics?

A: The IOC conducts testing at the Olympics. While the USADA and various international federations perform the actual athletic drug testing for the sports they have jurisdiction, it is important to remember that WADA does not test athletes.

8. Q: Can the owners or managers of professional teams use consent forms regarding drug-testing contract terms?

A: Under US federal labor law, the owners or managers of professional teams must negotiate players' consent by negotiating drug-testing contract terms and not by unilaterally imposing a consent form.

9. Q: What events led to congressional hearings on performance-enhancing drugs?

A: In 2005, Congress became concerned about the effect professional athletes who use performance-enhancing drugs might be having on impressionable young people. The decision to conduct a hearing also was sparked by the revelation that a high number of positive anonymous tests occurred among baseball players during the 2003 season.

10. Q: What substance was added to the list of banned substances in 2006?

A: In 2006, President Bush added gene doping to the list of banned substances.

11. Q: What sport joined the list of professional sport activities to enact a sweeping anti-doping policy in 2008?

A: NASCAR joined the list of professional sport activities to enact a sweeping anti-doping policy. Starting in 2008, crewmembers and racecar drivers were subject to random testing for banned substances and abuse of prescription medications.

12. Who received a TUE in 2007 and 2008, and why did it later come under fire?

A: According to the book *Blood Sport: Alex Rodriguez, Biogenesis and the Quest to End Baseball's Steroid Era*, during the 2007 and 2008 seasons, Rodriguez received a TUE to use testosterone, an otherwise banned substance under the doping rules of the MLB. Critics say the Rodriquez case demonstrates an abuse in the approval process for TUEs.

13. Q: What are typical punishments handed out by a sports body for violating prohibited substances or doping rules?

A: Punishments range from loss of medals and world titles to lifetime suspensions from competition for repeat offenders. At the Olympic level, a two-year ban is the norm.

14. Q: What are the most common methods for testing a prohibited substance?

A: Drawing urine is the most common method for testing for a prohibited substance. A procedure of drawing two samples is carried out when blood testing is used to detect such drugs as artificial oxygen carriers and the popular EPO used by endurance athletes.

15. Q: Which organizations do not adhere to WADA's list of banned substances?

A: Professional sports leagues, including the NFL, MLB, NBA, WNBA, and NHL, along with the NCAA, do not adhere to WADA's list of nearly two hundred banned performance-enhancing substances and methods.

16. Q: How does WADA identify prohibited substances?

A: Instead of identifying prohibited substances by name, WADA lists entire classes of drugs while providing some common names as examples.

17. Q: Which methods are banned at all times according to WADA?

A: The list of substances banned at all times includes blood doping, artificial oxygen carriers, tampering with samples and intravenous infusion, and gene doping.

Chapter Five

Governance and Labor Issues in Professional Sports

"If capitalism is fair then unionism must be. If men and women have a right to capitalize their ideas and the resources of their country, then that implies the right of men and women to capitalize their labor."—Frank Lloyd Wright

Historians point to the **Cincinnati Red Stockings**, organized in 1869, as the original professional sport team in the United States to pay its players for performance. Ballplayers shared gate receipts with team owners as they barnstormed across America.

By 1876, the Cincinnati baseball team was joined by teams from Chicago, Boston, Brooklyn, and other major cities to form the first North American professional sports *league*. Many components of this league's bylaws and constitution, including limits on a team moving from city to city, territorial rights for individual teams, and standard contracts for players, remain in place today at the **Major League Baseball (MLB)** level.

In contradiction to the general belief that Jackie Robinson broke the black color barrier in baseball in 1947, African Americans have a long history of playing major and minor league professional baseball, dating back to the late 1800s. Teams labeled them as Native American Indians, Latin Americans, or Mexicans. African American players also had their own barnstorming teams, and in 1920 organized the Negro League. Andrew "Rube" Foster, according to the Negro League Baseball Museum website, is acknowledged as the guiding force in creating a professional baseball league for African American ballplayers when they were barred from playing for MLB teams. Jackie Robinson was recruited to play for the Brooklyn Dodgers from the Kansas City Monarchs, a Negro League team. As more African American players were signed to MLB contracts, black fans began to follow their play, which led to the demise of the Negro League in the early 1960s.

In the early days of professional baseball, to wit, the 1900s, teams and leagues aggressively engaged in stealing each other's best players. At the same time, teams and leagues regularly folded for financial reasons. Ultimately, team owners unilaterally instituted and enforced changes meant to stabilize teams and leagues, which were not to the liking of the players. For instance, a player's contract could be bought and sold without a player's permission, and a restriction on a player's freedom to move from team to team, known as the **reserve clause**, was implemented.

Meanwhile, gamblers began to influence the game of baseball by bribing players. The team owners decided they needed a central authority to enforce league rules and penalize players for unsportsmanlike and illegal conduct. The issue came to a head in 1919, when players from the Chicago White Sox team attempted to "fix" the outcome of the World Series. In response to this infamous incident, MLB owners appointed the first *commissioner* in professional sports, Judge **Kenesaw Mountain Landis**. Initially, Landis refused the offer to serve as commissioner because he enjoyed his position as a federal judge. He accepted the appointment on two conditions: He could continue to serve as a judge, and he had the *exclusive authority* to act in the *best interests* of the game. Succeeding league commissioners in baseball and other professional sports leagues continue to rely on this implied, and now explicit, power embedded in their constitutions and bylaws.

Earlier attempts by the players to collectively push back against these unilaterally imposed employment conditions by the owners and the unrestrained authority of the commissioner were largely unsuccessful. In 1953, professional major league baseball players organized into the **Major League Baseball Players Association (MLBPA)**. By the mid-1960s, the players' union hired Marvin Miller as its executive director, who later negotiated the first-ever **collective bargaining agreement (CBA)** in professional sports. Immediately thereafter, ballplayers' salaries improved by more than 49 percent, pension benefits were implemented, arbitration of disputes was enacted, and the reserve clause was challenged under Miller's negotiating leadership. It has been written that the three most important people in the history of baseball are Babe Ruth, Jackie Robinson, and Marvin Miller.

The narrative events of baseball served as a model for professional football, hockey, soccer, and basketball in North America. For instance, in 1920, George Halas formed the first professional football league in Chicago. Professional basketball for white men began as a barnstorming activity, with players accepting whatever the spectators paid. While German, Irish, and Italian immigrants played organized soccer more than a century ago in the United States, it was not until 1968 that a formal professional soccer league was formed here known as the **North American Soccer League (NASL)**.

This league received a momentous popularity boast in the mid-1970s when international star Pelé joined the New York Cosmos. Professional hockey has enjoyed a rich and tumultuous history for men and women beginning in the 1800s and leading to the establishment of the **National Hockey League** in the first quarter of the twentieth century.

Title IX contributed to the growth of amateur and professional sports leagues for women. During the late 1970s, the first women's professional basketball league was founded. One of the first stars of the Women's Pro Basketball League was Nancy Lieberman. This league folded after three years. A few years later, after a handful of stop-and-go attempts to solidify a women's pro basketball league, the WNBA was formed. The other major professional sports league for women in the United States is the National Women's Soccer League (NWSL). Both leagues have a history of supplying top players to the US Olympic and national teams for basketball and soccer, respectively. The WNBA and NWSL are the only professional team sports organizations for women in the United States that have their games broadcast regularly on television.

SPORTS FRANCHISES

According to *Forbes* magazine, Manchester United's soccer team—a member of the English Premier League and Football Association—is the most valuable sports *franchise* in the world. Its worth tops off in excess of $2.2 billion. But what is a sports franchise?

At the professional sports level, a franchise is a legal entity, usually a corporation, limited partnership, or trust, that fields a club or team under the auspices of its league. The league, through a management council, constitution, and bylaws and under the leadership of a commissioner, determines the policies and procedures for adding teams, selling teams, relocating franchises, granting exclusive territorial rights, hosting championships, negotiating media contracts, executing sponsorships, and licensing deals. However, in general, local broadcasting rights, stadium revenue, and gate receipts are the purview of individual franchises.

In 2014, a fascinating legal and ethics question arose in the **National Basketball Association (NBA)**. The league commissioner, Adam Silver, fined and banned Donald Sterling, the owner of the Los Angeles Clippers basketball franchise, from NBA games and practices for life because of privately recorded insensitive racial comments that were publicly released. Silver then insisted that Donald Sterling, controlling owner of the Clippers franchise under a family trust, be ousted as an NBA franchise owner. A federal court ruled Sterling's wife had the legal authority to remove her husband as a trustee and sell the Clippers team.

According to the NBA's constitution, specifically article 13, the willful violation of league rules regarding immoral and unethical conduct that have a "material adverse effect on the league" are grounds for his removal. Silver, acting in his capacity as league commissioner, had sole authority to determine whether Sterling's bigoted remarks justify the forced sale of his franchise. Article 4.3 required an affirmative vote of three-quarters of the NBA owners before a franchise may be transferred, which occurred.

ROLE OF COMMISSIONER

As described earlier, baseball's first commissioner, Judge Kenesaw Mountain Landis, is well regarded for reestablishing the integrity of Major League Baseball by banning for life eight ballplayers who confessed to trying to fix the World Series despite their courtroom acquittal. In granting Landis sweeping administrative, investigative, and disciplinary powers, the owners established a pattern of executive authority that other major professional sports leagues have embraced.

As observed in the NBA scandal involving Sterling, a commissioner has discretionary power to discipline owners as well as club managers, office personnel, and players. The **National Football League's (NFL)** commissioner, Roger Goodell, suspended the starting quarterback of the Pittsburgh Steelers—Ben Roethlisberger—for six games because of his alleged indecent public intoxication. League commissioners do not always get it right when seeking to discipline players in the "best interest of the game" for misconduct. Goodell faced unprecedented public criticism and backlash from sponsors for initially suspending Baltimore Raven's running back Ray Rice for only two games for an off-the-field domestic violence "incident." Rice was captured on a video broadcast by TMZ knocking out his fiancée with a punch in an elevator at an Atlantic City casino. Later, the NFL commissioner admitted he "got it wrong" and implemented a new six-game suspension policy for first-time domestic abusers and banishment from the league for second-time offenders. Goodell's punishment of New England Patriots quarterback Tom Brady for his involvement in the "deflategate" episode that also included a $1-million team fine and loss of a first-round draft pick drew widespread criticism throughout New England for its harshness. These examples serve as a small sample of the types of authority owners grant commissioners to resolve club-versus-club disputes, determine player suspensions and fines subject to appeal, approve player contracts, and initiate rule changes.

The chief complaint for these broad powers is that individual commissioners, when acting "in the best interest of the game," have biases that invariably surface whenever one person is judge, jury, and executioner. In truth, though, a commissioner's authority and disciplinary actions in many situations are subject to review by owners, arbitrators, or judicial authorities. In the case of the Patriots' "deflategate" incident, Brady appealed his game suspensions without pay, whereas team owner Robert Kraft accepted the punishment leveled by the commissioner on the club.

On a different note, the NFL commissioner in conjunction with team owners is responsible for enforcing the Rooney Rule. This owner-imposed mandate requires an ethnic minority candidate to be interviewed for every head coach and general manager opening. To the embarrassment of the NFL, in the most recent off-season hiring period, all eight head-coaching and seven general-manager openings were filled by nonminorities. The soccer owners of the Football Association's Premier League in Europe are debating whether to install a similar rule requiring interviews of ethnic minority candidates for all team-manager openings.

ANTITRUST LAW

The seeds of recent labor discontent in professional sports surfaced in a long-ago US Supreme Court decision, *Federal Baseball Club of Baltimore v. National League of Professional Baseball Clubs* (259 U.S. 200, 1922). Justice Oliver Wendell Holmes, considered one of America's greatest jurists, writing for the court majority, ruled that the owners and operators of professional baseball were *not* engaged in "trade or commerce" as defined under federal *antitrust* laws. Holmes viewed the fact that, even though teams crossed state borders, an incident that normally constitutes "interstate," the transport was incidental to the actual playing of the game of baseball for money—the commerce or business.

Professional baseball team owners, alone among all organized professional team sports in the United States, are exempt from antitrust scrutiny for activities that otherwise might be viewed as illegal, collusive monopoly business practices. The court revisited the anomaly of baseball's exclusive exemption in *Flood v. Kuhn* (407 v. U.S. 258, 1972) as it related to whether the *reserve clause* is within the reach of the federal antitrust laws.

Justice Blackman penned the opinion of the court. He reached the following conclusion: "Professional baseball is a business and it is engaged in interstate commerce." This is not a surprising revelation. The court continued to acknowledge baseball's record as it relates to a team activity, like trading a player without a player's consultation, is not clean. Logic dictates that the court, having recognized the error of its original antitrust exemption for baseball was wrong, would then correct itself by reversing its prior ruling by Justice Holmes. No! Resting on the legal doctrine **stare decisis**, in which settled principles of law are given the greatest deference, the court said the duty to change the application of the law rests with Congress, not the courts.

Meanwhile, the court reiterated that all other professional sports leagues, teams, and governing bodies are subject to federal antitrust regulation of their business activities notwithstanding the "anomaly" of the Holmes decision for baseball. By all rational accounts, the opinion is incongruent and indefensible.

In a very limited capacity, Congress addressed a small aspect of baseball's unique antitrust exemption when it signed into law the **Curt Flood Act of 1988**. This statute gives players the right to sue their leagues for anticompetitive activities *after* they have decertified as a union or players' association.

Beyond the legal issue of whether antitrust laws apply to professional baseball, which was raised in the *Flood* decision, ballplayer Curt Flood did have a legitimate legal gripe against Commissioner Bowie Kuhn and all the other MLB clubs. Specifically, Flood complained that the St. Louis Cardinals should not be permitted to trade him to the Philadelphia Phillies without his knowledge or permission. Flood learned from a reporter that he had been traded. His protest to the commissioner was for naught, as Kuhn rejected Flood's request to become a free agent. The commissioner grounded his ruling on the notion that Flood was contractually bound to report to the Phillies because his Cardinals team reserved all player contract rights, and contracts can be assigned or traded freely without player approval.

The legal issue the court avoided in *Flood* was whether this reserve clause, which was found in all baseball contracts and had been part of the owners' contracts with players since the 1880s, was a collusive illegal restraint of the freedom of players to move from team to team in violation of the Sherman Antitrust Act. Federal antitrust laws exist to promote free competition and to prevent interstate business practices or activities that conspire or contract to illegally restrain trade or commerce. Baseball received a "pass" because of its special place in American culture. The judicial ruling explicitly was limited to baseball and did not extend to other professional sport activities.

At the time, baseball's rules permitted a team to reserve all contract rights to a player for a year after the contract expired—or so the players thought. However, three years after the *Flood* decision, two ballplayers, Andy Messersmith and Dave McNally, argued that they were free agents after they refused to sign new contracts upon the completion of the one-year period after their contracts had expired. The owners disagreed and maintained that the league's one-year unilateral reserve clause provision was renewed over and over again in perpetuity.

The two players elected to submit their grievance to arbitration, which was permissible under their collective-bargaining agreement. Arbitrator Peter Seltz ruled in favor of the players. He declared that baseball players are free agents after playing one year upon their expiration of the contracts. In response to the arbitrator's determination that the league's interpretation of the reserve clause was null and void, the owners appealed the arbitration award to the federal courts. Seltz's decision was upheld (*Kansas City Royals Baseball Corporation v. MLBPA*, 409 F. Supp. 233, 261, W.D. Mo. 1976, aff'd, 532 F.2d 615, 8th Cir. 1976). In 1976, the players and owners reached a new collective-bargaining agreement that gave players with six years of major league service the right to become free agents.

The question of free agency has served as a source of dispute between team owners and players in nearly all organized professional sports. For instance, in the sport of professional football, a similar reserve clause as was found in baseball was deemed an illegal restraint on the mobility of players when the express intent or conspiracy was to keep player salaries down. *Mackey v. NFL* (543 F. 2d 606, 8th Cir. 1976), a court decision four years after the Seltz baseball arbitration ruling, dealt with the league rule that stated, when a player's contract expired and he signed with another team, the new team had to compensate the former team. This rule, known as the **Rozelle Rule** and named after the then–NFL commissioner Pete Rozelle, was deemed an unreasonable restraint of trade. Economists for the players' union demonstrated that clubs were reluctant to sign other teams' free agents for fear of losing good players from their rosters, as transfer compensation was determined by the commissioner. This decision forced the league's owners to negotiate in good faith new rules regarding the movement of players, to wit, free agency, with the players' union.

The two broad federal anticompetitive statutes in play between the owners and players are the Sherman Antitrust Act and the Clayton Act. The first statute, which was used in the *Mackey* decision, prohibits monopolies, price rigging, and wrongful restrictions on trade. Not all monopolies are automatically illegal, however. The way in which the monopoly powers come about and its effect on its competitive market are two key factors that courts examine to determine legality. Violators of the Sherman Act are subject to criminal penalties by the government and civil damages, with an automatic provision that the prevailing party is awarded three times actual damages.

Under the Clayton Act, one business entity is prevented from acquiring another business if doing so substantially lessens competition in that field or creates a monopoly. The Clayton Act and another federal statute restricting the power of courts to issue injunctions in labor disputes, the **Norris-LaGuardia Act**, *statutorily exempt* labor unions, including players' associations, *from antitrust scrutiny*. This application of this legal principle means that federal courts cannot issue relief or orders in cases involving labor disputes. The term *labor disputes* includes broad controversies related to the term or length of employment and conditions of employment, along with attempts to change, fix, or negotiate the arrangement of terms and conditions of employment. The historical purpose of the act is to protect unions from charges of unfair labor practices by owners.

In *Smith v. Pro-Football, Inc.* (420 F. Supp. 738, D.D.C. 1976), the NFL was rebuffed for unilaterally imposing the college draft system outside the collective-bargaining process. The court rejected the owners' contention that they could automatically award draft choices in inverse order to a team's winning record as a necessity to maintain competitive league balance, and James "Yazoo" Smith was awarded treble civil damages. However, the full effect was not recognized because the commissioner of the NFL at the time, Paul Tagliabue, on behalf of the owners, negotiated a new collective-bargaining agreement that had the effect of sanctioning the college-to-pro draft system as the *Mackey* case was being heard on appeal. The new agreement as a *byproduct of the collective-bargaining process* protected the NFL from future lawsuits on the legality of the draft under the *nonstatutory exemption* from monopoly antitrust law.

Under federal labor and antitrust law, there exists two basic types of exemptions from charges of collusion, illegal restraint on trade, price fixing, and monopoly practices. The first is the basic recognition of the existence of a *statutory labor law exemption on **mandatory** matters related to the parties negotiating a collective bargaining*. It applies, though, when both parties actually negotiate in good faith and not when management unilaterally enforces upon the players a mandatory negotiating condition, such as what the owners attempted to do in implementing the draft without consultation and approval by the players. In the aforementioned *Mackey* decision, the second kind of exemption occurred, as described in the previous paragraph. Here the court noted that it grants the *byproduct of the collective-bargaining process a nonstatutory exemption from antitrust laws* based on the application of a three-prong test:

1. The collective bargaining agreement seeks to exempt a mandatory versus permissive negotiating subject;
2. The restraint on trade or commerce principally affects the parties to the collective-bargaining agreement; and
3. The final agreement is a product of bona fide good-faith arm's-length negotiations.

Another illustration of the nonstatutory antitrust exemption in action happened in a professional basketball decision, *Wood v. NBA* (809 F.2d. 954, 2d Cir. 1987). Wood, a college senior, challenged the legality of the NBA draft, salary cap, and free agency. The court denied his antitrust violation claim because the collective-bargaining provisions questioned were all *mandatory* subjects of bargaining that had been agreed upon by the union and owners in arm's-length negotiations.

A later decision, *Powell v. NFL, Inc.* (930 F.2d 1293, 8th Cir. 1989), extended the nonstatutory labor exemption from antitrust scrutiny beyond the expiration of a bona fide collective-bargaining agreement even after an impasse in labor negotiations occurs. The public policy reason for continuing the exemption is to encourage the parties to negotiate. Interestingly, after the *Powell* ruling, the football players' association decertified itself as a union so as to remove the nonstatutory labor exemption as a barrier to charges of illegal monopoly practices against the owners, as permitted to professional sports unions by the Curt Flood Act.

The application of antitrust laws applies to a variety of professional sport activities, including matters related to acquiring, owning, and selling a franchise; responses to the formation of a rival league; and limits on licensing rights. In 2010, the US Supreme Court handed down a fascinating unanimous decision that involved a challenge to the NFL's exclusive licensing agreement with Reebok. The court ruled that the NFL's league-wide apparel-licensing practices are subject to antitrust scrutiny under the Sherman Act.

The small privately owned equipment and apparel company American Needle claimed that the league used monopoly practices to prevent it from selling team-logo hats to individual teams. The NFL unsuccessfully argued that the league is a separate economic entity from its teams. Had the court accepted the NFL's position, the league could then have negotiated single licensing deals on behalf of all of its teams, as it did with Reebok before American Needle sued it. Justice Stephens, writing for the US Supreme Court, ruled that the NFL must be viewed as thirty-two separate teams and not a single entity for antitrust purposes. This decision paved the way for Under Armour, Nike, Reebok, adidas, American Needle, and other apparel companies to negotiate licensing agreements on a team, not league, basis. For more about the case, see: *American Needle, Inc. v. NFL* (560 U.S. 183, 2010).

More than forty years ago, Congress stepped in and reversed a similar antitrust defeat suffered by the NFL. The **Sports Broadcasting Act of 1961** gave professional, not intercollegiate, sports leagues antitrust exemption when negotiating television-broadcasting rights. The act enables a league commissioner to license a television package to ESPN, FOX, or any of the networks. The individual team franchises share the broadcast revenue equally.

The US Supreme Court ruled the NCAA's requirement that it negotiate broadcasting rights for its member schools was anticompetitive. Congress did not extend the antitrust broadcast exemption to the NCAA. In general, the pattern for college football and basketball teams is for individual conferences, like the SEC, Big Ten, and ACC, to negotiate television deals on behalf of its member schools, although schools, like the University of Texas and Notre Dame, have entered their own individual broadcasting contracts for their football programs.

COLLECTIVE BARGAINING IN PROFESSIONAL SPORTS

Two significant legal forces were beginning to work in players' favor. Outside of baseball, courts determined that antitrust rules apply to professional sports. Second, by virtue of players organizing into a union or professional association, they have the benefit of federal labor laws.

The **National Labor Relations Act** provides three basic rights for professional players engaged in interstate commerce:

1. The right to self-organize into a labor association or union;
2. The right to bargain collectively with management; and
3. The right to engage in collective activities for their mutual benefits (e.g., strike when no agreement is in place or picket).

The act created the **National Labor Relations Board (NLRB)** to serve as the administrative body to oversee the guarantee of rights granted to players.

Once the NLRB has certified a players' association as the exclusive bargaining agent for all the players in a particular sports league, the owners and players' union have a *legal duty to bargain in good faith* on the basic issues pertaining to wages, hours, and working conditions. The key issues typically negotiated that fall into the category of *mandatory* collective negotiating terms include minimum salary, salary cap, pension benefits, health benefits, free agency, salary arbitration, grievance process, reserve clause, revenue sharing, rookie salaries, standard player contract, and so on. The term *good faith* means the parties must exchange bargaining proposals of these key issues, they must respond timely to each other's proposals, they must meet regularly, and they must exchange pertinent financial and budgetary information.

The other category of relevant bargaining subject matter that the parties *may* consider in their negotiations is referred to as **permissive topics**. These issues are outside the mandated subject of wages, hours, and other terms and conditions of employment. No legal requirement for either party to negotiate in good faith exists for permissive subjects.

The distinction between mandatory and permissive categories can become confusing. Federal courts ultimately are the final arbitrators regarding whether team owners must or may negotiate with player union representatives over matters related to the length of the season, number of games in a season, players' uniforms, playing surfaces, dimensions of a field, concussion prevention, punishment for domestic abuse outside the game or homo-phobic comments, and so on.

Collective bargaining refers to the process whereby owners and the players' association engage in good-faith give-and-take negotiations to reach a written final contract, called a *collective-bargaining agreement*. This final document dictates the rules and regulations related to the relationship between the two negotiating parties. It typically lasts three or four years. The union promises during the term of the agreement not to *strike*, whereas the owners promise not to *lock out*, or prevent, the players from practicing or playing. After a collective-bargaining agreement has expired, the union is free to strike or engage in other concerted activities. The owners have the right to prevent players from reporting to training camps or playing. They are both economic weapons to coerce the other party to return to the bargaining table. Copies of collective-bargaining agreements for all the major professional sports in North America are found at the respective players' union or association websites.

UNFAIR LABOR PRACTICE

In the course of negotiating a collective bargaining, should either party not bargain in good faith, then an *unfair labor practice* charge may be filed with the NLRB. Then–New York judge Sonia Sotomayer, who now sits as a justice on the US Supreme Court, took this labor law requirement a step further. She ruled that MLB owners had engaged in bad-faith dealings with players when they unilaterally changed the rules governing free agency and salary arbitration after the then-current collective-bargaining agreement had expired. Upon appeal, *Silverman v. Major League Baseball Player Relations Committee, Inc.* (67 F. 3d 1054, 2d Cir. 1995), her determination was upheld that baseball owners do not have the right to change the terms on mandatory labor issues while they still had a legal duty to negotiate in good faith for a new agreement.

A quick recap of the interchange between labor and antitrust law is in order. Antitrust laws seek to force owners to maintain open, competitive markets by not illegally restricting the movement of players or engaging in collusive policies and practices that limit player salaries. Labor laws are designed to encourage players to organize and negotiate collectively. When the parties bargain in good faith and reach an accord, then the players lose their ability to challenge owners about limits on player mobility or salary restriction until the next round of collective negotiations.

DECERTIFICATION

But what happens when players elect to *decertify* their union once their agreement with management has expired?

In 2011, the **National Football League Players Association (NFLPA)** decided to decertify their union after negotiations and mediation attempts broke down. Led by two of the league's most outstanding and respected quarterbacks—Tom Brady and Peyton Manning—the union decertified and immediately thereafter filed an antitrust lawsuit against the owners. The eighteen-week-and-four-day lockout resulted in the longest work stoppage in NFL history. Before the start of the regular season, the parties reached a new ten-year collective-bargaining agreement after the players recertified their union. Key mandatory negotiated components of the deal cover free agency, salary caps, rookie compensation, minimum salaries, and franchise tags. The new agreement expires in 2021 and has an annual estimated value to the players in excess of $12 billion. Table 5.1 highlights some of the differences in pay between professional sports organizations.

STRIKES AND LOCKOUTS

In 1987, a fascinating sports law question arose after NFL players elected to strike over free agency—the owners wanted compensation when players were lost—after failing to reach a new collective-bargaining agreement. During the twenty-four-day strike that occurred at the start of the regular season, the owners hired replacement players. Was it legal? Yes. Because their collective-bargaining agreement had expired, the owners were free to hire new employees. Both sides quickly recognized the folly of their ways when the public was exposed to a near-laughable brand of pro football. Pressure from broadcasters, advertisers, and viewers influenced the players enough to quickly end their holdout.

The NHL lockout of players in 2004 resulted in the league ceasing operations. For the first—and only—time, a major sports league lost an entire season. The parties disagreed over management's request to institute a salary cap of 75 percent of league revenues, after they claimed that they lost around $275 million the prior year. The players preferred no salary cap but offered a form of revenue sharing, a luxury tax, and one-time 5-percent rollback in player salaries. In the end, the parties agreed on a league-wide team salary cap of about 54 percent of league revenues, a salary floor, and guaranteed salaries. The NHL lost its prime network broadcaster and a large part of its fan base after the 310-day lockout.

While strikes, lockouts, and hiring replacement players are legal, it is an unfair labor practice for team owners to retaliate by discriminating against

Table 5.1.

	NFL	NBA	MLS	MLB	NHL
Free Agency	Yes	Yes	No; uses reentry draft	Yes	Yes
Salary Cap	$133 million, with a salary floor of 88.8 percent of the cap	Soft cap of $63 million, which permits teams to exceed the cap up to the luxury tax of $76 million	$3.1 million per team for the first twenty roster spots	No salary cap; instead, teams have to pay a luxury tax if their payroll goes over a prede-termined figure by the league	$69 million
Arbitration	Yes	Yes	Yes	Yes	Yes
Minimum Salaries	$420,000	$490,180	$36,500	$500,000	$550,000
Rookie Salary	Pay and length of contract depends on position drafted (up to four years, with fifth-year option for first-round draft picks)	Two-year contract with pay dependent on position drafted	$36,500	$500,000	$925,000 maximum for all players under age twenty-five who are obligated to sign entry-level contract (three-year contract for eighteen- to twenty-one-year-olds)

players who strike, as occurred after the NFL's player strike in 1987. (See NFL Management Council, 309 NLRB 78, 1992.) The aftermath of the 1987 strike eventually led to the team owners granting free agency to veteran players, while the players agree to a hard salary cap that limited player salaries to no more than 64 percent of league revenues.

The NBA suffered labor strife in 2011 when the owners began a lockout after the expiration of their 2005 collective-bargaining agreement. The work stoppage occurred initially during the 2011–2012 season and reduced the number of regular-season games from eighty-two to sixty-six. Players were forbidden from practicing or playing at NBA facilities, although some signed

NBA lockout 2011 shortened Game Schedule

temporary contracts with foreign basketball teams. No trades or new contracts could be initiated during this period. The lockout extended into the 2012–2013 season. More games were canceled. The union dissolved itself. The players filed an antitrust lawsuit. By the end of 2012, both sides reached an agreement that gave the parties an almost-equal split in league revenues, a more flexible salary cap, and tougher luxury taxes on teams that exceed their salary caps.

SUMMARY

Over the years, players and owners have engaged in troublesome business and legal disputes stemming from management's unilateral imposition of restrictions on players' ability to change teams, called the reserve clause. In response, the players took advantage of federal labor law permitting them to organize into a union or players' association. By law, owners and unionized players are obligated to negotiate in good faith on the mandatory issues of wages, hours of employment, and conditions of work as part of the collective-bargaining-agreement process.

Congress passed a series of federal laws to prevent anticompetitive business practices. In an anomaly not shared by other professional team sports, professional baseball enjoys an exemption from antitrust scrutiny. Based on a series of legal opinions, players and owners are protected from antitrust charges during the collective-bargaining process and the final work product from the negotiations.

Strikes and lockouts continue to serve as economic tools that have contributed to dynamic changes in the landscape of professional team sports.

KEY WORDS

Cincinnati Red Stockings. Historians point to the Cincinnati Red Stockings, organized in 1869, as the original professional sport team in the United States.

Collective Bargaining Agreement (CBA). Collective bargaining refers to the process whereby owners and the players' associations engage in good-faith give-and-take negotiations to reach a written final contract.

Curt Flood Act of 1988. This statute gives players the right to sue its league for anticompetitive activities after they have decertified as a union or players' association.

Good-Faith Bargaining. The parties must exchange bargaining proposals of the key issues of mandatory and permissive topics, they must respond timely to each others' proposals, they must meet regularly, and they must exchange pertinent financial and budgetary information.

Landis, Kenesaw Mountain. Baseball's first commissioner, a former federal judge, is well regarded for reestablishing the integrity of Major League Baseball by banning for life eight ballplayers who confessed to trying to fix the World Series despite their courtroom acquittal.

Major League Baseball (MLB). The professional league of baseball in the United States and Canada comprised of teams in the American League and the National League.

Major League Baseball Players Association (MLBPA). The labor organization representing players in the MLB.

Mandatory Topics. Bargaining terms include minimum salary, salary cap, pension benefits, health benefits, free agency, salary arbitration, grievance process, reserve clause, revenue sharing, rookie salaries, standard player contract, and so on.

National Basketball Association (NBA). The national governing body for basketball in the United States, with thirty member teams, one of which is in Canada.

National Football League (NFL). National organization of American football that is comprised of thirty-two teams split between the American Football Conference (AFC) and the National Football Conference (NFC).

National Football League Players Association (NFLPA). The labor organization representing the players of the NFL.

National Hockey League (NHL). The premier ice hockey organization in the world, which has participating teams in the United States and Canada.

National Labor Relations Act. Provides three basic rights for professional players engaged in interstate commerce:

1. The right to self-organize into a labor association or union;
2. The right to bargain collectively with management; and
3. The right to engage in collective activities for their mutual benefits (e.g., strike when no agreement is in place or picket).

National Labor Relations Board. Serves as the administrative body to oversee the guarantee of rights granted to players.

Norris-LaGuardia Act. Restricts the power of courts to issue injunctions in labor disputes and statutorily exempts labor unions, including players' associations, from antitrust scrutiny.

North American Soccer League (NASL). The first major professional soccer league in the United States.

Permissive Topics. A category of relevant bargaining subject matter that the parties may consider in their negotiations is referred to as permissive topics. These issues are outside the mandated subject of wages, hours, and other terms and conditions of employment.

Reserve Clause. A player's contract could be bought and sold without a player's permission, and a restriction on a player's freedom to move from team to team was implemented.

Rozelle Rule. The league rule, which is named after the then–NFL commissioner, that, when a player's contract expired and he signed with another team, the new team had to compensate the former team. This rule was deemed an unreasonable restraint of trade.

Sports Broadcasting Act of 1961. This gave professional, not intercollegiate, sports leagues antitrust exemption when negotiating television-broadcasting rights. The act enables a commissioner to license a television package to ESPN, FOX, or any of the networks. The individual team franchises share the broadcast revenue equally.

Stare Decisis. The legal doctrine that states that settled principles of law are given the greatest deference.

DISCUSSION QUESTIONS

1. Q: What is the most valuable sports franchise in the world, and what is its value?

A: According to *Forbes* magazine, Manchester United's soccer team—a member of the English Premier League and Football Association—is the most valuable sports franchise in the world. It's worth tops off in excess of $2.2 billion.

2. Q: What is the Rooney Rule?

A: The Rooney Rule is an owner-imposed mandate that requires an ethnic minority candidate to be interviewed for every head-coach and general-manager opening in the NFL.

3. Q: What is the Curt Flood Act of 1988?

A: The Curt Flood Act of 1988 gives players the right to sue its league for anticompetitive activities after they have decertified as a union or players' association.

4. Q: What was at the heart of *Mackey v. NFL* (543 F. 2d 606, 8th Cir. 1976)?

A: *Mackey v. NFL* dealt with the league rule that, when a player's contract expired and he signed with another team, the new team had to compensate the former team. This rule, known as the Rozelle Rule and named after the then–NFL commissioner, was deemed an unreasonable restraint of trade.

5. Q: How does the Sherman Antitrust Act affect professional sport?
A: The Sherman Antitrust Act prohibits monopolies, price rigging, and wrongful restrictions on trade.

6. Q: How does the Clayton Act affect professional sport?
A: Under the Clayton Act, one business entity is prevented from acquiring another business if doing so substantially lessens competition in that field or creates a monopoly.

7. Q: What is the three-prong test used by the court to determine nonstatutory exemption from antitrust laws in the *Mackey* decision?
A: In the *Mackey* decision, the court noted that it grants the byproduct of the collective-bargaining process a nonstatutory exemption from antitrust laws based on the application of a three-prong test:

1. The collective-bargaining agreement seeks to exempt a mandatory versus permissive negotiating subject;
2. The restraint on trade or commerce principally affects the parties to the collective-bargaining agreement; and
3. The final agreement is a product of bona fide good-faith arm's-length negotiations.

8. Q: What does the Sports Broadcasting Act of 1961 enable a commissioner and individual teams to do?
A: The act enables a commissioner to license a television package to ESPN, FOX, or any of the networks. The individual team franchises share the broadcast revenue equally.

9. Q: What are the basic rights provided for professional players by the National Labor Relations Act?
A: The National Labor Relations Act provides three basic rights for professional players engaged in interstate commerce:

1. The right to self-organize into a labor association or union;
2. The right to bargain collectively with management; and
3. The right to engage in collective activities for their mutual benefits (e.g., strike when no agreement is in place or picket).

10. Q: What are the key issues in a mandatory collective negotiation?
A: The key issues typically negotiated that fall into the category of mandatory collective negotiating terms include minimum salary, salary cap, pension benefits, health benefits, free agency, salary arbitration, grievance pro-

cess, reserve clause, revenue sharing, rookie salaries, standard player contract, and so on.

11. Q: What caused the 2004 NHL lockout of players?

A: The parties disagreed over management's request to institute a salary cap of 75 percent of league revenues. The players preferred no salary cap. In the end, the parties agreed on a league-wide team salary cap of about 54 percent of league revenues. The NHL lost its prime network broadcaster and a large part of its fan base from the extended lockout.

Chapter Six

Sports Agents and Contracts

"No man can faithfully serve two masters whose interests are in conflict."—
Judge DeMascio, *Detroit Lions, Inc. v. Argovita*

The use of professional representatives or sports agents to negotiate contracts for professional athletes and entertainers is now commonplace. It has not always been this way. Historians point to the American entrepreneur **Charles Pyle** as one of the first sports agents. In the 1920s, this Chicago-based theater owner negotiated the first professional sports contract. His client, "Red" Grange, was a star running back for the University of Illinois when he elected to turn professional. Pyle convinced George Halas, owner of the Chicago Bears, to guarantee Grange up to $3,000 per game plus a share of the gate. Grange, who is considered one of the most talented running backs in the history of football, brought prominence and legitimacy to a league that was struggling for public recognition and acceptance. Pyle also is credited with starting the first professional tennis tour. The flamboyant French tennis player Suzanne Lenglen was the world's original female celebrity-athlete when Pyle signed her to a $50,000 contract to tour the United States and play against the leading female tennis players. Her decision to turn professional was widely criticized by the tennis establishment, including the All England Club at Wimbledon, which revoked her honorary membership even after she had won six single championships.

By the 1960s and 1970s, as professional sports teams gained in popularity, streams of revenue increased, and players became cultural icons, players' unions gained a greater role in collectively negotiating higher salaries and better benefits. However, the need for individual player representation in the form of player agents rose as salaries increased and endorsement and sponsorship income opportunities improved. Athletes who were now generating more revenue required expert tax, investment, and financial advice. Notwithstanding the early success of Charles "Cash and Carry" Pyle, most team owners and managers refused to negotiate with player agents.

In the modern pro team sports era, **Bob Woolf** is recognized as one of the early professionally trained lawyers to serve as a sports agent. Earl Wilson, the first acknowledged African American pitcher for the Boston Red Sox, retained Woolf in the 1960s initially for advice after an auto accident and then to negotiate baseball contracts on his behalf. Later on, Woolf became best known as the agent who represented legendary Celtic basketball player Larry Bird and scores of other renowned all-star athletes.

Around the same time as Woolf's entry into representing athletes, another attorney from the Midwest, Mark McCormack, began working with a young golfer, Arnold Palmer, on a handshake agreement. McCormack's ultimate contribution to the field of sports agency is twofold: He linked engaging athletes to marketing and sponsorship deals, and he ushered in a new negotiating business model—the sports agency firm—when he created **International Management Group (IMG)**.

By 1996, the business itself went west to Hollywood. In a now-famous movie scene that continues to capture the public's perception of agents, actor Tom Cruise plays a young, aspiring agent. In the film by the same name as the agent Jerry Maguire, Cuba Gooding Jr. was cast in the role of fictional football player Rod Tidwell. Speaking to his agent, Tidwell, after demonstrating frustration over the slow pace of his contract negotiations, yells, "Show me the money!"

Today's player agents do more than show clients dinero. Agents enjoy an often-prominent, glamorous, and occasionally notorious role in the sports and endorsement business. The commerce of sports has evolved into the entertainment business. Beyond signing players to multiyear, multimillion-dollar contracts, the daily fare for a top sports agent may include helping a client work with Nike or Under Armour to launch a new line of shoes, negotiate a guest television appearance, star in a music video, pen Tweets, or write a public relations press release to counteract negative publicity that results from a domestic-abuse criminal charge.

Sports agents no longer just represent professional team athletes. College and professional coaches, team managers, broadcasters, reporters, and Olympic stars hire agents to represent their interests when dealing with third-party marketers and employers. For instance, the renowned eighteen-Olympic-gold-medal-winning swimmer Michael Phelps turned pro in high school. Not long after his initial Olympic success, while still in high school, he hired sports agent Peter Carlisle of Octagon to help negotiate his endorsement, licensing, public relations, public-speaking, and merchandising deals.

CONTRACTS AND SPORTS AGENTS

Not all sports agents are lawyers, nor does the law require it. An advantage to retaining a lawyer in representing an athlete playing in a professional team sport is that he or she is trained in the elements of forming and negotiating contracts.

On the other hand, occasions exist when lawyers and accountants cannot personally connect with athletes the way fellow performers who want to expand their business affairs into the sports agency business might. Music and media mogul Jay Z recently entered into the sports agency world via his Roc Nation Sports firm, which is a subsidiary of his entertainment company Roc Nation. Jay Z's personal relationship with Yankee Alex Rodriguez, which led to him signing on as a client, and his desire to help professional athletes make money in the same way he has helped artists in the music business is an unprecedented aggressive and innovative move. To succeed, Jay Z or his associates will need to gain a skill set in negotiating sports contracts.

The skilled agent, lawyer or not, must become knowledgeable about how the athlete meets the needs of a team, recognizes salary and bonus money parameters, has familiarity with the terms of the collective-bargaining agreement, understands the athlete's strengths and weaknesses, has experience in securing personal services contracts, and is sufficiently personable to work with an adversary to negotiate a contract in the best interest of the athlete-client.

By way of an example, on the narrow issue of negotiating a baseball contract for a high school or college player who was drafted by a major league team, these are aspects of the collective-bargaining agreement that an agent must understand. Teams may no longer immediately sign a drafted athlete to a major league contract. Each major league team has a limited bonus pool that they can spend on signing bonuses for newly drafted players in addition to the negotiated annual salary. Bonus pools fluctuate depending on the number of draft selections a team has during the first ten rounds of the June draft. In the most recent draft year, the bonus pool ranged from more than $17 million to less than $4 million. Each individual draft slot is assigned a recommended bonus amount. The current recommended signing bonus for the first pick of the draft is around $9 million, whereas the last choice in the first round is slotted at around $2 million. However, a team may pay more than the slot-recommended bonus for an individual player so long as the total paid does not exceed that team's bonus pool. A team that exceeds its signing bonus pool limit must pay a financial penalty depending on the dollar amount of the overage. A team has until July 15 to sign a drafted player; otherwise the team loses the right to sign the player to a contract, which in the first instance must be a minor league contract. The unsigned player may not sign with another major league team until the following year's draft, when he is reeligible for the draft. For more information on the rookie player draft in baseball, see www.baseballamerica.com/draft.

In this baseball illustration, the term *contract* is used multiple times. But what is a *contract*? A **contract** is a legally binding agreement between two or more parties. In the business of sports, a common contract is a standard player agreement that nearly every professional team requires their players and their players' agents to use. Book deals, publicity appearances, and licensing of publicity rights for a product endorsement necessitate different contracts.

All contracts, including a *standard player agreement* found in a sport's collective-bargaining agreement, must include the following elements for it to be legal and enforceable:

- The contract involves an *offer* that the other party must *accept*.
- The parties must exchange something of mutual value, also known as **consideration**. At the most basic level, the athlete promises to practice and perform to his or her highest level, and in return, the team promises to compensate the player for performance.
- There must be a *meeting of the minds* over what the material or key terms and conditions of the agreement cover.
- There must be the *actual performance or delivery* of the duties or promises the parties considered in the agreement.
- The agreement must be for a *legal purpose*.
- The parties who sign the agreement must be of *sound mind* and of *legal age* (generally the age of eighteen or older; otherwise a parent or legal guardian must sign).
- The parties acted in *good faith* and *honest dealings* throughout the negotiations.

Sports contracts are different than many business-related agreements, as Jay Z and other non–legally trained agents learn. Player-team contracts are *employment* contracts. Each individual athlete brings to his or her sport a unique skill set and personality. Agents assist players in leveraging their extraordinary contributions and stature by adding to standard player contracts bonus conditions for exceptional performance or no-trade clauses after significant years of service to the same club.

The flip side of the exceptional talent–negotiating position a professional athlete enjoys is a reciprocal acknowledgment that more is expected on and off the field by management. Past publicized player incidents of gambling abuse and illicit use of performance-enhancing drugs led to a modification of the *integrity* condition found in today's standard players' agreements.

Players promise in writing not to *breach* these material conditions without being subject to punishment by the league commissioner.

Increasingly significant in a world sensitive to disparaging remarks and domestic violence is an express contract duty on the part of players to maintain good moral character and citizenship, even on their social media sites, consistent with the best interest of their sports. Three examples stand out. The Kansas City Chiefs suspended and later released star running back Larry Johnson for Tweeting an antigay slur. The NBA's New York Knicks fined starting guard J. R. Smith for posting seminude photos of a woman on his Twitter account. Baltimore Ravens running back Ray Rice was initially suspended two games for knocking his then-fiancée unconscious in a hotel elevator and later released by his team for conduct detrimental to the team's best interests.

Appendix B includes a copy of the standard player contract used in the NFL by management, players, NFLPA, and player-agents acting on behalf of their clients. Keep in mind: Agents negotiate the unique performance bonus terms in the addendum to the basic agreement.

Professional athletes engaged in action sports not associated with teams utilize the services and expertise of sports agents, too. For example, besides Olympic gold-medal swimmer Michael Phelps, young athletes, such as snowboarder Keegan Valaika, pro surfer Alana Blanchard, and X Games skateboarder Mitchie Brusco, all rely on the vast pool of Octagon agents for contract negotiations, endorsement programs, public relations responses, and charity foundation involvement.

Not all professional athletes depend on the services of an agent all the time. When Matt Bonner was one of the few NBA players without a formal sneaker endorsement, he decided to negotiate his own shoe contract via Twitter. After a few back-and-forth Tweets, he thought that he might have landed a sponsorship deal with New Balance, until New Balance stopped Tweeting. Ultimately, he signed a shoe deal with adidas. In an even more unusual situation, the New York Giants' 2015 first-round draft pick, Ereck Flowers, elected to negotiate his own player contract alone while hiring a lawyer to double-check the contract language.

In contrast to the league-mandated standard player contracts that agents typically negotiate, *endorsement* contracts are different because they do not involve an employer-employee relationship. The endorsing athlete is deemed an **independent contractor**, or someone who is not subject to the complete control or manner and means of performing the agreed-upon sponsorship services. Similarly, the legal relationship between an agent and athlete is regarded as a **contractor–independent contractor** association, not an employer-employee connection.

AGENT CERTIFICATION

Once the NLRB recognizes a players' association or union as the official collective-bargaining agent for players in a league, then that union is recognized as the *exclusive bargaining agent or representative*. In theory, a players' union is *the* entity that bargains for stronger rights, free agency, pension plans, injury protection, and higher salaries for its players. In reality, leading sports agents for players were strong advocates for players unionizing and have always had a significant role in individual, or microcontract, negotiations, even when management was reluctant to acknowledge them. Today, the typical sports collective-bargaining agreement contains language that recognizes the right of players to negotiate player contracts with the assistance of their own agents. Put another way, the unions have *delegated* their exclusive authority to negotiate individual player agreements to agents. However, each players' association has set forth rules and regulations required for *certification* as a sports agent or contract advisor, as the NFLPA refers to agents, before the authority to negotiate can exist.

In legal terms, sports agents are authorized *subagents* of players' associations. Individual players are permitted to select agents to represent them in negotiating compensation packages consistent with the league's collective-bargaining parameters. Complaints from athletes about agents egregiously stealing from them, inducing them to accept gratuities that jeopardized college eligibility, or failing to use due care in managing funds has led to across-the-board changes in regulating agents by players' associations to protect players.

The players' associations for professional football, baseball, hockey, and basketball teams have each put into place a procedure and process for agent certification. For instance, the NFLPA requires prospective contract advisors to demonstrate negotiating experience or receipt of a postcollege degree prior to seeking certification. Once a person is certified to serve as a contract advisor, the agent must negotiate at least one NFL player contract over a three-year period to retain NFLPA certification.

Attendance at a union-sponsored annual education conference, passage of a skills and knowledge test, disclosure of felony convictions and malfeasance findings, promises not to provide a player with misleading information to induce a player to sign as a client, purchase of malpractice insurance, and compliance with the mandated maximum-percentage compensation fee (3 percent in the NFL, 4 percent in the NBA, 5 percent in the MLB) for negotiating a player contract are among the many agent certification and compliance conditions imposed by various players' unions.

Effective 2015, the international governing body for soccer, FIFA, changed its agent-*licensing* system to require US Soccer, the national governing body, to put into place a process for licensing player agents. Licensure, which is similar to certification, requires an agent to obtain indemnity insurance, pass an exam, not have a relationship with FIFA, agree to have a written contract between the agent and the soccer player, and have an "impeccable reputation" before FIFA will allow an agent to represent a player.

SPORTS AGENT FEES

Sports agents who perform client services beyond negotiating a player-team salary-related contract are not limited in pay by the union-mandated caps. Players and agents are free to negotiate a fee-for-services arrangement based on an hourly rate for tax, financial, and accounting services and a percentage arrangement for publishing, recording, marketing, and endorsement contracts. Fee arrangements paying an agent between 10 and 25 percent of the dollar value of an endorsement deal are not unusual.

Forbes estimates the average professional athlete earns an additional 1 to 2 percent of their player contracts in endorsements. An example of an athlete who falls outside this parameter is NFL quarterback Drew Brees. Annually, he earns about $40 million from his team contract, along with an additional $11 million from endorsements, which is a staggering 27.5 percent of his team contract. LeBron James every year earns twice as much from sponsorship deals as his contract pays him for playing for the Cleveland Cavaliers in the NBA.

The exceptions to a general rule frequently create interesting narratives. So continuing along, megastar soccer legend Lionel Messi pockets as much on sponsorship deals with Nike, EA Sports, and Turkish Airlines as he does from competing for his FC Barcelona team in Spain. Roger Federer's endorsement contracts with Nike, Gillette, Rolex, and NetJets pay him around $60 million a year, more than six times his annual tennis winnings. The top three annual endorsement winners for female professional athletes are all tennis players: Maria Sharapova, Serena Williams, and Li Na. They each snare more than $20 million a year in endorsement earnings, sums that substantially exceed on-the-court prize money earnings. On average, agents for professional athletes and celebrities are paid 10 to 25 percent of the total negotiated endorsement earnings in fee compensation, which indeed is a tidy sum.

STATE REGULATION OF SPORTS AGENTS

Beginning in the early 1980s, states with prominent college athletic programs began to regulate agents for selfish reasons. California, the home state to UCLA; USC; University of California, Berkeley; Stanford; and San Diego State, enacted the first statute that required nonlawyer agents to register with the state, pay a licensing fee, post a surety bond, file a fee schedule, maintain accounting records, and agree to arbitration of any player-agent disputes. The statutes were a direct response to colleges losing elite athletes before their eligibility had expired. In many cases, too, the colleges were forced to forfeit their wins for playing games with an ineligible player in violation of NCAA bylaws prohibiting a student-athlete from signing a contract with an agent.

In an attempt to uniformly regulate agents on a state-by-state basis, the National Conference on Uniform State Laws and the NCAA encouraged states to adopt its proposed legislation. The vast majority of states did when they enacted the **Uniform Athlete Agents Act (UAAA)**. The statute civilly and criminally penalizes agents for impermissible conduct. Wrongful conduct includes initiating or inducing a student-athlete to enter into an agency contract without warning in conspicuous language that a student-athlete may lose his or her amateur eligibility for signing. An intriguing punitive component to these statutes is a civil remedy permitting schools to sue agents for financial losses incurred as a result of penalties imposed by the NCAA for playing with an ineligible student-athlete. In light of the staggering sums paid college teams by media broadcasters and bowl participation revenue, the amount owed could be in the millions.

Florida, Louisiana, and Texas have all charged agents for failing to register or not timely informing the school's athletic director, as required by state law, after meeting with student-athletes regarding potential representation. Despite media attention focusing on high-profile agency-abuse cases, civil penalties and criminal indictments under UAAA are rare.

FEDERAL REGULATION OF SPORTS AGENTS

In 2004, President George W. Bush signed into law federal legislation that regulates sports agents. The statute, **Sports Agent Responsibility Trust Act (SPARTA)**, mirrors the UAAA insofar as it seeks to protect student-athletes. It requires agents to conspicuously notify student-athletes of potential loss of eligibility for signing with an agent, prohibits the use of illegal inducements to sign a student-athlete, and requires both the agent and the student-athlete to notify the athlete's athletic director when the parties enter into an agency agreement.

Federal compliance of the three principal duties of a sports agent under SPARTA—disclosure, truthfulness, and not buying student-athletes—are regulated by the Federal Trade Commission (FTC). Once a student-athlete's college eligibility has expired, SPARTA and UAAA no longer apply.

FIDUCIARY DUTIES AND RESPONSIBILITIES OF A SPORTS AGENT

In addition to the statutory and union-imposed agency standards of conduct, a *fiduciary* relationship exists between a sports agent and an athlete upon the signing of a representation agreement. This contract is separate and different from the previously discussed player-team standard contract and endorsement contract. Each players' association has its own basic player-agent agreement that agents must use as a condition precedent for representing an athlete in team contract negotiations. An agent is free to draft his or her own agreement to cover nonteam affairs, such as licensing and merchandising the athlete's publicity rights. A sports agent is legally obligated to always act in the *best interest* of his or her athlete. A sports agent acting as a fiduciary is *duty bound* to act in *good faith* with *due care* and *loyalty* at all times.

Disputes, however, do occur between a player and agent over a variety of contentious matters. In Europe, a soccer player sued his agent, alleging a breach of fiduciary duty. This civil lawsuit led to an appeals court addressing the broad fiduciary duties required of all sports agents (*Imageview Management Ltd. v. Kelvin Jack*, EWCA Civ. 63, 2009). In this particular case, while negotiating a team-player contract for his client, the agent made a secret deal with the team benefiting the agent, not the player. After the player discovered what had occurred, he stopped paying the agreed-upon commission. The agent sued to recover his fees. The court held that, because the sports agent failed to *disclose* the private arrangement, it raised the real possibility of a *conflict of interest*, which is a *breach* of an agent's duty of *good faith*.

Furthermore, the court determined that an agent who is guilty of some breach of fiduciary duty forfeits any right to remuneration. All commissions paid the agent by the player were remanded or returned back to the player. The court reminded all sports agents of the need for *open, transparent*, and *honest* dealings when representing athletes.

A similar situation arose in a well-documented case in the United States. An agent employed by Mark McCormack's IMG sports firm negotiated a memorabilia deal for NFL Pro Bowl running back LaDainian Tomlinson. The company that retained Tomlinson gave the agent a kickback worth more than twenty thousand dollars. The agent failed to disclose the clandestine deal benefiting the agent to Tomlinson and the agent's employer, IMG. In the absence of the player's consent to this arrangement, the sports agent violated a fiduciary duty owed the player-client. The agent's dishonest actions are grounds for dismissal from IMG employment, which is what happened.

The list of cases demonstrating financial improprieties by sports agents is quite long. The legal theories allowing wronged athletes to seek recovery for misappropriation of funds or mismanagement of investments starts with breach of fiduciary duty but frequently expands to include *breach of contract* and tort-based *negligence* or *fraud* causes of action.

For instance, Tank Black was a well-established certified sports agent for NFL players. He operated a sports agency firm known as Professional Management, Inc. A rival agent tipped off the NFLPA that Black was illegally supplying money to college football players before their eligibility had expired. Among the college athletes who received money were players on the University of Florida football roster. The state of Florida charged Black with failing to register and comply with its agency regulation statute.

Further investigations into Black's dealing with drug dealers and Ponzi (pyramid) schemers resulted in federal criminal charges. Black pled guilty to laundering money for drug dealers and, in a separate Florida lawsuit, conspiring to commit mail and wire fraud. Black was sentenced and served time in a federal penitentiary for his crimes. Besides defrauding the federal government, he was convicted of fraudulently mismanaging nearly $14 million in client-athlete funds. The NFLPA decertified Black as an agent. Black's misdeeds occurred before the "civil recovery for loss of revenue penalties" component of the UAAA was in play.

The situations described in these cases are not unique in the world of professional sports. Put together, the vulnerable, financially well-off professional athletes who are skilled at their sports but not schooled in investment theory, financial controls, banking, or management practices blindly trust unscrupulous agents serving as financial advisors or tax planners, and the worst outcomes can be expected.

Sports Illustrated reported that nearly 80 percent of all former NFL players are either bankrupt or nearly bankrupt two years after hanging up their cleats. In the NBA, 60 percent fall into that same category within five years of leaving pro ball.

Former University of Miami collegiate star and NFL standout Warren Sapp purportedly earned about $40 million during his career. He is now nearly $7 million in debt. Ex-NBA player Antoine Walker earned more than $100 million during his career. He, too, is broke. Family members estimate Walker supported around seventy friends and family during his Boston Celtic–playing days. Both Sapp and Walker left college early before earning degrees. Bad financial management practices and poor lifestyle decisions contribute to these unfortunate and preventable occurrences.

Additionally, conflicts can arise between sports agents, and not merely between a player and his or her agent. A common fact pattern is one where an agent leaves the employ of one firm and joins another sports agency, taking his or her clients. The lawsuits raise issues of misappropriation of trade secrets, breach of fiduciary duty to the original firm, nonpayment of commissions, and breach of an employment contract.

LAWYER–SPORTS AGENTS SPECIAL DUTIES

Sports agents who are lawyers and operate their sports agency business as a law firm operate under a special attorney-client fiduciary relationship. The typical sports agent is regulated publicly by SPARTA and UAAA and privately by the certification or licensing process of players' unions. The lawyer–sports agent is also governed by a state bar association's *Code of Ethics*, especially in the area of soliciting clients and the state's highest court. Trust and confidentiality are cornerstone ingredients to an effective athlete-lawyer relationship, in addition to avoiding conflicts of interest, communicating openly and honestly, and maintaining professional competence and skill in the field of sports business and law.

SPORTS AGENCY FIRMS

The viewing public was first introduced to the world of sports agents when **Creative Artist Agency (CAA)** client Tom Cruise starred as Jerry Maguire. A firm that began as a talent agency for Hollywood films morphed into one of the largest sports agency firms in the world. CAA operates as a full-service agency firm representing professional hockey, basketball, football, and baseball players.

Scott Boras, considered the most successful and feared sports agent ever, limits his practice to representing professional baseball players. By last count, Boras has negotiated contracts valued well over $1.6 billion to CAA's $5.3 billion. Despite his reputation as a tough, skilled negotiator, his loss of Alex Rodriguez as a client to Jay Z's now-rival agency firm working in conjunction with CAA sent reverberations throughout the professional sports world.

Some athletes prefer representation by smaller sports agency firms, largely because they are ensured more personal attention. Athletes drafted in later rounds or who are less-established free agents may experience difficulty in finding qualified, experienced agents. Smaller firms frequently subcontract tax accounting, prenuptial advice, public relations, and financial advice and focus exclusively on contract negotiations.

Established sports agents, like David Falk, whose star client was Michael Jordan, represents so many NBA players that at times it appears as though he controls the market for signing players. Occasionally, professional athletes understand the business well enough to break off from their agency relationships and create their own firms. Golfers Nick Price and Greg Norman left IMG, the late Mark McCormack's firm, and formed their own management companies to serve their own business needs.

SAMPLE NFLPA CONTRACT ADVISOR AND ATHLETE REPRESENTATION CONTRACT

The players' associations for each of the team sports require certified agents to use its standard representation agreement for basic team salary contract negotiations, as mentioned earlier. An additional contract is generally used when sports agents provide further professional services. Appendix C contains the required NFLPA representation contract. The players' associations' websites contain similar representation contracts and certification requirements.

SUMMARY

From modest historical beginnings, sports agents now play a significant role in representing professional athletes in contract negotiations, media relations, financial management, and endorsements. Sports agents are governed by public and private law regulations. UAAA and SPARTA are legislative mandates at the state and federal levels, respectively, that regulate the relationship between an athlete and a sports agent. The players' associations for professional football, hockey, basketball, and baseball register, supervise, and discipline agents through a certification process.

All sports agents are held to a high standard of conduct. Specifically, they have a duty to act in the best interests of the players they represent and not in any self-serving manner. A sports agent acts as a fiduciary for a client-athlete. Instances of egregious misconduct and bad-faith dealings by agents on unsuspecting athletes are numerous. In some cases, civil and criminal charges are appropriate remedies for the harm caused.

KEY WORDS

Boras, Scott. Considered the most successful and feared sports agent ever, he limits his practice to representing professional baseball players. By last count, Boras has negotiated contracts valued well over $1.6 billion to CAA's $5.3 billion.

Consideration. In a contract, the parties must exchange something of mutual value, also known as consideration.

Contract. A contract is a legally binding agreement between two or more parties. In the business of sports, a common contract is a standard player agreement that nearly every professional team requires their players and their players' agents to use. Book deals, publicity appearances, and licensing of publicity rights for a product endorsement necessitate different contracts.

Contractor–Independent Contractor. The legal relationship between an agent and athlete is regarded as a contractor–independent contractor association.

Creative Artists Agency (CAA). A firm that began as a talent agency for Hollywood films morphed into one of the largest sports agency firms in the world. CAA operates as a full-service agency firm representing professional hockey, basketball, football, and baseball players.

Independent Contractor. In an endorsement contract, the endorsing athlete is deemed an independent contractor, or someone who is not subject to the complete control or manner and means of performing the agreed-upon sponsorship services.

International Management Group (IMG). Sports agency firm created by Mark McCormack, an attorney from the Midwest who began working with a young golfer, Arnold Palmer, on a handshake agreement. McCormack's contribution to the field is twofold: He linked engaging athletes to marketing and sponsorship deals, and he ushered in a new negotiating business model—the sports agency firm.

Offer. A contract involves an offer that the other party must accept.

Pyle, Charles. One of the first sports agents. In the 1920s, he was a Chicago-based theater owner who represented "Red" Grange when he signed him to a player's contract with the Chicago Bears. Pyle also is recognized for starting the first professional tennis tour starring Suzanne Lenglen.

Sports Agent Responsibility Trust Act (SPARTA). Signed into law in 2004 by President George W. Bush, the statute mirrors the UAAA insofar as it seeks to protect student-athletes. It requires agents to conspicuously notify student-athletes of potential loss of eligibility for signing with an agent, prohibits the use of illegal inducements to sign a student-athlete, and requires both the agent and the student-athlete to notify the athlete's athletic director when the parties enter into an agency agreement. Federal compliance of the three principal duties of a sports agent under SPARTA—disclosure, truthfulness, and not buying student-athletes—are regulated by the FTC.

Uniform Athlete Agents Act (UAAA). The statute civilly and criminally penalizes agents for impermissible conduct. Wrongful conduct includes initiating or inducing a student-athlete to enter into an agency contract without warning in conspicuous language that a student-athlete may lose his or her amateur eligibility for signing. An intriguing punitive component to these statutes is a civil remedy permitting schools to sue agents for financial losses incurred as a result of penalties imposed by the NCAA for playing with an ineligible student-athlete.

Woolf, Bob. Recognized as one of the early professionally trained lawyers to serve as a sports agent. Earl Wilson, the first acknowledged African American pitcher for the Boston Red Sox, retained Woolf in the 1960s initially for advice after an auto accident and then to negotiate baseball contracts on his behalf. Later on, Woolf became best known as the agent who represented legendary Celtic basketball player Larry Bird.

DISCUSSION QUESTIONS

1. **Q: Who is considered to be one of the first sports agents?**
A: Historians point to Charles Pyle as one of the first sports agents.

2. **Q: Who is recognized as one of the early professionally trained lawyers to serve as a sports agent?**
A: Bob Woolf is recognized as one of the early professionally trained lawyers to serve as a sports agent.

3. **Q: Who created IMG, and what was this person's contribution to the field of sports agents?**
A: Mark McCormack's contribution to the field is twofold: He linked engaging athletes to marketing and sponsorship deals, and he ushered in a new negotiating business model—the sports agency firm—when he created IMG.

4. **Q: In addition to professional athletes, whom do sports agents represent?**
A: Sports agents no longer just represent professional team athletes. College and professional coaches, team managers, broadcasters, reporters, and Olympic stars hire agents to represent their interests when dealing with third-party marketers and employers.

5. **Q: What is an advantage to retaining a lawyer to represent an athlete?**
A: An advantage to retaining a lawyer in representing an athlete playing in a professional team sport is that he or she is trained in the elements of forming and negotiating contracts.

6. **Q: What is one major difference between endorsement contracts and standard player professional services contracts?**
A: Endorsement contracts are different from standard player professional services contracts because they do not involve an employer-employee relationship.

7. **Q: What led to the modification of the integrity condition in today's standard player agreements?**

A: Past incidents of gambling abuse and illicit use of performance-enhancing drugs led to a modification of the integrity condition found in today's standard players' agreements. Players promise in writing not to breach these material conditions without being subject to punishment from the commissioner.

8. Q: What must an agent do to remain certified to serve as a contract advisor in the NFLPA?

A: Once a person is certified to serve as a contract advisor, the agent must negotiate at least one NFL player contract over a three-year period to retain NFLPA certification.

9. Q: What state regulation is involved in becoming a sports agent, and why were they implemented?

A: California enacted the first statute that required nonlawyer agents to register with the state, pay a licensing fee, post a surety bond, file a fee schedule, maintain accounting records, and agree to arbitration of any player-agent disputes. The statutes were a direct response to colleges losing elite athletes before their eligibility had expired and, in some cases, forfeiting wins for playing games with an ineligible player because the player had signed an agent contract in violation of NCAA bylaws.

10. Q: What are the three principal duties of a sports agent under SPARTA?

A: Federal compliance of the three principal duties of a sports agent under SPARTA—disclosure, truthfulness, and not buying student-athletes—are regulated by the FTC.

11. Q: What is the financial status of nearly 80 percent of NFL players two years after leaving the sport? What is it in the NBA for players five years after leaving the sport?

A: *Sports Illustrated* reported that nearly 80 percent of all former NFL players are either bankrupt or nearly bankrupt two years after hanging up their cleats. In the NBA, 60 percent fall into that same category within five years of leaving pro ball.

12. Q: What are examples of the things required of a sports agent to become certified by a players' association?

A: Attendance at a union-sponsored annual education conference, passage of a skills and knowledge test, disclosure of felony convictions and malfeasance findings, promises not to provide a player with misleading information to induce a player to sign as a client, purchase of malpractice insurance, and compliance with the mandated maximum-percentage compensation fee (3 percent in the NFL, 4 percent in the NBA, 5 percent in the

MLB) for negotiating a player contract are among the many agent certification and compliance conditions imposed by various players' unions.

Chapter Seven

Intellectual Property and Sports Law

"We prefer to battle our competitors in the marketplace and on the field of play."—Kevin Plank, Under Armour CEO, after suing Nike for appropriating the phrase "Protect this house" in its online and social media sites

The term *intellectual property* refers to the exclusive intangible property rights of the mind granted to those who creatively express an idea. The laws of intellectual property encompass familiar topics, such as *patents, trademarks, trade names, trade dress,* and *copyrights.* Closely related to these areas of interest and significance in sports are the *rights of publicity, freedom of the press* to publish newsworthy information, and the tort or civil wrong of *defamation,* which are more fully addressed in the following chapter.

One of the reasons intellectual property is so relevant to the study of sports law is because these property rights can be *sold, assigned,* or *licensed* for a fee. Collectively, the IOC, NCAA, NASCAR, WNBA, FIFA World Cup, and professional sports teams and leagues around the world generate billions of dollars in revenue from diverse sources. The right to broadcast a game on television, by radio, or over the Internet includes licensing of copyrighted material, team logos, and brand names (trade names), along with negotiated advertising and sponsorship contracts.

Recently, NBC, CBS, and FOX renewed their NFL television-broadcasting contracts. Annually, the league receives about $2 billion split evenly between its thirty-two teams. By the 2022 season, the broadcasting licensing fees jump to more than $3 billion a year. In a separate deal, ESPN paid for the privilege of retaining exclusive television rights for "Monday Night Football" through 2021. Annual payments by then will reach $1.9 billion, up from the present $1.1 billion.

The NFL is the premier league for generating sports revenue in the United States. Advertisers are willing to pay on average more than $3.5 million a minute during Super Bowl broadcasts because the game draws an unsurpassed diverse male and female audience. In a typical fall television season, more than 90 percent of the most-watched shows are NFL games.

The Spanish-language media giant Univision paid $325 million to broadcast the last two FIFA World Cups in Spanish throughout the United States and Puerto Rico. Meanwhile, ABC and ESPN paid $100 million for the English-broadcasting media rights, including Internet.

NBC won the broadcast licensing rights in the United States for Rio 2016, the first summer Olympic Games hosted by a South American country, Brazil. The network paid $1.226 billion, about the same as it paid in licensing fees to the IOC for similar broadcasting rights to the London Games in 2012 but more than double what it spent for the 2000 Sydney Olympics domestic-broadcasting rights.

Broadcast licensing enables teams, leagues, and sporting events to generate brand recognition and consumer awareness. Licensing also occurs when the manufacturers of products, such as Under Armour, Nike, adidas, and Electronic Arts, pay for the right to sell T-shirts, jerseys, shoes, mascots, emblems, and video games bearing the names of teams, jersey colors, and logos; in most cases they are all registered as protected trademarks under federal statutory law.

Under three different types of legal doctrine—common law, statutory law, and foreign treaties and conventions—the various forms of intellectual property receive protection from those who might use the product, brand name, or broadcast without authorization or permission (see table 7.1). The business of *protecting* the legal rights of sports organizers, governing bodies, leagues, and teams from illegal infringement or unfair competition from counterfeiting of their exclusive economic ownership rights is a big business. At stake is the potential loss of billions of dollars in revenue and even damage to the reputations of the owners and managers of sports enterprises and their branding.

COPYRIGHT OWNERSHIP AND PROTECTION OF BROADCASTS

A **copyright** gives the owner of a creative work the right to prevent others from using the work without permission or license. In an early case dealing with who owns the property rights to the broadcast of a sporting event, the Pittsburgh Pirates baseball team sued a local radio station that broadcasted play-by-play descriptions of home games relying on paid observers located outside the ballpark. The Pirates, by written contract, had granted the exclusive rights to broadcast account of the games to competing radio stations for compensation.

Table 7.1.

	Copyright	Trademark	Patent
Subject Matter Protected	Works of original authorship fixed in tangible mediums of expression, such as writing, music, paintings, photos, literature, software, games, sculpture, and sound recordings.	Word, phrase, letter, number, taste, smell, sound, shape, logo, mark, emblem, name, picture, sign, and design used to distinguish the goods and services of one organization, event, team, or league from another.	An exclusive right for an invention—a product or process that provides anything new or a useful improvement.
Examples	Team photo, rule books, visual image and audio recording of a game (e.g., NFL broadcast or NFL film), team playbooks, advertisements, published results of an event, databases, technical drawings, scripted choreographed moves (such as World Entertainment Wrestling match), and Madden NFL Mobile.	Word: *Kentucky Derby*. Symbol: Nike's swoosh. Number matched with name and color. Term: *March Madness*.	Products: Use of lighter-weight materials in wheelchairs for Paralympic athletes, prosthetic carbon-fiber blade for such amputees as Oscar Pistorius, replacement of natural materials (aluminum for wood in baseball bats, nylon for cow's intestine in strings for tennis rackets, polyurethane foam blank and epoxy for redwood in surf boards). Methods or processes (highly controversial): Sports training techniques, such as a method for putting a golf ball, a method for fitness training, a method for training baseball players. Arena Football teams contest a "rival free game" under its newly patented method and rules of play.

Term of Protec-tion	Life of author plus 70 years, or work for hire—95 years from publication or 120 years after creation, whichever expires first. All for works created after January 1, 1987. Under international law, not less than 50 years from creation.	20 years plus renewable under federal statute (Lanham Act). World Intellectual Property Organization (WIPO) enables global registration.	20 years from effective date of filing design patents; 14 years from issuance.
Manner of Acquiring	Common law—automatic, no registration required, or may file with US Copyright Office for enhanced statutory protection (Lanham Act). Berne Convention internationally.	In the United States, automatic registration with use; federal statute grants stronger protection (Lanham Act). International registration via Madrid treaties administered by WIPO.	Application to US Patent and Trademark Office; globally WIPO enables inventors to file single international application.
Grant	Exclusive ownership of right to reproduce, publicly exhibit, broadcast, translate, and adapt and may assign, sell, or license.	Exclusive ownership of right to use the marks to identify goods and services or to authorize others to use for payment.	Exclusive ownership conferring a right to exclude others from using or selling the product or process.
Infringe-ment	Copying a substantial portion of work without license or permission.	Unauthorized use likely to cause confusion, mistake, deception, or dilution of the value of the mark.	Unauthorized use.

Defenses to Infringement	Fair use: not commercial, limited in amount and substantiality of portion used to whole work, criticism, news reporting, in public domain, parody.	Fair use, nominal use, parody.	Showing that a patent owner misused the patent, invention does not work, prior art affects the novelty or nonobviousness of invention so it did not qualify for patent, failure to fully disclose the invention in the application.

In sweeping language, the court determined the property right in disseminating, publishing, selling, or licensing the play-by-play descriptions of the baseball game is vested exclusively in the Pirates. Consequentially, the unauthorized broadcasting of real-time game information constituted unfair competition calculated to interfere with the economic licensing rights of the team (*Pittsburgh Athletic Co. v. KQV Broadcasting Co.*, 24 F. Supp. 490, W.D. Pa. 1938).

The *Pirates* court case relied on pre-1976 copyright law. It was decided under common-law theories of unjust enrichment. The original foundation for copyright recognition is found in article 1, section 8, clause 8, of the US Constitution, known as the **Copyright Clause**. The express purpose of granting inventors and authors a property right is to encourage and protect the creative process to advance the sciences and arts. By 1976, the United States had enacted its fourth generation of federal copyright law, which codified the principle decided in the *Pirates* decision by providing express copyright protection for broadcast of an athletic event.

While the **Copyright Act of 1976** grants the owners of a copyright the exclusive right to capture a sporting event and distribute it over the airways, a key legal question is, Who actually owns the copyright to broadcast a sporting event? In *Baltimore Orioles, Inc. v. MLBPA* (805 F.2d 663, 7th Cir. 1986), the court ruled that the telecasts of baseball games rely on the performance of the players; however the players are employees of the team, and their performances before broadcast audiences fall within the scope of their employment obligations. In legalese, the club owners are the *authors* and own the copyrights associated with the telecast of the games.

Similar judicial decisions acknowledge that the NFL owns the copyright in all of its game telecasts, not the players; promoters of boxing matches, not the boxers, own the copyright in the film distribution of fights.

Typically, within a professional sports league, the owners contractually parcel out local and national broadcast rights working with various media networks. Connected to antitrust law as discussed in chapter 5, the **Sports Broadcasting Act** grants professional sporting teams a limited exemption from antitrust scrutiny to allow for the pooling of broadcast rights and entering into broadcast-licensing deals with networks and media outlets.

Astute students are asking themselves how it is possible that local news stations can broadcast brief highlights to games or students can upload for viewing videos containing copyrighted graphics, sound recordings, and images on social media sites featuring outstanding or outlandish athletic performances without infringing on or violating the copyrights of the broadcast owners. Herein lies the rub in copyright law.

In answering the initial question about news organizations showing team or event highlights, the clubs forward action clips in many instances to the stations for that specific use. When the recorded broadcast events are truly *newsworthy*, such as the sudden death of a prominent athlete or announcement of the first transgender player in a league, then the First Amendment rights of freedom of speech, press, and information serves as a broad exception to the restrictive copyright rules.

As to the second inquiry, unfortunately, none of the language or terms in existing or past copyright statutes supply a precise self-evident means for determining when the public can fairly use parts or components of a copyrighted work without infringing on the private property interests of the owner of the work.

Technology and the Internet make it easier than ever for the public to record, appropriate, distribute, reproduce, modify, edit, mash up, collage, mock, or exploit for fun or commerce sounds and images produced and transmitted by sporting-event owners. Teams and leagues attempt to ward off potential infringers by noting before or after event broadcasts that "any rebroadcast, retransmission or other use of the events of this game, without the express written consent of the owner, is expressly prohibited" by law. The effectiveness of this warning is debatable and perhaps even false in light of the fair-use exception to infringement, which is further described next.

Fair Use

The most significant defense to a claim of copyright infringement is *fair use*, which is codified in section 107 of the federal copyright statute. This defense is the basis for nearly every conversation and deliberation about how society should strike a balance between a private-property right available for license or sale that carries enormous revenue potential and the public's interest in the free flow of learning and sharing the expression of ideas found in the broadcast.

ESPN commentators, *New York Times* sports columnists, *Sports Illustrated* writers, non-media-credentialed bloggers, and just about anyone else are all free to publicly report the outcomes of games, comment on referees' calls, criticize coaching decisions, and conduct scholarly research on statistical aspects of the sporting game free from restriction under the fair use doctrine.

For instance, in *NBA v. Motorola, Inc.* (105 F.3d 841, 2d Cir. 1997), the court ruled that the reproduction of real-time statistics from a basketball game does *not* constitute a copyright infringement, even when the statistical information is gathered from watching a televised copyright broadcast. The real-time game information was keyed into a computer and ultimately transmitted to purchasers of paging devices that displayed real-time scores, time of possession, names of teams playing, and so on.

There are some important points to consider from this case. The first is that copyright does not prevent parties from gathering and reporting *facts* or statistical data from game broadcasts. There is no copyright for the underlying facts of the game, such as LeBron James hitting the game-winning three-point shot at the end of regulation play.

However, let us distinguish this fact pattern from a situation where a blogger watches a game on TV and simultaneously reports blow-by-blow game accounts over the Internet or Tweets the full event sequentially in real time. In this circumstance, the reporting may constitute a broadcast, placing the case squarely on all fours with the *Pirates* judgment.

While we are toying with facts, the fair-use doctrine could have been used as a defense in the *Pirates* decision had the court found that the fact-finding process was protected by copyright. Fair use guards the public's *right of access to information*, such as game statistics.

In contrast, many decades ago, the US Supreme Court held that a local television broadcast of an *entire* circus performance, to wit, a fifteen-second human cannonball act, violated the right of the owner of the event to control the broadcast distribution. Media claims of First Amendment newsworthy protection were denied. Consequentially, this landmark decision stands for the proposition that, whenever a broadcaster publishes or depicts an athlete's entire performance without permission or license, the athlete's publicity rights trump any First Amendment protection claim. (See *Zacchini v. Scripps-Howard Broadcasting*, 433 U.S. 564, 1977.)

In another significant case, ESPN unsuccessfully argued statutory fair use and First Amendment newsworthiness defenses when it contended that its *rebroadcast* of taped highlights of sporting events is permissible. The court determined that ESPN wrongly appropriated the owner's *expression* of that information by copying highlights of the original film broadcast (*New Boston Television, Inc. v. ESPN, Inc.*, 215 U.S. P.Q. 755, D. Mass 1981).

The ESPN decision highlights an important distinction regarding protected interests in the land of copyrights that is worth repeating. Copyright protects the way an owner or author expresses him- or herself; it does not protect the facts, information, or idea conveyed in the broadcast or publication.

Quite frankly, the findings of many of the fair-use decisions, especially when applied to music and fine arts cases, where an argument is made that the new work or publication *transforms* the original copyrighted material, are frequently subjective. A clear example of the nonclarity of the application of the fair-use doctrine one could argue is found in the court's *New Boston Television* case mentioned earlier. Unlike in *Zacchini*, where the entire performance was transmitted to the public over the airways, ESPN broadcasted substantially less than the whole sporting event, and it did so after the event occurred live.

To fully understand the distinction between infringement and fair use requires an analysis of the four crucial factors outlined in *section 107*:

1. The purpose and character of the use, commercial or not (e.g., educational);
2. The nature of the copyrighted work;
3. The amount and substantiality of the portion used in relation to the copyrighted work as a whole; and
4. The effect of the use on the market or potential market for, or value of, the copyrighted work.

Keep in mind that there is no safe-harbor rule that guarantees that reproducing a limited portion of a copyrighted work will always qualify as a protected fair use. That is, there is no specific number of words, lines from a publication, or portion of a broadcast that could be safely used or republished without permission or license.

In general, in applying these four factors, judges evaluate them one by one to determine whether a particular use of a copyrighted work falls within the exception to the infringement rule. The concept of transformative use mentioned earlier focuses on the third factor. Justice Souter, in a 1994 decision that reviewed whether a rap band's borrowing of the opening lines from the song "Oh, Pretty Women" by Roy Orbison fell within the fair-use defense, emphasized the necessity of examining whether the new song transformed the purpose and character of the original song. In this instance, Justice Souter determined the lyrics or material taken were given new meaning and, therefore, were protected (*Campbell v. Acuff-Rose Music*, 510 U.S. 569, 1994).

Of course, the safest course to avoid litigation and the possibility of the copyright holder filing an injunction to prevent further use or to stave off a request for financial remuneration for lost revenue is to seek permission. Ironically, in the "Oh, Pretty Women" case, the rap band, 2 Live Crew, originally sought to purchase the right to use portions of the Orbison hit song. The copyright holder denied the licensing request because it did not want any of his lyrics used in a rap song. In any event, let's return to the ESPN decision for further analysis.

Examples of false defense

ESPN is a commercial for-profit media enterprise, but that fact alone does not prohibit the application of the fair-use defense. Fictional or highly expressive copyrighted works tend to receive greater copyright protection. Television game broadcasts do require technical skills even though they are depicting live factual events. The statutory language that protects owners of the games requires an examination of the amount or *quantity* of the whole taken. A twenty-second highlight from a full-length professional sporting event is a small amount of the whole game. The policy of courts in judging these cases, though, is to consider the *quality* or significance of the highlighted broadcast. Showing the game-winning ninth-inning homerun in a 1–0 score argues against the fair-use defense. A brief visual clip of a quarterback sack that did not influence the outcome of the game may support the defensive argument. The last factor looks to whether ESPN's unauthorized use harms the market or economic value of the original broadcast. An argument can be made that the media outlet that paid the licensing fee to broadcast the game could edit and distribute its own highlights. Therefore, ESPN's action has damaged the market or potential market for rebroadcast. On the other hand, ESPN's highlights may serve as a teaser, encouraging viewers to watch the entire rebroadcast.

This analysis demonstrates the complexity in applying the fair-use doctrine as a defense to charges of copyright infringement.

A 1983 US Supreme Court decision, *Sony Corporation of America v. Universal City Studios, Inc.* (464 U.S. 417), made it clear that recording a sports' broadcast for noncommercial, in-home personal use is not a copyright infringement. Charging your friends even a nominal sum, to wit, chips and soft drinks, to watch a prerecorded game on your personal high-definition flat-screen television in theory may violate an owner's broadcast copyright. The commercial versus noncommercial use distinction can be an important factor in fair-use analysis, as described earlier, especially when the entire game is rebroadcast, not short snippets.

On the heels of World Cup fans uploading thousands of short-action soccer clips on social media platforms, such as Twitter and even YouTube, within seconds of the action being broadcast, more and more professional leagues and teams around the world are concerned about the unauthorized sharing of copyrighted game broadcasts.

The Premier League in the United Kingdom licenses its soccer broadcast rights to BT and Sky Television for about $1.4 billion annually. The publishers of two prominent British papers pay nearly $30 million a year for the right to broadcast Premier League game *highlights* on the papers' video websites. To protect these commercial interests, some clubs are reminding paying fans that it is a violation of ticket-sale restrictions to film and post live game footage on social media sites for nonpersonal use. Another affirmative step is to prohibit the use of stadium Wi-Fi for uploading game footage to the

Internet. Both steps may sound reasonable but undoubtedly are unpopular among fans.

Sports leagues and traditional broadcast networks are watching a rising tide of viewers who are canceling their cable subscriptions and watching games and major sporting events streamed online. In 2012, an upstart enterprise, Aereo, attempted to establish a new viewing service that required subscribers to pay a less-than-twelve-dollar-a-month fee to rent a small antenna that captured over-the-air signals.

Using modern technology, Aero sought to mimic the primitive model of the '50s, '60s, and '70s, where a rabbit-ear antenna sat atop a television box, allowing for free viewing of publicly broadcast shows. After two years of legal squabbling, the US Supreme Court ruled that the retransmission of public performances, including sporting events, requires permission of the copyright owner, which Aereo did not have.

Readers who are interested in examining the subject of fair use further will find many valuable sources online, including the US Copyright Office at www.copyright.gov.

TRADEMARKS

The business of sports marketing, advertising, and retailing is centered on the law of *trademarks*, which is codified by US statute in the **Federal Trademark Act of 1946 (Lanham Act)**. Trademarks are different from copyrights and patents, which have fixed terms. Trademarks can last forever unless they fall into the *public domain* from nonuse and abandonment or become a generic term. Trademarks are *symbols*, *words*, *names*, or *devices* that help to identify and distinguish one product or service from a competing product or service. In addition, *shapes*, *fragrances*, *sounds*, and *colors* may also be trademarked. The law of trademarks has expanded to include **trade dress**. Trademark owners possess the legal authority to stop others from using the same or similar symbols or marks when their unauthorized use creates a likelihood of deception or confusion, subject to important exceptions.

David Moore is an artist who specializes in painting iconic sports figures and historic scenes from memorable college football games, including those from the University of Alabama. Moore is in the business of selling his sports paintings, prints, and even calendars. The University of Alabama sued Moore for failing to pay a licensing fee. The university argued that the team's uniform colors and designs depicted in his art are trademarked and Moore's use of the uniforms confuses the public into thinking that the school endorses his paintings.

Hogwash, ruled the Eleventh Circuit Court of Appeals in announcing that Moore never marketed the paintings as "endorsed" or "sponsored" by the university. More importantly, the court noted that the trademarked colors and designs are needed by Moore to realistically portray the famous football scenes. In sweeping language, the court held that the works are "embodiments of artistic expression, and are entitled to First Amendment protection" (*University of Alabama Board of Trustees v. New Life, Inc.*, 683 F. 3rd 1266, 11th Cir. 2012).

This decision is significant because it stands for the proposition that video-game designers, graphic artists, filmmakers, graphic artists, and other artists in some situations might be able to use trademarks in their works so long as they do not create a connection in the minds of the consumer of a link between the artists and the trademark holder.

The Sixth Circuit Court of Appeals, a few years before, reached a similar conclusion when it determined that a well-known sports artist who painted and sold collages of artistic depictions of Tiger Woods golfing was protected by the First Amendment against a claim of false endorsement under the Lanham Act. In this instance, the artist not only featured a likeness of Woods in his art works but also included his name in the print. The court further noted that the artist does not lose First Amendment protection of the idea or concept communicated in the visual art when the work is offered for sale (*ETW Corporation v. Jireh Publishing, Inc.*, 332 F.3d 915, 6th Cir. 2003).

The electrifying former Texas A&M Heisman-winning quarterback, now attempting to play football in the NFL, Johnny Manziel, has filed ten trademark applications with the **US Patent and Trademark Office (USPTO)**. Manziel's intent in registering the moniker "Johnny Football"; "The House That Johnny Built" (referencing the renovated A&M stadium); and now his new nickname, "Johnny Cleveland," is to use these marks on licensed athletic apparel and footwear. However, while federal trademark law protects marks used in interstate commence and allows for federal court jurisdiction in the event of a dispute, existing common-law recognition of trademarks or names and state trademark legislation provide nearly identical protection. An entire 2015 law review article found at http://www.scholarlycommons.law. northwestern.edu is devoted to Manziel's trademark registration and how it might affect the intellectual property rights of NCAA student-athletes.

On a related note, in 1997, the original case that recognized the protection of an athlete's nickname occurred when Elroy "Crazylegs" Hirsch successfully sued a company for marketing a moisturizing shaving cream under the name of "Crazylegs." At the time, Hirsch was a "rock star" football player of national prominence who acquired his nickname because of his unique running style that was described as looking "something like a whirling eggbeater." The court ruled that the unauthorized commercial use of the name "Crazylegs" violated Hirsch's personal right of publicity in his nickname and infringed on his common-law trade name rights (*Hirsch v. S. C. Johnson & Sons, Inc.*, 90 Wis. 2d 379, 1997).

Manziel is not the first modern sports figure to commercially capitalize on a distinctive name or series of words the public draws an association with. NBA coach Pat Reilly owns four trademarks associated with the word *Three-Peat*. In a recent registration filing with the USPTO, Riley's company filed a trademark to use the number-word combination *3-Peat* on sports memorabilia, rings, and other jewelry.

In 2003, Lance Armstrong launched the LIVESTRONG brand, to re-sounding success, for his philanthropic foundation that provides assistance for those suffering from cancer. Among the foundation's thirty-nine federal trademark registrations is the well-known yellow wristband. A sample of the familiar wristband mark that was registered for protection with the USPTO is shown in figure 7.1.

Sometimes, though, marketers that rely on an athlete's positive projections of doing "good" for the public can suffer when that athlete falls into disgrace. By way of example, the LIVESTRONG Foundation saw donations sink by 35 percent less than a year after Armstrong publicly admitted to his extensive use of performance-enhancing drugs in contravention of the rules of his sport. In a familiar situation when a brand becomes too closely connected to a public figure who now conjures up a negative image, the foundation was forced removed Armstrong from its board leadership in an attempt to rebrand itself.

Trademark protects more than team logos, names of athletes, sports teams, and slogans. Such sporting goods equipment as Rawlings baseball bats, K2 snowboards, Trek bicycles, Hobie surfboards, Tubbs snowshoes, and Abu Garcia fishing rods are all recognized branded consumer goods. Fans who attend sporting events frequently eat Oscar Meyer hotdogs and munch on Frito-Lay-branded Cracker Jack popcorn and nuts while drinking Coca Cola or Pepsi beverages. These are all examples of branded products and goods protected under the trademark or name intellectual property umbrella.

Figure 7.1.   Livestrong trademark bracelet. Photo courtesy Lexi Jones.

In 2014, the Trademark Trial and Appeals Board of the USPTO took a long-awaited courageous vote when it canceled the Washington Redskins' federal trademark on the basis that it is "disparaging to Native Americans." Eight years earlier, five Native Americans representing four tribes had filed a case against the Washington football franchise on the grounds that the name and logo, which involved six different uses of the "Redskins" trademark, are an offensive slur to Native American people. *Section 2(a)* of the **Lanham Act** prohibits the registration and allows for the cancellation of any mark that is "disparaging, scandalous, contemptuous or disreputable."

This administrative law decision, which has been appealed to a federal district court, does not mean the owner of the team, Daniel Snyder, can no longer use the name *Redskins* when referring to his NFL franchise. It does mean, though, that the team and the other NFL clubs that share in team-licensing revenue cannot collect royalties or licensing fees from the use of the name and logo. In effect, any fan is free to produce and sell previously protected Washington Redskins–logoed apparel and equipment without having to pay a licensing fee. It is not clear whether, under the common law and state trademark law, the Redskins' mark might still be protected. In any event, this ruling adds to the considerable political weight in Congress and moral pressure from civil rights activists to encourage Mr. Snyder to change the name of his Washington professional football franchise.

TRADE DRESS

In addition to the standard recognition of protecting names, words, services, symbols, and devices under trademarks, the law has expanded to protect distinctive identifying features, commonly called *trade dress*. In this regard, Nike won a permanent order enjoining a company called Not For Noth'N from designing and selling shoes strikingly similar in looks to the ever-popular and famous line of Air Jordan (also a registered-trademark name) shoes. Nike has protected every new variation of the shoes by obtaining design patents, trademarks, and trade dress rights.

In an interesting sidebar to the Nike decision, design patents last fourteen years. The original Air Jordan debuted in 1985, and therefore, the design patent for this shoe has expired. Nike was successful in stopping the copying of this particular shoe design because the *trade dress* rights still exist.

The trade dress rights of university sports teams became a thorny issue when a company called Smack Apparel began selling T-shirts containing colors, images, and slogans that were strikingly similar to the color schemes of the teams that were competing in championship bowl games. None of the T-shirts actually contained any of the teams' registered trademarks. Nonetheless, the Fifth Circuit Court of Appeals held that the unlicensed sale of the T-shirts violated the schools' trade dress. The court determined that the color schemes of the universities' football uniforms were extremely strong marks known to the public, had acquired a distinctive secondary meaning (associating the school colors with the universities), and were nonfunctional, and given the overwhelming similarity of the marks and the apparel company's intent to profit from the universities' reputations, to permit their sale would likely cause confusion in the minds of consumers (*Board of Supervisors for Louisiana State University v. Smack Apparel Co.*, 550 F. 3d 465, 5th Cir. 2008).

PATENTS

In a world where our mobile phones do far more than what consumers even ask of them, it is not shocking that the public now expects more from their sporting equipment. A major growth industry is the combination of technology with athletic equipment. Innovative firms, such as Nike, Samsung, and Google, are designing wearable devices that monitor an athlete's activity. In response to lawsuits from former football players for brain injuries related to concussions, such companies as Riddell, the licensed helmet company for the NFL, has designed headgear that measures the impact of a tackle and transmits that data to a wireless sideline device. There are soccer balls that can measure the strength of a kick, golf clubs designed to analyze a swing, electronic devices that use global positioning technology and sonar displays to help catch fish, basketball shoes that measure vertical leap, and running shoes that increase foot and ankle stability to minimize injury. The NFL began installing devices that track every player's movement through shoulder-pad sensors. The device enables teams to chart via data points every player's location, speed, and distance traveled. The information collected makes it possible for teams to calculate everything from a running back's acceleration speed to how quickly a safety can tackle a wide receiver.

In the cases described here, there is legal infighting over who owns the right to make, use, and offer for sale *each* of these inventions. For instance, in 2015, a firm called Zynx System Developers, Inc., filed suit against the company that piloted the NFL's on-the-field sensor tracking devices, alleging it stole the proprietary technology. In all of these cases, the intellectual property right in question is referred to as a *patent*. By federal statute (Patent Act), the USPTO is responsible for thoroughly reviewing a patent application before determining whether it meets the legal standard for issuing a patent. Patents exist to protect those who devise a new, nonobvious, novel, useful invention (*utility*) or design an original and new ornamental feature found on a manufactured product (*design*). Depending on whether a patent is designat-

Patent

ed a utility or design patent, its term of protection lasts either twenty years after application or fourteen years from date of issue, respectively.

Unfortunately, patent litigation in the sports arena also is becoming a growth industry as the new technology moves from the field of play to the courtroom. The fitness-tracking company Jawbone has filed multiple lawsuits against Fitbit, accusing the company of infringing on a patent for a "wellness application using data from data-capable band." Fitbit is best known for manufacturing wearable devices that act as heart-rate monitors, sleep monitors, and pedometers. Jawbone's principal business includes fitness trackers and audio speakers. Both companies have developed and protected hundreds of fitness-related patents and expect lengthy and costly court battles.

In an intriguing twist to the fitness tracker controversy, Jawbone has recognized that there might be an international aspect to the dispute that it could leverage. The International Trade Commission, a quasi-judicial body, has the authority to block the importation of any component parts used in the manufacture of Fitbit's products should it determine that Fitbit has engaged in the *unfair trade practice* of patent infringement.

For the advanced reader, there are other international regulatory bodies and agreements that might have application to global intellectual property disputes involving sport-related entities. One of the best known is the General Agreement on Tariffs and Trade, which created the World Trade Organization to enforce compliance with free-trade agreements. The Paris Convention is a treaty that regulates trademark relations between the United States and other countries. Another crucial accord for sports businesses doing business outside the United States is the Berne Convention. It is an international treaty that standardizes basic copyright protection throughout the world. Finally, the Patent Cooperation Treaty is an international agreement that streamlines procedures for obtaining patent protection among its member countries.

SUMMARY

Innovation and creativity play a crucial role in helping to push the boundaries of athletic success and can make a sport safer to play. The law of patents encourages inventors to employ technological advances to develop and sell better sporting goods equipment. By adding a distinctive name or logo to sporting gear or a team name, a trademark can help develop brand awareness. The "look" of a product can be protected by trade dress. The graphic design, advertising copy, and sound recordings used to promote the equipment, league, team, or brand name in advertising and marketing can be a subject of copyright protection. A copyright statute specifically protecting the owners of a game from unlawful infringement by unlicensed broadcasters governs the broadcast of sporting events containing play-by-play announcements and colorful graphic images of real-time performance. Collectively, these intellectual property rights provide legal protection to the economic value of sports.

KEY WORDS

Copyright. A copyright gives the owner of a creative work the right to prevent others from using the work without permission or license. Copyrights are works of original authorship fixed in tangible mediums of expression, such as writing, music, paintings, photos, literature, software, games, sculpture, and sound recordings.

Copyright Act of 1976. Grants the owners of a copyright the exclusive right to capture a sporting event and distribute it over the airways.

Copyright Clause. A section of the US Constitution that grants Congress the power to promote the arts and sciences by granting exclusive property right to their original writings and inventions.

Fair Use. The most significant defense to a claim of infringement is fair use, which is codified in section 107 of the federal copyright statute. This defense is the basis for nearly every conversation and deliberation about how society should strike a balance between a private property right available for license or sale that carries enormous revenue potential and the public's interest in the free flow of learning and sharing the expression of ideas found in a broadcast.

Federal Trademark Act of 1946 (Lanham Act). The act that codified the business of sports marketing, advertising, and retailing and is centered on the law of trademarks.

Intellectual Property. The exclusive intangible property rights of the mind granted to those who creatively express an idea. The laws of intellectual property encompass familiar topics, such as patents, trademarks, trade names, copyrights, and domain names.

Lanham Act. *See* Federal Trademark Act of 1946 (Lanham Act).

Patent. Patents exist to protect those who devise a new, nonobvious, novel, useful invention (utility) or design an original and new ornamental feature found on a manufactured product (design). Depending on whether a patent is designated a utility or design patent, its term of protection lasts either twenty years after application or fourteen years from date of issue, respectively.

Sports Broadcasting Act. A federal statute that grants professional sports teams an exemption from antitrust laws to pool broadcasting rights.

Trade Dress. A term that describes distinctive identifying features that cannot be infringed on, such as the unique designs of Nike's sneakers.

Trademark. A symbol, word, name, or device that helps to identify and distinguish one product or service from a competing product or service. Trademarks are different from copyrights and patents, which have fixed terms. Trademarks can last forever unless they fall into the public domain from nonuse and abandonment or become a generic term. Trademark owners possess the legal authority to stop others from using the same or similar symbols or marks when their unauthorized use creates a likelihood of deception or confusion, subject to important exceptions.

US Patent and Trademark Office (USPTO). Agency within the US Commerce Department that handles the issuance of patents for inventions to businesses and inventors and all trademark registration for product identification.

DISCUSSION QUESTIONS

1. Q: What is the relevancy of studying patents, trademarks, trade names, and copyrights in sports law?

A: One of the reasons patents, trademarks, trade names, and copyrights are so relevant to the study of sports law is that these property rights can be sold, assigned, or licensed. Collectively, the IOC, NCAA, NASCAR, FIFA World Cup, and professional sports teams and leagues around the world generate billions of dollars in revenue from diverse sources.

2. Q: What is the cost of retaining exclusive television rights for "Monday Night Football"?

A: ESPN paid for the privilege of retaining exclusive television rights for "Monday Night Football" through 2021. Annual payments by then will reach $1.9 billion, up from the present $1.1 billion.

3. Q: What are the most-watched shows during the fall television season?

A: In a typical fall television season, more than 90 percent of the most-watched shows are NFL games.

4. Q: What was the importance of *Pittsburgh Athletic Co. v. KQV Broadcasting Co.*, 24 F. Supp. 490 (W.D. Pa. 1938)?

A: The Pittsburgh Pirates baseball team sued a local radio station that broadcasted play-by-play descriptions of home games relying on paid observers located outside the ballpark. The Pirates, by written contract, had granted the exclusive rights to broadcast accounts of the games to competing radio stations for compensation. In sweeping language, the court determined that the property right in disseminating, publishing, selling, or licensing the play-by-play descriptions of baseball games is vested exclusively in the Pirates. Consequentially, the unauthorized broadcasting of real-time game information constituted unfair competition calculated to interfere with the economic licensing rights of the team.

5. Q: What is the Copyright Clause, and what is its purpose?

A: The original foundation for copyright recognition is found in article 1, section 8, clause 8, of the Constitution, known as the Copyright Clause. The express purpose of granting inventors and authors a property right is to encourage and protect the creative process to advance the sciences and arts.

6. Q: What does the Copyright Act of 1976 grant to owners?

A: The Copyright Act of 1976 grants the owners of a copyright the exclusive right to capture a sporting event and distribute it over the airways.

7. Q: What case determined that club owners are the authors and own the copyrights associated with the telecast of baseball games?

A: In *Baltimore Orioles, Inc. v. MLBPA* (805 F.2d 663, 7th Cir. 1986), the court ruled that the telecasts of baseball games rely on the performance of the players; however, the players are employees of the team, and their performances before broadcast audiences fall within the scope of their employment obligations. In legalese, the club owners are the authors and own the copyrights associated with the telecast of the games.

8. Q: Who owns the rights to telecasts of NFL games?

A: Based on judicial decisions, it has been acknowledged that the NFL owns the copyright in all of its game telecasts.

9. Q: What was the importance of *NBA v. Motorola, Inc.* (105 F.3d 841, 2d Cir. 1997) in regards to the reporting of statistics from live games?

A: In *NBA v. Motorola, Inc.* (105 F.3d 841, 2d Cir. 1997), the court ruled that the reproduction of real-time statistics from a basketball game does not constitute a copyright infringement, even when the statistical information is gathered from watching a televised copyright broadcast. The real-time game information was keyed into a computer and ultimately transmitted to purchasers of paging devices that displayed real-time scores, time of possession, names of teams playing, and so on.

10. Q: What are the four factors of the second part of the fair-use doctrine?

A: The second part of the fair-use doctrine requires an analysis of four factors:

1. The purpose and character of the use, commercial or not (e.g., educational);

2. The nature of the copyrighted work;
3. The amount and substantiality of the portion used in relation to the copyrighted work as a whole; and
4. The effect of the use on the market or potential market for, or value of, the copyrighted work.

11. Q: What was important about the Supreme Court's decision in *Sony Corporation of America v. Universal City Studios, Inc.* (464 U.S. 417)?

A: A 1983 US Supreme Court decision, *Sony Corporation of America v. Universal City Studios, Inc.* (464 U.S. 417), made it clear that recording a sports broadcast for noncommercial, in-home personal use is not a copyright infringement.

Chapter Eight

Privacy, Publicity, and Defamation

"Who steals my purse steals trash; 'tis something, nothing
'Twas mine, 'tis his, and has been slave to thousands;
But he that filches from me my good name
Robs me of that which not enriches him,
And makes me poor indeed."

—William Shakespeare, *The Tragedy of Othello, the Moor of Venice* III:iii

In 1890, two former classmates from Harvard Law School wrote an article published in the *Harvard Law Review* titled "The Right to Privacy." In response to the tabloid journalism of their era, they stirred the legal community with a call to arms to protect ordinary citizens against the exposure of their personal affairs on the public pages of the press. They dubbed this new right the **right to privacy,** or the right to be left alone.

Closely related to the right to privacy is the notion that there is commercial value in a person's name or likeness. This cognate right is called the **right of publicity.** In some ways this right is similar to a privacy right but differs insofar as it is a *property* interest that can be bartered, assigned, or transferred for consideration. A product or service endorsement by an athlete is an example of an exercise of a public person's publicity rights.

Unlike copyrights and other forms of intellectual property law that are largely governed by federal statutes, privacy and publicity rights are the product of common-law cases and state statutes.

A third right of interest is the reputation right of **defamation.** Quite prevalent in sports today are lawsuits filed against reporters and bloggers for publishing statements or images that may be unflattering, untrue, or malicious.

The challenge for society is to harmonize each of these rights with *free speech* protection. For instance, Tiger Woods closely guards his private life

129

while accepting millions of dollars from such companies as Nike, General Motors, Gatorade, and Titleist for the privilege of associating his name with their products. News stories about his marriage infidelities led to publication of pictures of Tiger and his alleged mistresses, with screaming headlines, such as "I Slept with Tiger Woods the Night His Dad Died." These reports may have held Tiger up to ridicule, embarrassment, and public contempt, but to the extent that they spoke the truth, the words and images are protected by the First Amendment.

Late-night comedians joined in on the cheating scandal conversation, too. Jay Leno of the *Tonight Show* joked, "Gatorade has officially ended their relationship with Tiger Woods. He was seeing at least five other sports drinks."

Comedy in the form of **parody** enjoys equally strong legal protection under freedom-of-the-press case law standards. Woods hired a public relations firm to help him reestablish his reputation.

THE RIGHT TO PRIVACY

Some years after the publication of the famous *Harvard Law Review* article by Samuel Warren and Louis Brandeis, the right-to-privacy interest gained traction from the scholarly writings of Dean William Prosser. He identified four separate and distinct privacy *torts*. He suggested that the right to privacy is invaded when one of the following occurs:

1. Unreasonable intrusion into the private affairs or activities of a person;
2. Appropriation of a person's name or likeness;
3. Unreasonable publicity given to a person's private life; or
4. Publicity that places a person in a false light.

Notwithstanding the public's increasing concern about government and private entities encroaching on a person's right to privacy, as the common law and state statutes relate to supporting a celebrity-athlete's privacy rights, the record is mixed. Most of the successful cases argued are grounded in right-of-publicity language because they tend to involve the unauthorized use of an athlete's likeness or name, which are considered property claims, in advertising.

For instance, in a Ninth Circuit Court of Appeals case, *Motschenbacher v. R. J. Reynolds Tobacco Co.* (498 F.2d 821, 1974), the court refused to find a privacy violation under California law. Reynolds, the tobacco company, had produced a television commercial that altered a photograph containing Motschenbacher's racing car without being able to identify him as the driver. The court indicated the interest at stake was the economic value of his identity, which is under the rubric of a *property* interest.

Former heavyweight boxing champion of the world Muhammad Ali, however, was successful in asserting a violation of privacy claim against *Playgirl* magazine. The magazine depicted a nude black man seated in the corner of a boxing ring that was unmistakably recognized as Ali. The magazine included the tagline "The Greatest" with the caricature image. The court relied on a New York civil rights privacy law that makes it illegal to use a person's name, portrait, or picture for purposes of commerce without written consent. The court was careful to distinguish between the protected media interest in disseminating news or information from the commercialization of Ali's personality without his approval (*Ali v. Playgirl, Inc.*, 447 F.Supp. 723, S.D.N.Y. 1978). *Playgirl* was enjoined from distributing any more copies of the magazine worldwide. It was also required to remove all copies for sale at newsstands.

RIGHT OF PUBLICITY

Many states but not all recognize a right of *publicity*. California and New York are two states that stand out for *statutorily* accepting a celebrity's or an athlete's right to use his or her "name, likeness, or voice" in commerce for advertising or trade purposes. In other situations, this right is viewed as a derivative right from the *common law tort* of the invasion of privacy first articulated by Warren and Brandeis. In those states that do not acknowledge a right of publicity, the federal Lanham Act, section 1125(a), protects against unauthorized use of a person's identity to falsely advertise a product.

The financial significance of the recognition of publicity rights is quite apparent to anyone who reads the news, listens to the radio, watches television, or browses the Internet. Every year *Sports Illustrated* publishes a list of athletes who earn the most endorsement income. The list is valuable for identifying the names and sports of professional athletes who make more money from endorsement income than from their sport earnings.

Tony Stewart, Jimmie Johnson, Jeff Gordon, Kyle Bush, and Dale Earnhardt Jr. easily earn three to four times more by peddling diet soft drinks, tires, energy drinks, and life insurance than they do from sprinting around a racetrack. Former INDYCAR star, and now Sprint Cup racer, Danica Patrick doubles her race earnings in endorsements.

While celebrity athletes are enjoying unprecedented riches and exposure from endorsements, many leading athletic apparel and footwear companies are becoming concerned about risks associated with athletic endorsements. Nike suspended its licensing contracts with Olympic sprinter Oscar Pistorius and NFL running backs Ray Rice and Adrian Peterson after highly publicized legal proceedings.

JUDICIAL RECOGNITION, FANTASY SPORTS LEAGUES, AND SPORTS VIDEO GAMES

In 1953, a US court first recognized an athlete's common-law personality right in his name or likeness that is independent of a right to privacy. In *Haelan Laboratories, Inc. v. Topps Chewing Gum, Inc.* (202 F.2d 866, 2d Cir. 1953, *cert. denied*, 346 U.S. 816, 1953), the dispute occurred when a chewing-gum manufacturer knowingly induced a baseball player to sign a contract to use the player's photograph on a baseball card when it knew the player had already *exclusively* assigned this right in connection with the sales of gum to a rival company. The court determined that a celebrity athlete has a right to damages and other relief for the *unauthorized commercial appropriation* of the athlete's persona under New York law.

The issue of privacy linkage is important because publicity rights are considered a distinct property entity and, therefore, like most property rights are transferrable or assignable. Privacy rights, in contrast, are more closely associated with the right to be left alone and are not assignable.

Forty-three years after *Haelan*, the Tenth Circuit Court of Appeals held that a *parody* baseball card producer did not violate an athlete's publicity rights. Parody is the creative mimicking of an original protected work or interest. The company produced trading cards that used the names and cartoon caricatures of famous baseball players, such as Treasury Bonds parodying Barry Bonds (see figure 8.1). The First Amendment free-expression right outweighed the ballplayer's property rights to publicity (*Cardtoons L.C. v. MLBPA*, 868 F. Supp. 1266, N.D. Okla. 1944, *aff'd* 95 F.3d 959, 10th Cir. 1996).

The case law related to using statistical data or information about players is not always consistent and difficult to rectify. In a decision that preceded *Cardtoons*, a federal court in Minnesota found that an athlete's identity is wrapped up in his "name, likeness, statistics and other personal characteristics," which are the fruit of his or her labor and a type of property. Consequentially, a private manufacturer of baseball parlor and table games was prohibited from using information about a player's team, uniform, playing position, and game statistics (*Uhlander v. Hudrickson*, 316 F.Supp. 1282, D. Minn. 1970).

In a similar decision, a 1967 New Jersey court ruled that the manufacturer of a board golf game that contained a profile of the professional golfing career of Arnold Palmer violated his right of publicity (*Palmer v. Schonhorm Enterprises, Inc.*, 96 N.J. Super. 72, 1967).

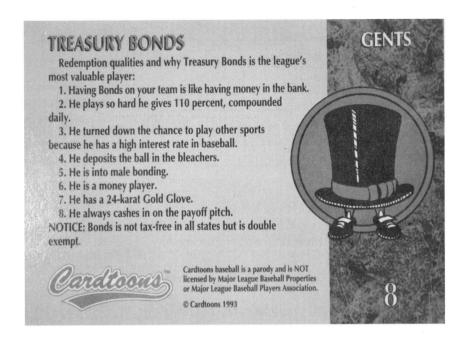

Figure 8.1. "Treasury Bonds" parody card. Photo courtesy Lexi Jones.

A state appeals court denied the claims of former baseball players that their prior employer, MLB, violated their rights of publicity when it rebroadcast games in which they appeared over the Internet. This case was resolved under California's statutory and common-law right of publicity standards (*Gionfriddo v. MLB*, 94 Cal. App.4th 400, 2001).

In a complete reversal to these findings, the Eighth Circuit Court of Appeals concluded that the First Amendment trumped an athlete's right to license game statistics and names for use in popular online *fantasy sports games*. This court noted that the state of Missouri's publicity rights were implicated. These rights, though, must give way to the protection afforded the public to use information that is readily found in the public domain, such as players' names and historical game statistics. In addition, the court rejected MLB's claim that it owned a copyright in the compilation of players' names and statistics (*C.B.C. Distribution and Marketing, Inc. v. Major League Advanced Media, L.P.*, 505 F.3d 818, 8th Cir. 2007).

The implication for online fantasy game creators is profound. This case stands for the proposition that a person can use the names of players and game statistics in a *fantasy sports league* without the need for prior approval or a license from the players or professional sports leagues.

According to a recent report by *Medill Reports*, an online publishing newsletter by graduate journalism students at Northwestern University, Yahoo!, CBSSports.com, and ESPN.com are the three leading online fantasy sports hosts. Research by the fantasy sports trade group industry has revealed that fantasy participants attend more sporting events, watch more sports on television, and purchase more sports-related gear than non–fantasy fans.

In the last reported year, more than 42 million people over the age of twelve participated in fantasy leagues in the United States and Canada. More than 5 million adults in the United Kingdom play in fantasy soccer leagues online. This growth industry is estimated to have an annual economic impact of more than $3 billion.

So while the Eighth Circuit opinion meant the loss of 9 percent royalties in licensing fees to the various professional sports leagues, the decision opened up an entirely new field of play. The majority of those who participate in fantasy sports leagues pay to play. A New Jersey court ruling held the pay-to-play format is not an illegal gambling activity under the federal **Unlawful Internet Gambling Enforcement Act of 2006.**

ELECTRONIC ARTS, VIDEO GAMES, AND COLLEGE ATHLETES

The complex issue of whether the First Amendment shields *video game makers* from lawsuits for failing to obtain a license from current and former college athletes depicted in college football video games was addressed in two separate federal appeals cases. Both cases reached similar outcomes that are hard to distinguish from the aforementioned *C.B.C. fantasy sports league* decision.

In a Third Circuit Court of Appeals case, *Hart v. EA, Inc.* (No. 11-3750, May 21, 2013), former University of Miami and later Rutgers University quarterback Ryan Hart sued Electronic Arts (EA), a video game producer. Hart sued on grounds of misappropriation of his right of publicity when EA used his player avatar, team number, and actual physical description, including height, weight, skin tone, and hometown, without his permission. EA countered that the video games are a form of expression protected by the First Amendment.

One-time Nebraska University and then Arizona State University quarterback Sam Keller also sued EA for using his likeness and personal information and athletic performance data without a license in violation of his right of publicity (*Keller v. EA, Inc.*, No. 10-15387, July 3, 2013). Keller's suit was merged with a similar lawsuit brought by former UCLA basketball player Ed O'Bannon.

Hart was the lead plaintiff in a class-action lawsuit brought under New Jersey's right of publicity state law. Keller and O'Bannon sued in California

U.S. Fantasy Sports Participation by Sport

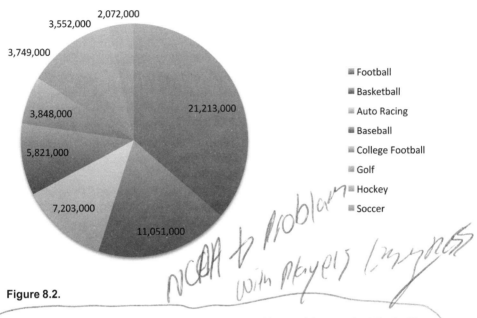

Figure 8.2.

and, like Hart, were joined by other former college athletes. The Ninth Circuit *Keller* opinion relied on California's statutory and common-law right of publicity.

Factually, it is significant to note that EA had obtained a license to use trademarks from the NCAA and individual universities whose teams appeared on the NCAA football video games. NCAA student-athletes assign broad publicity and media rights to their member institutions during their college-eligibility years. Once the players' college eligibility is over, the NCAA and the players' colleges have no claim to use their images commercially. However, in this instance, neither the NCAA nor EA obtained a specific license to use their images in these video game cases while the players were attending college. The NCAA claimed EA agreed not to use the athletes' likenesses in the video games.

Both courts determined that the use of the players' avatars, including their personal data and jersey numbers, while placing the players in virtual versions of their actual stadiums in the context of a video football game, the very sport where the players gained fame and recognition, was not a protected creative use under the First Amendment. Had EA creatively *transformed* the game environment, the result may have been different. In both rulings, the courts relied on language derived from the *fair-use* cases in *copyright*, an intellectual property right, in tipping the balance in favor of the athletes' commercial interest in their personal game likenesses.

Agreed-upon postjudgment settlement damages from EA, the College Licensing Company, and the NCAA resulted in an award in the neighborhood of $60 million. EA has put NCAA Football video games in hiatus. It stopped manufacturing the NCAA Basketball video games in 2010.

In an attempt to provide clarity in a confusing area of the law, the California federal appeals court stated the EA video game case is different from the C.B.C. fantasy sports league opinion because the avatars were derived from the players' personal identities and were not statistical game data readily found in the public domain.

Not long after these decisions, in 2014, the NCAA was dealt a crushing blow to its principle of amateurism once more by the Ninth Circuit Court of Appeals. The before-mentioned Ed O'Bannon successfully sued the NCAA on *antitrust grounds* as an *unreasonable restraint of trade* for not allowing college athletes to negotiate and receive compensation for their publicity rights, to wit, their names, images, and likenesses. The court did allow the NCAA to cap the maximum amount college athletes can receive from publicity licensing starting in 2016. However, this decision is on appeal.

The Collegiate Licensing Company, a party to the *EA* lawsuits, handles about 80 percent of the licensing by colleges largely through the NCAA. It is estimated that the licensing of college brands generates annual revenue in excess of $4 billion.

These decisions recognize the limited right of college athletes to monetize their names and likenesses. It is quite plausible that current college athletes under these judicial rulings could enter into video game licenses with EA and other commercial licensing entities subject to judicially recognized NCAA restrictions to avoid commercial exploitation of student-athletes. A postcollege athlete is free to directly market his or her name, likeness, and image.

MICHAEL JORDAN'S SLAM DUNK

In 2009, *Sports Illustrated* devoted an entire issue of its magazine to Michael Jordan. A Chicago-based grocery store was offered free advertising in exchange for agreeing to sell the commemorative magazine in its stores. The grocery store accepted the offer and ran a full-page advertisement, shown in figure 8.3. The ad displayed shoes featuring the familiar "#23" associated with Jordan, along with congratulatory references to his selection into the Naismith Basketball Hall of Fame. The store's logo appeared in the middle of the ad, saluting a fellow Chicagoan. Jordan sued the store for violating his right of publicity under Illinois statute and the unauthorized appropriation of his identity under *section 1125(a)* of the Lanham Act.

MJ Logo Being associated w/ those shoes w/ his concerts

Five years after the case began, the Seventh Circuit Court of Appeals reversed the finding of the lower federal trial court. In sending the case back to the trial court for further review and to award damages, the higher court

Figure 8.3.

determined that the ad was not a welcome celebratory gesture, rather a wrongful exploitation of Jordan's public image to promote the store's brand. The court rejected the store's assertion that the advertisement was fully protected under the First Amendment as noncommercial speech.

PUBLICITY RIGHTS AFTER DEATH

A notable distinction between a right to privacy and a right of publicity is that an individual's right to privacy ends when the individual dies. In some states, publicity rights associated with a person's commercial value may survive death. In these cases the estate or heir of a famous public person, including an athlete, may continue to control and license the deceased's image, name, and likeness.

Currently, more than twenty states by statute or common law recognize a right of publicity after death. Tennessee—the state where Elvis Presley died—places no limit on the length of the postmortem right as long as the deceased's representatives are still using it.

One might expect the celebrity- and entertainment-rich state of New York to extend the right of publicity beyond a person's lifetime. It does not. In contrast, California does recognize a seventy-year property-right term after a public person's death. The seventy-year term is identical to the familiar term length of a copyright that extends seventy years after the death of the copyright author. California's celebrity protection act grants protection to any person whose name, voice, signature, photograph, or likeness has commercial value at the time of death.

The domicile of a celebrity or an athlete at the time of death is important. A federal judge in California determined that the late Marilyn Monroe's rights of publicity were not protected in California because she was domiciled in New York when she died.

DEFAMATION

Defamation cases, much like misappropriation right-of-publicity cases, are plentiful in the world of sports and the media. In the context of amateur and professional sports, the law of *defamation* is concerned with the *reputation* of an athlete, coach, or general manager. In recent years, there has been a shift in viewing the two forms of defamation—libel and slander—from the common-law tort tradition to the constitutional law freedom-of-expression structure.

Libel is a tort, or civil wrong. It refers to a statement that impairs a person's reputation through written words. **Slander** is the twin of libel. An impairment of a person's reputation through spoken words is called slander. Increasingly, the term *libel* is used as substitute for the word *defamation*.

In 1964, the law of defamation changed dramatically. The US Supreme Court in *New York Times Co. v. Sullivan* (376 U.S. 24, 1964) was asked to determine the extent to which the constitutional protections for free speech and the media limit a state's power to award damages in a libel action brought by a public figure against those who criticize his official conduct.

Before *Sullivan*, it was possible to create liability for defamation simply by proving four things: a false and hurtful statement was made; the statement was not privileged, and it was made to a third party; the party who published the statement was negligent; and there was some harm. After *Sullivan*, for *a public official* to prevail in a libel suit, there must be proof of *"actual malice"* by the publisher, frequently the news media. For a public official to prevail in a defamation lawsuit, he or she must demonstrate that the statement was published with a *known falsehood* or published with a *reckless disregard for the truth*.

The effect of this opinion, written by Justice William Brennan, is immense for bloggers, newspapers, Internet chat rooms, advertisers, and other forms of communication that cover athletes and their professional and personal lives. The court's decision eliminated the previous "chilling" effect of traditional state-derived defamation laws. Wiggle room for minor errors in publishing factual news articles, making inaccurate statements in advertising, or misspeaking on talk shows now exists.

The First Amendment protects a publisher's right to state an *opinion*, even when the comments may be perceived as hurtful to an athlete's reputation. For instance, MLB Hall-of-Famer Orlando Cepeda unsuccessfully sued a magazine company for remarking that he was "not a team player" and "unproductive." The comments were opinions, not malicious factual statements. In any event, *truth is always a defense to defamation*.

PUBLIC FIGURE

The *Sullivan* case involved a public official in the course of his public duties. It did not take long for this same court to extend the "actual malice" standard of proof to a football coach who was deemed a **public figure**.

In *Curtis Publishing Co. v. Butts* (388 U.S. 130, 1967), a famous football coach at the University of Georgia was accused of fixing a game with legendary Alabama football coach Paul "Bear" Bryant. The *Saturday Evening Post* magazine received a tip about the purported sharing of game strategies to Bryant by Butts. In reporting the story as told to the *Post*, the court noted it made no effort to actually confirm the tip, which was given to them by a known unscrupulous individual. Butts was forced to retire because of the

Athletes are considered public figures

publication. In awarding a large reputational financial award for Butts, the court determined that a college football coach is a public figure and that this football coach met the *Sullivan* standard of proving "actual malice" to overcome the magazine's free-speech assertions.

Since *Butts*, courts have consistently ruled that athletes are public figures. Included in this list are racecar drivers, horse jockeys, and professional athletes in the sports of baseball, soccer, basketball, hockey, cricket, cycling, and football. In some cases, well-known amateur athletes also have been deemed public figures.

In another US Supreme Court decision not involving a coach or an athlete, a distinction was made between a private and a public figure. For **private figures**—those who do not achieve fame or notoriety for their public actions—the defamed party does not have to demonstrate that the communication was published to a third party with actual malice.

However, the court created a new category: **limited public figure**. A benchwarmer on a field hockey team could thrust or inject herself into a particular public controversy and thereby become a public figure for a limited time on a limited issue. For example, assume a female field hockey player who is not a team starter decides to speak at a public forum in support of the right of same-sex couples to marry. She more than likely would qualify as a limited public figure. Further, assume a news publication covering the event prints an unflattering image of her. Inside the article it states that, based on her appearance, she must be a lesbian. For her to win a defamation suit for damage to her reputation, she must prove the article was published with a reckless disregard for the truth or with actual malice.

KEY CASES

Demonstrating that a communication directed at an athlete or coach was defamatory is difficult. The public figure must convince a judge or jury by *clear and convincing evidence* that the publication meets the legal standards of defamation.

In 2014, the US Supreme Court rejected a defamation lawsuit filed by former Chicago Bulls basketball player Scottie Pippen. The former teammate of Michael Jordan had filed a defamation lawsuit against several websites for failing to correct an erroneous story stating that he had filed for personal bankruptcy. A lower court tossed out his lawsuit because he failed to prove the story originally reported by NBC and CBS was published knowing it was false or published with a reckless disregard for its truth.

Internet posters need to be careful about republishing information that later proves to be published recklessly. They, too, may be held liable for defaming an athlete or coach as though they were the original publisher.

The infamous basketball-player-turned celebrity Latrell Sprewell sued the *New York Post* for defamation when the paper reported that the player had broken his finger in a fight. The New York state court noted that the paper did not report the incident as incontrovertible fact. Unlike in *Butts*, the reporter cautioned readers that the story was based on two confidential witnesses and its accuracy was denied by Sprewell. The court ruled Sprewell could not proceed because, as a public figure, he failed to prove that the reporter knew the material was probably false or that he had serious doubts that it was true.

In a novel 2014 decision, a federal court held that an international sporting goods supplier is not a public figure or a limited public figure. HBO's *Real Sports with Bryant Gumble* ran a television segment that showed a subcontractor of the sporting goods company Mitre using child labor in India to sew its soccer balls. The report acknowledged that Mitre denounced the use of child labor and was working to address the issue. In ruling that Mitre is a private figure, the company can move forward in its defamation lawsuit for damages under a lower burden-of-proof standard.

SUMMARY

The interests of privacy, publicity, and defamation frequently intersect but are different from each other. Unlike intellectual property rights, which are protected by federal law, the recognition of privacy and publicity occurs at the state level. While many professional athletes are protective of their personal spaces and lives, they have a different relationship with the media and commercial licensing entities. The law of publicity protects them from the unauthorized commercial use of their names, likenesses, and images. Public-figure athletes who fall from grace may find that they lose endorsements and are the subject of unflattering news reports that may be false and damage their reputational rights.

KEY WORDS

Comedy. Comedy or parody enjoys equally strong legal protection under freedom-of-the-press case law standards.

Defamation. A third right of interest is the reputation right of defamation. Quite prevalent in sports today are lawsuits filed against reporters and bloggers for publishing statements or images that may be unflattering, untrue, or malicious.

Libel. Libel is a tort, or civil wrong. It refers to a statement that impairs a person's reputation through written words. Increasingly, the term *libel* is used as substitute for the word *defamation*.

Limited Public Figure. Someone who could thrust or inject himself or herself into a particular public controversy and thereby become a public figure for a limited time on a limited issue.

Parody. Parody is a humorous form of public comment or criticism of an original work or interest.

Private Figures. Figures who do not achieve fame or notoriety for their public actions.

Public Figure. Included in this list are racecar drivers, horse jockeys, and professional athletes in the sports of baseball, soccer, basketball, hockey, cricket, cycling, and football. In some cases, well-known amateur athletes also have been deemed public figures.

Right of Publicity. Closely related to the right to privacy is the notion that there is commercial value in a person's name or likeness. This cognate right is called the right of publicity. In some ways, this right is similar to a privacy right but differs insofar as it is a property interest that can be bartered, assigned, or transferred for consideration. A product or service endorsement by an athlete is an example of an exercise of a public person's publicity rights.

Right to Privacy. In 1890, two former classmates from Harvard Law School wrote an article published in the *Harvard Law Review* titled "The Right to Privacy." In response to the tabloid journalism of their era, they stirred the legal community with a call to arms to protect ordinary citizens against the exposure of their personal affairs on the public pages of the press. They dubbed this new right the right to privacy, or the right to be left alone.

Slander. Slander is the twin of libel. An impairment of a person's reputation through spoken words is called slander.

Unlawful Internet Gambling Enforcement Act of 2006. The majority of those who participate in fantasy sports leagues pay to play. A New Jersey court ruling held that the pay-to-play format is not an illegal gambling activity under the federal Unlawful Internet Gambling Enforcement Act of 2006.

DISCUSSION QUESTIONS

1. Q: How does the right of publicity differ from the right to privacy?

A: The right of publicity is similar to a privacy right but differs insofar as it is a property interest that can be bartered, assigned, or transferred for consideration. A product or service endorsement by an athlete is an example of an exercise of a public person's publicity rights.

2. Q: Does comedy or parody have any legal protection?

A: Comedy or parody enjoys equally strong legal protection under freedom-of-the-press case law standards.

3. **Q: According to Dean William Prosser, what are the four separate and distinct privacy torts?**

A: Dean William Prosser identified four separate and distinct privacy torts. He suggested that the right to privacy is invaded when one of the following occurs:

1. Unreasonable intrusion into the private affairs or activities of a person;
2. Appropriation of a person's name or likeness;
3. Unreasonable publicity given to a person's private life; or
4. Publicity that places a person in a false light.

4. **Q: According to a federal court in Minnesota, how is an athlete's identity important?**

A: A federal court in Minnesota found that an athlete's identity is wrapped up in his "name, likeness, statistics and other personal characteristics," which are the fruit of his or her labor and a type of property.

5. **Q: What was the implication for online fantasy games in *C.B.C. Distribution and Marketing, Inc. v. Major League Advanced Media, L.P.* (505 F.3d 818, 8th Cir. 2007)?**

A: The implication for online fantasy game creators is profound. This case stands for the proposition that a person can use the names of players and game statistics in a fantasy sports league without the need for prior approval or a license from the players or professional sports leagues.

6. **Q: What are the three leading online fantasy sports hosts?**

A: According to a recent report by *Medill Reports*, an online publishing newsletter by graduate journalism students at Northwestern University, Yahoo!, CBSSports.com, and ESPN.com are the three leading online fantasy sports hosts.

7. **Q: Which sport has the largest participation in US fantasy sports?**

A: Football has the largest participation in US fantasy sports, with 21,213,333 participants.

8. **Q: How did the California federal appeals court differentiate between the *EA video game* case and the *C.B.C. fantasy sports league* opinion?**

A: In an attempt to provide clarity in a confusing area of the law, the California federal appeals court stated that the *EA video game* case is different from the *C.B.C. fantasy sports league* opinion because the avatars were derived from the players' personal identities and were not statistical game data readily found in the public domain.

9. Q: What is a notable distinction between a right to privacy and a right of publicity?

A: A notable distinction between a right to privacy and a right of publicity is that an individual's right to privacy ends when the individual dies. In some states, publicity rights associated with a person's commercial value may survive death. In these cases, the estate or heir of a famous public person, including an athlete, may continue to control and license the deceased's image, name, and likeness.

10. Q: What was the major change to come out of the US Supreme Court in *New York Times Co. v. Sullivan* (376 U.S. 24, 1964)?

A: In 1964, the law of defamation changed dramatically. The US Supreme Court in *New York Times Co. v. Sullivan* (376 U.S. 24, 1964) was asked to determine the extent to which the constitutional protections for free speech and the media limit a state's power to award damages in a libel action brought by a public figure against those who criticize his official conduct. The effect of this opinion written by Justice William Brennan is immense for bloggers, newspapers, Internet chat rooms, advertisers, and other forms of communication that cover athletes and their professional and personal lives. The court's decision eliminated the previous "chilling" effect of traditional state-derived defamation laws. Wiggle room for minor errors in publishing factual news articles, making inaccurate statements in advertising, or misspeaking on talk shows now exists.

11. Q: At what level does the recognition of privacy and publicity occur?

A: Unlike intellectual property rights, which are protected by federal law, the recognition of privacy and publicity occurs at the state level.

Chapter Nine

Sports Liability: Torts

"Some restraints of civilization must accompany every athlete onto the playing field."—Illinois Court of Appeals, *Nabozny v. Barnhill*

Tort is a branch of private law. Unlike in criminal law, where a case is brought and prosecuted by the state, a tort action is strictly the province of a private party filing a fault-related lawsuit in court. The judgment usually sought by a harmed party is financial compensation for the injury suffered.

The subject of torts in sports is a relatively new phenomenon. For many years, patrons who attended games and people who played games or joined a sports team were presumed to assume all risks associated with watching or participating. The business of torts, as so ably described by Justice Oliver Wendell Homes, is to "fix the dividing line between those cases in which (a person) is liable for harm which he has done and those in which he has not." It was not until the 1970s that society, and more particularly the judicial system, began to impose civil penalties for egregious conduct in sports.

It is well recognized that a violent hit or at least bodily contact can be a normal component of contact sports. Historically, teams and leagues accepted the notion that fines and suspensions imposed by game officials on behalf of the owners of a sport are sufficient punitive actions to curtail harm to spectators or participants. Society, though, began to impose liability for nonexcusable and unforeseeable behavior that caused severe physical and emotional harm. There are instances, though, when conduct may constitute a crime, which is a societal wrong, and a tort, which is a civil wrong, at the same time. The subject of crime in sports is explored in the last chapter of this book.

In general, torts are divided into three major categories: *negligence*, *intentional*, and *strict liability*. By far, the most common tort claims in sports, whether the harm occurs at a local workout facility, on a community rock-climbing wall, or during practice before a volleyball game, are based on a theory of negligence. Claiming the conduct of a coach, fellow player, or facility manager is careless, reckless, or purposeful so as to lead to an injury and proving it, as the cases illustrate, is still a high burden to overcome even in the simplest negligence fact patterns.

A less common tort is what is referred to as an intentional tort. They can arise when one party knowingly acts in a fashion to cause harm or offense to another. It is not a defense to argue that the offending party did not intend to cause the particular harm suffered. The term *assault and battery*, as individual or interrelated charges, is another name for an intentional tort.

Product liability claims for defective sporting equipment, such as hockey helmets, trampolines, or soccer goals, may arise under any of the three tort categories. However, a claim for strict liability arguably makes the manufacturer of sports equipment the insurer and therefore absolutely liable for all harm that flows from the defective product. Strict liability civil lawsuits are rare causes of action in the sports industry.

Understanding the various theories of tort law is an integral component of successfully managing recreation and athletic complexes. The filing of lawsuits for product or equipment defects and personal injury claims by sports participants and spectators has steadily increased. A seasoned grasp of the legal issues related to torts can assist facility managers in reducing the risk of harm through prevention and intervention of known or foreseeable hazards.

NEGLIGENCE

Liability for the tort of *negligence* only occurs when some person fails to follow the degree of care that a *reasonably prudent person* would follow to avoid *foreseeable* harms. Negligence is known as an unintentional tort. It happens by *omission* or *commission* of an act that causes harm to a person with whom he or she owes a *duty to act with care*.

In analyzing sports-related negligence claims, the relationship between the party who is injured and is seeking monetary damages and the person responsible for failing to act responsibly who owed the injured party a duty of care is key. Negligence also extends to a *duty not to act carelessly*.

Depending on the relationship between parties, there are different standards of care or duties imposed. For instance, participants in a professional sporting activity voluntarily agree to play and abide by the rules of the sport. In many, if not most, instances, the athletic *participants assume the risks inherent in the play*. It is what was once referred to as the "implied license of the playground." These risks tend to be known and *foreseeable* and therefore nonactionable for recovery in the event an injury occurs. Participants whose conduct falls below the *reasonable-prudent-person standard* based on the rules and culture of the game, however, may find himself or herself responsible for *gross, reckless, or willful negligent actions.*

Frequently, the law of negligence levies a *special duty of care* on individuals who have specialized training or skills. A team physician who fails to properly screen, diagnose, or treat an athlete, and the *actual harm suffered* is a *consequence* of this failure, may be sued for *medical malpractice*, a special type of negligence claim.

Facility managers responsible for operating and managing arenas and stadiums owe different duties, depending on the legal status of the harmed person. For instance, a season ticket holder who pays for the privilege of sitting in box seats is owed a higher level of care than a nonpaying, uninvited trespasser who jumps over a fence to enter onto the field of play.

While torts are private actions, individual states can mandate minimum levels of care owed the public. For example, a state might legislatively mandate that all public gymnasiums have automated external defibrillators (AEDs) on site. A high school that fails to install AEDs, as required by law, may be deemed negligent. Similarly, architects who design athletic structures have a legal duty to comply with relevant building codes, industry standards, and statutes that require compliance with nondiscriminatory treatment for the disabled and handicapped. In the latter two cases, it is state or federal law that dictates the minimum standard of care.

The five elements that an injured person or plaintiff must prove in a typical negligence case are as follows:

1. The defendant owed a duty of care to the plaintiff;
2. The defendant breached that duty;
3. The defendant failed to act as a reasonable person would under the circumstances;
4. The defendant's action or failure to act was the proximate cause of the harm; and
5. The plaintiff suffered damages.

Case Examples: Negligence

Although this chapter subsection is titled negligence, the simple fact is that a claim and finding of *simple negligence* is rarely sufficient to impose player-to-player liability. The collective history of the line of cases in this area of the law demonstrates that *recklessness* is the standard of conduct for participants in recreation and athletic activities to establish liability and recovery. *Negligence plus* is another way to view the concept of recklessness.

Player-to-Player Liability

Before the mid-1970s, state and federal courts consistently denied liability claims for injuries that arose out of another participant's failure to follow game rules during a sporting event. Immunity from liability was based on the application of the legal defense that, no matter how egregious the game contact, all the players assumed the risks inherent in playing that sport.

In 1975, however, the state appeals court in Illinois broke away from this line of reasoning in the case of *Nabozny v. Barnhill* (Ill. App. 3d 212, 1975). The facts from this high school soccer match are quite dramatic. The plaintiff was a goalie bent over and reaching for the ball when the defendant, a forward, ran into the penalty area and kicked the goalie in the head. The plaintiff's skull was fractured, and he suffered brain trauma. The court held that a "player is liable for injury in a tort action if his or her conduct is such that it is either *deliberate, willful or with a reckless disregard for the safety* of another player so as to *cause injury* to that player." By acting in a *reckless* fashion, the player *breached* his *duty* to obey the rules of the game and *cause* no bodily harm to the opposing player.

In a larger context, the *Nabozny* decision stands for the major proposition that, when a player recklessly or wantonly violates a safety rule—such as no contact with a goalie who is holding the ball in the penalty area—causing bodily injury, then liability incurs. In the aftermath of this decision, some state courts began to rule that participants in noncontact sports owe a greater duty of care not to harm fellow players than exists in contact sports. Consequentially, a number of states have imposed a simple negligence standard for noncontact sports. Kick-the-can, intramural softball, touch football, and pick-up baseball are activities that have been deemed contact sports. Hence, the recklessness standard applies to these and other commonly defined contact activities. These decisions are largely based on state law, so there is no universal national standard to follow.

At the professional level, an injury that transpired during a football game between the Denver Broncos and the Cincinnati Bengals broke new legal ground. Acting out of anger and frustration but without a specific intent to injure the player, the Bronco player, Charles "Boobie" Clark, used his right forearm to strike the kneeling and defenseless Bengal player, Dale Hackbart. The referees missed the play, so no personal foul was called. After the game, Hackbart began to complain of discomfort. It was later determined by a team physician that he suffered a serious fracture to the neck.

The court rejected the notion of refusing to find liability for player injury when the action takes place during the course of a professional contact sport. Instead, the court found culpability because of Clark's *reckless disregard* for the safety of another player (*Hackbart v. Cincinnati Bengals, Inc.* 601 F.2d 516, 10th Cir. 1979; also known as *Hackbart II*).

These two sports cases from the 1970s provide the legal foundation for more modern cases dealing with athlete-to-athlete sports-related liability. The variety in participant-related sports injuries is nearly endless, but here are a few cases to consider. The state supreme court in Wisconsin dismissed a cheerleader's claim that a fellow cheerleader was negligent in failing to catch her properly, when she fell while he was holding her on his shoulders. The court found that his failure to catch her was not a reckless act, merely inadvertent. Interestingly, cheerleading was deemed a contact sport, and by agreeing to participate in this high school activity, she *assumed the risk* of known dangers, to wit, falling.

In a well-publicized California decision, the court in *Shin v. Ahn* (165 P.3d 581, Cal. 2007) dealt with an occasional occurrence on golf courses— dodging or failing to dodge errantly hit golf balls. Golf is decidedly not a contact sport. Still, injuries do occur to spectators and other golfers who are struck by carelessly hit balls. The California high court determined that getting hit by an unintended ball strike is an *inherent risk* that spectators and golfers assume.

Coaches

The violent nature of the sport of football has led to a large number of lawsuits related to whether coaches have properly instructed or warned their players. Frequently, the outcome of these cases turns on the age, physical attributes, and experience of the players and coaches; level of play; and "how to play the game" instructions given by coaches. A high school coach taught his running backs to keep their heads up while running. A jury determined that he failed to properly warn his young players about the dangers of making contact with the head when meeting a tackler.

Coaches who match players of unequal size and experience in practice drills have been held negligent for improper supervision because of the inherent common-sense hazards. In a high-profile media case, former standout USC football player Stafon Johnson sued an assistant strength coach for allegedly carelessly and recklessly placing a weight-lifting bar into Johnson's hand when he was not prepared to hold the barbell. The 275-pound bar dropped and landed on his neck and throat, causing severe life-threatening injury. The case was eventually settled out of court.

The range of responsibilities for coaches is nearly endless. Coaches have been held liable for not selecting the most appropriate equipment for their players. Failing to pull a team off a soccer field in the midst of a thunderstorm that carries the inherent weather risk of lightning led to a lawsuit when a player was struck by lightning. A coach who attempts to diagnose an on-the-field injury beyond his scope of experience and training was found liable for neglecting to immediately contact qualified medical assistance. The more dangerous the sporting activity, the greater the duty imposed on a coach to warn and inform players about *foreseeable* risks and how to avoid them.

In general, the crucial areas in determining negligent coaching deal with improper instruction or teaching, supervision, and maintenance, to wit, practice and playing environment. A general rule, for instance, is that a coach cannot force an injured athlete who has not been medically cleared to practice or play. In 2015, a University of Illinois soccer player sued her school for failing to follow its own concussion protocol. She maintained that during a game she collided head-on with an opposing player. She collapsed to the ground and struggled to get up. Instead of pulling her off the field, she alleged, her coach and the university's medical staff continued to allow her to play. After the game, she was diagnosed with a concussion.

A high school gym instructor was held responsible for lack of instruction and supervision when she had a student attempt to instruct another student on how to swing a golf club as part of a mandatory health class. A fellow fourteen-year-old student who had no experience with the game of golf and was not warned of any dangers because he missed the instructional class was struck in the head when he stood too close. He died from the incident. A coach can avoid liability by taking all reasonable steps to exercise reasonable care.

Medical Malpractice

The *American Journal of Sports Medicine* not long ago published a study on the severity of high school sports injuries by gender, injury area, and sport. It found that, with more young people participating in sports, there has been a rise in the number of reported injuries. According to the latest findings of the Youth Sports Safety Alliance, since 2010, high school athletes have undergone an average of 2 million injuries, 200,000 doctor visits, and 30,000 hospitalizations annually. Football is the most dangerous activity that boys play. Girls suffer the most severe injuries from playing basketball, followed by soccer. Nearly 15 percent of all high school sports-related injuries result in the loss of twenty-one or more days of practice and competition time. By far, injuries to the knee were the most common severe injury for young female athletes.

Health care professionals, including doctors, nurse practitioners, athletic trainers, and physical therapists, are responsible for caring for the injured athlete. Professional teams are fortunate to have a full medical staff ranging from skilled cardiologists to orthopedic physicians. At the college level, a federal appeals court decision, *Stineman v. Fontbonne College* (644 F2d 1082, 8th Cir. 1981), held that a university has a duty to refer an injured player to the appropriate health care provider for medical assistance. While professional teams and colleges regularly use athletic trainers as first responders for evaluating and treating injuries, only about 55 percent of high schools across the United States have access to certified athletic trainers. Hawaii is the sole state to require that every high school employ an athletic trainer on staff. The lack of skilled professionals available to evaluate and treat athletes injured at practice and competition increases the risk of improper or delayed diagnosis and care.

Medical professionals owe athletes a *special duty of care* based on their training and experience. The specific imposed duty is to exercise reasonable skill and care as is common for those practitioners performing similar services in that particular medical field. Failures to evaluate, advise, diagnose, treat, or prescribe properly to fulfill that duty is deemed *medical malpractice*.

Baseball icon Alex Rodriguez filed a medical malpractice claim against a Yankees team physician for reportedly giving him clearance to play when an MRI purportedly showed that his left hip was seriously injured and did not inform him of the injury. This case resembles a case brought by a Red Sox infielder Marty Barrett against his Boston team. The team's physician was found negligent for failing to alert the player to serious cartilage and ligament knee damage that would require extensive reconstruction surgery. Instead, the physician told Barrett that he could return to the lineup in time for the playoffs following a few weeks of physical therapy and rehabilitation.

Barrett received a substantial jury award because of the doctor's *breach* of his *duty to disclose* and *properly treat*. The incident drew additional scrutiny because the team physician was also a part owner of the team. Pundits questioned whether this relationship to the team created an inherent *conflict of interest* that was impossible to avoid and should have disqualified him from serving the team in dual capacities.

In an extremely sad and complicated medical malpractice lawsuit connected with a wrongful death charge, the wife of Pro Bowl right tackle Korey Stringer sued the Minnesota Vikings' training camp physician and an assistant trainer. She alleged they were grossly negligent when caring for her husband, who collapsed in training camp from a heat-related stroke.

The claim raises two vital defenses. The first is that Stringer *contributed* to his death because he purportedly came to camp out of shape and used a dietary substance linked to heart attacks, stroke, and high blood pressure, which was found in his locker. In many jurisdictions, the **contributory negligence** defense that bars recovery for even the slightest degree of fault by an athlete has been replaced with a **comparative negligence** standard. Under this test, recovery is barred only when the athlete contributes more than half of the reason for the injury.

The second defensive assertion is one that arises when there is an *employment relationship* between the affected parties. In most employee-and-employer situations, state *workers' compensation statutes* govern compensation for job-related injuries. Korey Stringer's wife originally sued a host of team officials, coaches, and other medical service providers. These defendants were removed from her case because the incident occurred in the course of their employment and they were immune from suit by Minnesota's workers' compensation statute. The training camp physician and assistant trainer apparently were not employees but independent contractors. An out-of-court settlement was eventually reached for far below the $100 million damages she sought.

In an isolated and unique medical malpractice claim, again linked to a wrongful death action, the mother of former Kansas City Chiefs linebacker Jovan Belcher filed suit against his team for failing to educate him about concussions, failing to monitor and treat him for neurological dysfunction, failing to provide appropriate counseling, and failing to remove him from games after sustaining repetitive head trauma. Belcher made headlines after killing his girlfriend and then committing suicide in 2012.

Good Samaritan state statutes have been used to protect the actions of medical health care providers who provide assistance to an injured athlete in an emergency situation, even though they may not have the requisite special skill or training. The public policy reason is to encourage trained medical personnel to provide assistance free from fear of lawsuit for unintended injury or death.

Finally, for the uninitiated, medical malpractice claims are extremely expensive and difficult to win. They require legions of expert witnesses by both the plaintiff(s) and defendant(s), which drive up the cost of litigation. More than 90 percent of medical malpractice cases that reach the jury stage are unsuccessful.

Spectator Harm

Regardless of the level of competition, spectators can suffer injury from attending literally any sporting event. At every MLB game, there is at least one significant spectator injury usually caused by foul balls. Fans attending hockey games are at risk from flying-saucer-like pucks. Racecars' wheels hurdle over protective barriers into the stands at NASCAR events. Teams seek to insulate themselves from liability by publicly warning spectators not to reach over walls and to stay alert for known dangers. Disclaimers are printed on game tickets. Signs are plastered on walls telling fans to beware of special risks. Attempts to absolutely absolve a team from all spectator harm are not always successful.

In legal terms, spectators are considered **public invitees**. By virtue of advertising and inviting fans to attend a game or event, the owners of a sporting or recreation facility are under a duty to prevent harm by creating a reasonably safe environment. Any unreasonable breach of this duty that causes harm or injury to a spectator may lead to liability.

In determining the standard of care, courts focus on the facility owner's knowledge of unsafe conditions and whether the dangerous conditions are foreseeable and, therefore, largely preventable. For instance, it is reasonably foreseeable in the course of a baseball game that a hit ball will deflect into the stands, potentially injuring a fan. The facility is obligated to take reasonable protective measures to avoid liability. This may include installing screening behind home plate, where most of the foul balls land, or posting warning signs.

The traditional rule that baseball facility owners are free from all liability for injuries to spectators has its limits. The state supreme court of Pennsylvania upheld a judgment against the owners of Three Rivers Stadium in Pittsburgh when it ruled that a person who attends a baseball game cannot be properly expected to anticipate as an inherent risk being struck by a foul ball while using a walkway and not sitting in the stands. In the event the game hosts special guests, such as a significant number of invited visitors from a foreign country, then the owner may have a special duty to warn the visitors or invitees in their native language of these foreseeable risks. The standard of care may change whenever minors are invited to a game because they may not have the experience and reasoned judgment to appreciate what adults otherwise know as risks.

In *Silva v. Woodhouse* (356 Mass. 119, 1969), the court "wrestled" with how to treat damages to a fan when a 290-pound "professional" wrestler became a "deadly projectile." During the course of a match, one wrestler was tossed out of the ring by another wrestler. He landed on a spectator, causing severe injury. The court held that the spectator did not *assume this risk* because it was not a known risk, even though the spectator had attended prior wrestling matches at this arena. On the other hand, the court said that the facility owner was aware of the fact that wrestlers could become human projectiles. It, therefore, was under a duty to move the front-row seat to a safer distance from the wrestling ring or post a warning of the potential risk.

A recent study by the *Charlotte Observer* determined that forty-six spectators died at motorsport events between 1990 and 2010. Cars leaving the track and careening into spectators or debris from car crashes traveling in excess of one hundred miles per hour flying into the grandstand are known causes of personal injury at race venues throughout the world. Besides compensating victims, this area of tort law has led motorsport owners to adopt better safety measures, including extending protective barriers higher to protect fans.

This same newspaper report singled out unsafe soccer facilities as one of the leading, if not the leading, cause for spectator death and injury. Older European soccer stadiums used terraces or standing-room sections for overflow fans. In one incident, ninety-six spectators died when a stampede prevented people from safely exiting. The terraces were replaced with fixed seats to prevent overcrowding.

In Ohio, a thirteen-year-old girl became the first spectator to die at an NHL game after being struck in the temple at a Columbus Blue Jackets game. An out-of-court settlement in excess of $1 million was reached with the NHL, the team, and the arena owners. In the aftermath of this tragic event, the NHL implemented a rules change that required high netting over the ends of each rink to prevent stray pucks from harming spectators. In many cases, once professional leagues impose new facility safety requirements, these improvements trickle down to the college and eventually high school levels.

Facilities and Waivers

There are sports, like scuba diving, rock climbing, skiing, and snowboarding, that are inherently dangerous and risky. As such, resort facilities, where visitors frequently partake in these kinds of action sports, rely on written **waivers or releases** with boldly printed language on the back of tickets explaining the dangers to limit exposure from personal injury claims. For the most part, these explicit releases are effective. However, an appeals court in Pennsylvania ruled that an exculpatory release that required waiving claims based on allegations of reckless and intentional conduct by the facility or a fellow skier was in violation of *public policy* because it encouraged parties to adhere to the most minimal standards of care and public safety.

A waiver or release is a *legal document* voluntarily signed to inform facility users, or their parents or guardians in the case of minors, of known risks involved in various activities and to shield the facility or organization from liability from personal harm or loss of property. Incorporated into the waiver or release document is language to the effect that the releasing person is responsible for his or her conduct and expressly assumes the risks of participation. Community organizations and schools frequently rent park or recreation facilities. The institution or organization sponsoring an event may require their participants or their parents or guardians to sign a *hold-harmless* document to limit its legal exposure from any loss of property or personal harm, as well.

Another common technique used by facility owners and mangers to limit damage exposure is to place highly visible *warning signs* throughout a facility. The signs serve the purpose of both informing "invitees"—ticket purchasers and spectators—of the potentially dangerous nature of these activities and that as participants they assume all foreseeable risks associated with engaging in these activities. Popular resorts in major ski areas of the United States and Canada have turned to state or province legislative bodies to provide additional protection by statutorily limiting liability.

The estate of a twenty-four-year-old woman who tragically died while snowboarding at the Alpine Meadows ski resort in California filed a wrongful death tort action for failing to properly warn her of certain dangers. In ruling against the claim, the Ninth Circuit Court of Appeals upheld a lower court's determination that a large sign cautioning her of the dangers at the entrance to the slope and the fifteen to twenty orange-and-black signs marking the boundaries were sufficient warnings. She died after she slipped on firm snow, lost her balance, and slid uncontrollably down an icy slope past posted ski boundaries. Further, the court held that the waiver signed by the adult decedent, which indicated that she had agreed to assume the risk of injury from the activity, was valid (*Gregorie v. Alpine Meadows Ski Corp.*, 2010 U.S. App. Lexis 26328, 9th Cir.).

In the aftermath of this incident, the father of the deceased snowboarder launched a public awareness campaign to require all children in California to wear a helmet to ski or snowboard. The state of California already mandates that minors must wear a protective helmet to bike, skate, or skateboard.

INTENTIONAL TORT

When a player or coach purposefully, knowingly, and wantonly places another person in fear of bodily harm or actually causes bodily injury, it is possible that that person has committed an *intentional tort*. The *apprehension* of imminent offensive physical contact is deemed the intentional tort of **assault**. The intentional tort of *battery* occurs when there is actual impermissible offensive *physical contact*. For instance, a hockey player who purposefully strikes a defenseless player from behind with a hockey stick commits a battery. A hockey goalie who picks up a puck and throws it in the direction of an opposing player for the purpose of frightening him, even when it misses, commits an assault. Should the goalie hit another player by mistake, the law *transfers* his or her *intent* to the innocent party. The goalie is still liable for battery.

Football cases are where intentional tort actions most commonly arise. University of Arizona football coach Frank Kush, known for a physically demanding coaching style, successfully defended himself against charges of battery and assault by a player. In the aftermath of a poor punt during a game, Kush grabbed the player's facemask and shook it so hard the player suffered physical and emotional pain. Kush also reportedly punched the player in the face. The court dismissed the player's claims (*Rutledge v. Arizona Board of Regents*, 660 F. 2d 1345, 9th Cir. 1981).

Nowadays, it is unlikely that courts would view the *Rutledge* decision in the same light because, in part, society's sense of "consent" has changed. An Ohio court held that a golfer whose intentional conduct in hitting a golf ball was to strike another golfer could give rise to battery because it would be the result of an unforeseeable act unlike an errantly hit golf ball. The revelation a few years ago that players from the New Orleans Saints professional football team contributed cash into a "bounty" pool that rewarded "knockout" hits at $1,500 and "cart-offs" at $1,000 raises the specter of potential personal intentional tort liability. Apparently, the Saints rewarded players more for injuring top-tier opponents, such as Brett Favre, over benchwarmers, in violation of the competitive spirit and rules of the game. Despite the contact nature of football, these are not risks that players should assume, nor are they foreseeable. And coaches who were aware of or condoned these bounty payments or should have known what was going on and did not stop it very well may be culpable to the injured parties under a negligence or intentional tort theory. Ironically, but not necessarily surprisingly, many of the football players who were targeted considered the bounty hits an assumed risk of the game of football. Fortunately, none of the players suffered any serious career-ending injuries.

As a side note, the NFL's commissioner, Roger Goodell, suspended numerous players who were allegedly part of the bounty scheme; however, an arbitrator later vacated them. The commissioner imposed sanctions against coaches and front-office personnel, including fines and loss of draft picks against the Saints.

PRODUCTS LIABILITY

A *product liability* claim for injury because of a defective product can proceed under a number of legal theories: *negligence, breach of warranty (contract)*, and *strict liability*. In a strict liability claim, a manufacturer of a product in a *defective condition* that is *unreasonably dangerous* to the user is liable for any physical harm or property damage. The user in a strict liability case does not have to be the purchaser of the product. Improper use and assumption of risk may serve as defenses thereby limiting the manufacturer's liability, although some jurisdictions, such as New York, frown upon its application.

In general, proving a strict liability claim requires demonstrating that a defect in design or manufacture is "unreasonably dangerous." Examples of sporting goods whose product manufacturers were sued for design defects include trampolines, diving boards, and tumbling devices. Increasingly, though, plaintiffs are arguing that a *failure to warn of known dangerous conditions is also a defect*. A gymnast who suffered a significant head injury while attempting a backflip was able to proceed on a "failure to warn" strict liability theory. Experts testified that size and location of the warnings on the apparatus were insufficient in explaining how to safely use it.

A physical therapist in New York was awarded $65 million in damages when a Cybex weight machine fell on her. The therapist was paralyzed for life after she used the machine as a stretching device, not as a leg extension piece of equipment as the manufacturer intended. The defective condition, again, was not in faulty design or broken equipment but in failure to warn of known dangers. Intriguingly, the court was not persuaded by Cybex's argument that, because she used the equipment in a manner that was not intended (i.e., stretching against the machine rather that pushing the weights), it should not be liable for her harm. Frequently, though, this defense is successful.

So in a slight twist of traditional strict liability law, many courts are ruling that, although the design, material, and workmanship may be flawless, the equipment might still be defective where the manufacturer fails to properly warn or instruct with respect to known dangers in the use of the equipment. A manufacturer, then, may be liable for producing an unreasonably dangerous product because of its defective condition (failure to warn of known dangers), even though the manufacturer is not negligent in designing and manufacturing the product.

The introduction of high-performance composite baseball and softball bats at the high school and college levels has raised questions regarding player safety versus schools attempting to save costs from constantly replacing broken bats. A legal issue is whether these new bats are "defective" because a ball comes off a bat at a much faster speed, therefore making it harder for infielders to react. A court in Oklahoma held a bat manufacturer liable for a high school pitcher's injuries under this theory. The case law in this area is still unsettled.

In what is arguably the largest sports-related products liability claim ever, beginning in 2011, more than 3,500 former NFL players have filed 160 lawsuits against the sport's premier helmet manufacturer, Riddell, seeking recovery for concussions and traumatic brain injuries. The two most common brain injuries suffered from repeated impact to the head are sudden impact syndrome (SIS) and chronic traumatic encephalopathy (CTE).

The Riddell helmet liability theories focus on three claims: design defects, manufacturing defects, and failure to warn. The cases' outcomes may turn on what Riddell knew beforehand about the long-term effects of concussions on football players wearing their helmets. In theory, the players are asking whether Riddell had superior knowledge and therefore was under a duty to warn players of possible side effects. Additionally, the players will inquire as part of the discovery process whether Riddell could have easily and inexpensively designed a safer helmet. Around 80 percent of all NFL players wear Riddell brand helmets, so the pool of potential litigants is large.

To date, different courts have reached contrary conclusions on Riddell's culpability. A Colorado jury found that the helmet manufacturer was *contrib-*

utory negligent by failing to properly warn a brain-injured high school player about concussion danger. This same court rejected assertions of helmet design defects. The player's coaches were also sued for negligent supervision. In Mississippi, a jury denied all product liability claims filed against Riddell by a high school football player who suffered a stroke after practice.

Related to the product liability claims by NFL players, these same individuals also brought a tort suit against the NFL for failing to disclose the dangers of concussions. After years of contentious legal battles, in 2015, a federal judge approved a settlement that provides up to $5 million to each player who has suffered from certain severe neurological diseases. However, the settlement is on hold because a handful of players have appealed the decision on the grounds that the settlement fails to include financial recovery for a common degenerative brain disease associated with head trauma in football, CTE. A year earlier, the NCAA settled its negligence class-action head injury lawsuit by agreeing to create a $70 million fund to diagnosis current and former college players to determine whether they suffered brain trauma while playing soccer, hockey, and football.

The ice hockey helmet manufacturer Bauer is facing similar lawsuits across North America. All Canadian organized amateur ice hockey players are required by law to wear a Canadian Standards Association (CSA)–approved helmet. The CSA standards are considered the bare-minimum safety requirement for impact-resistant wear. Undeniably, it is a foreseeable risk that hockey players will hit the ice or boards at hockey rinks. The negligence argument is that Bauer has a duty to protect players from the risk of serious head injury from impact. By failing to design and manufacture a helmet that provides sufficient protection from concussion injuries and by not warning players of potential known dangers, Bauer should be held strictly liable.

In the lawsuit filed in Canada by a head-traumatized ice hockey player, the court determined that, as a manufacturer of a consumer product, Bauer has a duty to take *reasonable design* steps to make sure that its helmets are *safe for their intended use* and to *minimize any loss from foreseeable harm*. This theory falls more so under a *breach of warranty* contract cause of action than negligence. The court was careful to note that Bauer is under no duty to design the safest helmet possible. It is required to design a helmet that provides reasonable protection for foreseeable risk under normal use.

The specific head injury suffered by the player, SIS, was due to rotational forces that, under current state-of-the-art conditions, is impossible to design and manufacture a helmet to protect against. The court also determined that the warning stickers within the helmet and on the chinstrap were sufficient for the player to make an informed choice about whether to use this CSA-approved helmet under the circumstances.

Finally, in language that may give helmet manufacturers some hope from expensive tort litigation, the court ruled that Bauer is not an insurer, nor is it held to a standard of perfection. The user, too, has an obligation to handle the equipment properly, and coaches have a duty to properly instruct and supervise their players.

AMERICANS WITH DISABILITIES ACT OF 1990

A dozen plus years ago, a former Stanford University teammate of Tiger Woods made history when he sued the PGA for failing to reasonably accommodate him so that he would have an opportunity to compete at the highest level of professional golf. Casey Martin was Tiger Woods's college teammate. Martin sought to convince the PGA that because of his rare circulatory disorder he was unable to walk an eighteen-hole golf course three or four times over a tournament weekend. The accommodation he wanted from the golfing establishment was the use of a golf cart, which would require a rules exemption from the requirement that all golfers must walk the course during tournament play.

Martin's case against the PGA reached the US Supreme Court. In *PGA Tour, Inc. v. Martin* (532 U.S. 661, 2001), the court, over a vociferous dissent by Justice Anthony Scalia, held that the waiver of the PGA walking rule was a *reasonable accommodation that did not fundamentally alter the game* of professional golf. The legal basis for the holding was a federal statute known as the **Americans with Disability Act (ADA), Title III**. Scalia believed it was not the role of any court, even the Supreme Court of the United States, to dictate "individualized" rules for talented disabled athletes while nondisabled athletes compete under a different set of rules.

A reoccurring question in this area of the law is, What does the term *disability* mean under ADA? The statute states that it includes any individual who has a *physical or mental impairment* that *substantially limits* one or more *major life activities*, has *a history* of such impairment, or is *perceived* as having such impairment. Examples are a person who is blind, deaf, or disfigured; has a loss affecting body functions; or suffers from a mental or psychological disorder but excludes drug addiction. Under Title III of the ADA, the federal statute applies to organizations or facilities that provide a *place of public accommodation*.

The law does respect some limits. For instance, a request by a disabled individual that places an *undue burden* on an organization, *compromises* the *safety* of others, or *fundamentally changes the nature of the activity or sport* are permissible grounds to deny an accommodation.

A Massachusetts court denied a wheelchair-restricted paraplegic's attempt to compete in a men's racquetball league by altering the rules of the game to allow for two bounces in a game rather than one bounce. The court, relying on dicta language from the *Martin* decision, held that varying the sport's official rules in this instance was an *unacceptable rules modification request.*

Rather than addressing a rules modification demand, a Florida court had to decide whether the owners of the Miami Dolphins, Florida Marlins, and ProPlayer Stadium, a private place of accommodation under the ADA's definition, operated the facility in a discriminatory fashion. The stadium was built prior to passage of the ADA.

The issue before the court was whether the stadium presented architectural sight barriers to a wheelchair-bound quadriplegic. Specifically, the disabled spectator sought additional handicapped parking spaces, better accessibility to restrooms and food service areas, and improved sight lines for wheelchair seating. The court held that, while the plaintiff was denied the full opportunity to enjoy the stadium because of his disability, the law did not require the owners to incorporate the architectural changes and overall improvements suggested because it was already meeting their legal obligations (*Access Now, Inc. v. South Florida Stadium Corp.*, 161 F. Supp.2d 1357, S.D. Fla., 2001).

The Florida stadium decision stands in contrast to a consent agreement reached between the US government and the owners of Madison Square Garden in New York City. This multiuse entertainment and sports facility was built in 1968, before passage of the ADA, but substantially renovated thereafter. The Garden owners agreed to remedy hundreds of architectural barriers; install wheelchair-accessible seats at floor level; and ensure that disabled patrons have full access to food service, drinking fountains, and bathrooms.

A few years ago, a federal court ordered the owners of FedEx stadium, where the Washington Redskins play, to provide auditory information assistance so the deaf and hard-of-hearing could "hear" messages broadcast over the public address system, referee calls, and half-time entertainment.

More than 30 million Americans suffer from a defined disability under the ADA. Following a best-practices policy toward compliance is a way to help all patrons experience a more fulfilling life by expanding the opportunity to participate and attend sporting and recreation activities, while reducing defensive litigation costs and unwanted negative publicity.

SUMMARY

Many years ago, the esteemed legal scholar Karl Llewellyn remarked that our society is honeycombed with disputes, and it is the task of the law to resolve these disputes. Competitive athletes, coaches, spectators, administrators, medical professionals, equipment manufacturers, and facility owners are all subject to a variety of risks. The business of the law of torts deals with how to allocate these risks and determine liability from harm suffered. In many instances, state and federal courts are tasked with the responsibility of resolving civil disputes grounded in the legal theories of negligence, intentional harm, products liability, and failure to comply with a federal statutory requirement of opportunity and ccommodation for the disabled.

KEY WORDS

The Americans with Disability Act (ADA), Title III. The statute states that it includes any individual who has a physical or mental impairment that substantially limits one or more major life activities; has a history of such impairment; or is perceived as having such impairment. Examples are a person who is blind, deaf, or disfigured; has a loss affecting body functions; or suffers from a mental or psychological disorder but excludes drug addiction. Title III of the ADA applies to organizations or facilities that provide a place of public accommodation.

Assault. The apprehension of imminent offensive physical contact is deemed the intentional tort of assault.

Comparative Negligence. Under this test, recovery is barred only when the athlete contributes more than half of the reason for the injury.

Contributory Negligence. In many jurisdictions, the contributory-negligence defense bars recovery for even the slightest degree of fault by an athlete.

Intentional Tort. Intentional torts happen when one party knowingly acts in a fashion to cause harm or offense to another. It is not a defense to argue that the offending party did not intend to cause the particular harm suffered. Assault and battery is an example of an intentional tort. For example, when a player or coach purposefully, knowingly, and wantonly places another person in fear of bodily harm or actually causes bodily injury, it is possible that that person has committed an intentional tort.

Medical Malpractice. Medical professionals owe athletes a special duty of care based on their training and experience. The specific imposed duty is to exercise reasonable skill and care as is common for those practitioners performing similar services in that particular medical field. Failures to evaluate, advise, diagnose, treat, or prescribe properly to fulfill that duty is deemed medical malpractice.

Negligence. The most common tort claim. Liability for the tort of negligence only occurs when some person fails to follow the degree of care that a reasonably prudent person would follow to avoid foreseeable harms. Negligence is known as an unintentional tort. It occurs by omission or commission of an act that causes harm to a person with whom he or she owes a duty to act with care.

Product Liability. Product liability claims for defective sporting equipment, such as hockey helmets, trampolines, or soccer goals, may arise under any of the three tort categories.

Public Invitees. In legal terms, spectators are considered public invitees.

Strict Liability Theories. Strict liability theories make the manufacturer of sports equipment the insurer and, therefore, absolutely liable for all harm that flows from the defect. Strict liability cases are rare.

Torts. Torts are divided into three categories: negligence, intentional, and strict liability. The business of torts, as so ably described by Justice Oliver Wendell Homes is to "fix the dividing line between those cases in which [a person] is liable for harm which he has done and those in which he has not." It was not until the 1970s that society, and more particularly the judicial system, began to impose civil penalties for egregious conduct in sports.

Waiver (or Release). A waiver or release is a legal document voluntarily signed to inform facility users, or their parents or guardians in the case of minors, of known risks involved in various activities and to shield the facility or organization from liability from personal harm or loss of property.

DISCUSSION QUESTIONS

1. Q: Torts are divided into which categories?

A: Torts are divided into three categories: negligence, intentional, and strict liability.

2. Q: What type of tort is negligence, and how does it occur?

A: Negligence is known as an unintentional tort. It occurs by omission or commission of an act that causes harm to a person with whom he or she owes a duty to act with care.

3. Q: How can a team physician be sued for medical malpractice?

A: Frequently, the law of negligence levies a special duty of care on individuals who have specialized training or skills. A team physician who fails to properly screen, diagnose, or treat an athlete, and the actual harm suffered is a consequence of this failure, may be sued for medical malpractice, a special type of negligence claim.

4. Q: What are the five elements crucial to a negligence case?

A: The five elements that an injured person or plaintiff must prove in a typical negligence case are as follows:

1. The defendant owed a duty of care to the plaintiff;
2. The defendant breached that duty;
3. The defendant failed to act as a reasonable person would under the circumstances;
4. The defendant's action or failure to act was the proximate cause of the harm; and
5. The plaintiff suffered damages.

5. Q: What was important in the case of *Nabozny v. Barnhill* (Ill. App. 3d 212, 1975)?

A: *Nabozny v. Barnhill* (Ill. App. 3d 212, 1975) was important because it broke away from the common practice before the mid-1970s of state and federal courts consistently denying liability claims for injuries that arose out of another participant's failure to follow game rules during a sporting event.

6. Q: Which sports do the majority of injuries for boys and girls come from?

A: Football is the most dangerous activity that boys play. Girls suffer the most severe injuries from playing basketball, followed by soccer.

7. Q: Under which legal theories can a product liability claim proceed?

A: A product liability claim for injury because of a defective product can proceed under a number of legal theories: negligence, breach of warranty (contract), and strict liability.

8. Q: What is the legal issue with high-performance composite materials used in baseball and softball bats for high school and college athletes?

A: The introduction of high-performance composite baseball and softball bats at the high school and college levels has raised questions regarding player safety versus schools attempting to save costs from constantly replacing broken bats. A legal issue is whether these new bats are "defective" because a ball comes off a bat at a much faster speed, therefore making it harder for infielders to react.

9. Q: What are the two most common brain injuries suffered from repeated impact to the head?

A: The two most common brain injuries suffered from repeated impact to the head are sudden impact syndrome (SIS) and chronic traumatic encephalopathy (CTE).

10. Q: What are some limits placed on the Americans with Disability Act (ADA), Title III?

A: The law does respect some limits. For instance, a request by a disabled individual that places an undue burden on an organization, compromises the safety of others, or fundamentally changes the nature of the activity or sport are permissible grounds to deny an accommodation.

11. **Q: What is the only state that requires every high school to employ an athletic trainer on staff?**

A: Hawaii is the sole state to require that every high school employ an athletic trainer on staff.

Chapter Ten

Crime, Justice, and Sports

"No sports league, no matter how well organized or self-policed it may be, should thereby render the players in that league immune from criminal prosecution."—Judge Carter, *Regina v. Maki*, 14 D.L.R.3d 164, 1970

Football star O. J. Simpson is responsible for helping the major media outlets achieve some of the highest prime-time television ratings on record. The featured event was not pictorial images of him winning the Heisman Trophy as a senior running back at USC or becoming the first professional football player to rush for 2,000 yards in a season. Viewers were glued to their televisions as they watched Simpson's slow ride in the back of a Ford Bronco with a gun pointed to his head on an LA freeway as he was trying to escape from the horrors of his murdered ex-wife and her friend.

In what is generally considered the most publicized criminal trial in American jurisprudence, Simpson was acquitted on the criminal charges of killing them. Throughout the judicial proceedings, the public watched, talked, and learned about *domestic violence.* Beating a spouse or ex-spouse at home would no longer be treated as a family spat, even when committed by an athlete-turned-celebrity-superstar.

The Simpson affair stands as a pivotal moment in sports. Once upon a time, to follow sports meant keeping track of team standings and box scores. It then evolved into discussions about long-term contracts, free agency, salary caps, licensing rights, drug testing, and endorsements. Player misconduct on and off the athletic field and charges of bullying, sexual harassment, and assault, coupled with spectator violence, are now part of the daily fare for the sports junkie.

Athletes being role models

ATHLETES AS ROLE MODELS

In an oft-quoted remark, former NBA star and television commentator Charles Barkley, appearing in a Nike commercial, stated, "I'm not a role model. I'm not paid to be a role model. I'm paid to wreak havoc on the basketball court. Parents should be role models. Just because I dunk a basketball doesn't mean I should raise your kids."

Contrast Barkley's comments that personal privilege bestowed on exceptional athletes does not lead to personal responsibility with observations by another NBA all-star. Karl Malone believes that athletes do not have to behave perfectly all the time. By virtue of their public prominence, whether they like it or not, the public views them as role models and sometimes heroes. Athletes have a duty to accept that responsibility. Why else, Malone contends, do players receive lucrative endorsement deals other than to hope fans will follow their lead and buy a certain shoe brand or box of cereal?

But here is the rub. After studying moral judgments for dozens of years, Professor Sharon Stoll of the Center for Ethical Theory and Honor in Competitive Sports at the University of Idaho has discovered that athletes invariably score lower on moral reasoning than nonathletes. Athletes who compete in sports that generate revenue score even lower than non-revenue-producing sports athletes. Female athletes do score significantly higher than male athletes.

Athletes learn early in life that society values success on the athletic pit or pool almost regardless of how it is achieved. Institutionally, coaches and athletic administrators coddle and protect extraordinary athletes as privileged members of a tribe. According to Stoll, the environment of elite sports fails to teach and model moral reasoning and moral valuing. Fairness, honesty, and responsibility on and off the athletic turf take a back seat to winning.

Apparently this same lack of moral judgment is not limited to elite professional and college athletes. According to the Josephson Institute of Ethics, more than a quarter of all high school athletes believe that playing dirty is not a big deal. Deliberately throwing a pitch at a batter who homered the prior time up was viewed as okay by 20 percent of all female high school softball players and 30 percent of all male high school baseball players. Presumably, this is a culture practice and belief that is passed on from the observed play of MLB players.

Journalist Jeff Benedict's investigation on the prevalence of crime in the NBA culminated in a well-publicized book, *Out of Bounds: Inside the NBA's Culture of Rape, Violence and Crime*. In his view, the lifestyle of the NBA, especially for younger players, contributes to a culture of reckless behavior.

Is it any wonder, then, that so many gifted college and professional athletes demonstrate little sense of acceptable behavior and personal responsibility? Poor judgment and lack of a moral compass can lead to excessive

aggression on the mat or playing field, bullying in the locker room, domestic violence at home, impaired driving, punching a woman at a bar, or sexual assaults in dorm rooms and hotels. These are all examples of offenses that may lead to criminal charges. As one media pundit noted, for some athletes, orange is becoming the new uniform color.

NFL Quarterback Michael Vick Convicted of Dog Fighting

Penn State Coach Jerry Sandusky Jailed for Child Sex Abuse

Second Drunk Driving Charge Leads to 6 Months Swimming Suspension for Michael Phelps

Puma Drops Patriots Tight End Hernandez From Endorsement Deal after Facing Charges of Murder and Illegal Firearms Possession

Ray Rice Suspended by the NFL for Assaulting His Girlfriend

NASCAR Driver Tony Stewart Cleared of Criminal Charges for Striking and Killing Sprint Car Driver Kevin Ward Jr.

Court Rules for Sanders in Her Sexual Harassment Suit against New York Knicks Executive Isaiah Thomas

CRIMINAL LAW BASICS

As a starting point, it is safe to say that, as a general rule, most injuries that occur in sports, especially contact sports, do not trigger criminal culpability. Some degree of violence is known and expected in many sports. Players assume these risks, especially in such contact sports as ice hockey, football, basketball, and wrestling. In those situations where one player's conduct is deemed reckless and the harm is foreseeable or intentional, then a civil tort action may be an appropriate remedy to recover damages.

A crime is different from a civil law tort. Tort law allows an individual to seek compensation for a loss suffered within the scope of a legally recognized interest. A **crime** is *an offense against the government that is prosecuted by the government.* Society through its legislative bodies defines conduct that is illegal and punishable. Each state and province has its own set of criminal statutes that define impermissible conduct and the appropriate punishment. At the national level, Canada and the United States, for instance, both have numerous federal agencies that investigate federally defined crimes.

Crimes, therefore, refer to the body of state, province, and national statutes that prohibit conduct the government deems harmful. Another important distinction between a crime prosecuted in criminal court by the government and a private tort filed in civil court by a harmed person is the *standard of proof.* In *criminal cases*, the government must prove each and every element of an alleged offense *beyond a reasonable doubt.* In contrast, the level of proof in most *private tort* lawsuit jurisdictions is a *preponderance of the evidence. Crimes*, unlike torts, carry the possibility of *incarceration as punishment.*

Consider, too, that the facts in a particular case may give rise to both civil actions and criminal charges. The aforementioned O. J. Simpson was acquitted on criminal charges of murder but found liable in separate trials for civil monetary damages arising from the murder.

Depending on the severity of an offense against the public, there are different ways to classify a crime. In general, crimes that carry the possibility of incarceration of a year or more and involve serious offenses, such as embezzlement, theft by force, child abuse, assault and battery, kidnapping, illegal gambling, bribery, statutory rape, and murder, are identified as **felonies.** Less serious crimes, such as first-time driving while impaired, shoplifting, public intoxication, hazing, bullying, and selling alcohol to a minor, that carry a maximum sentence of a year or less in jail along with a fine and/or community service are called **misdemeanors.** In many jurisdictions, even less serious offenses, such as operating a car without a driver's license, speeding, underage possession of alcohol, or loitering, are not classified as crimes. Instead, they are deemed **violations** and cannot result in incarceration. A first-time charge of driving under the influence of a controlled substance or alcohol is an example of an offense that may result in a misdemeanor or a violation, depending on the laws of the jurisdiction where the incident occurred.

ASSAULT AND BATTERY

A policy issue facing society is whether to impose criminal liability for outrageously aggressive or violent activity that occurs on the playing court or field. Historically, punishment for injurious conduct committed by an athlete during a sporting event is the purview of the league and sports-governing body. The exceptions are rare. The game of professional hockey relies on "enforcers." Their conduct has led to criminal prosecutions in Canada for violence far beyond the rules and culture of the sport, where the *defense of implied consensual* force breaks down.

The most common criminal charge applicable in such sports contests as ice hockey is the offense of *assault and battery.* Purposefully or willfully placing another player, coach, referee, or spectator in fear of imminent bodily injury is an **assault.** Actually physically harming a player, coach, referee, or spectator by force is a **battery.** Committing an assault or battery when using a weapon, to wit, a hockey stick, tennis racket, or baseball bat, constitutes **aggravated assault** or **battery**. Despite these legal definitions, their application in sporting events to player misconduct does not always constitute criminal behavior.

A successful prosecution of the crime of assault requires the government to prove beyond a reasonable doubt that the player had the **requisite state of mind** to commit the threatening offense and then carried out that intent. The mental intent is referred to as *mens rea*. The actual carrying out of the intent to knowingly place another person in imminent fear is called *actus reus*. Both elements must occur for a successful assault criminal conviction.

The crime of battery requires the additional elements of a *physical contact or touch* that *causes* the *bodily injury*. A successful criminal battery conviction obligates the government to demonstrate the requisite *mens rea* and *actus reus*. Proving the player had a reckless disregard for the safety of the victim is sufficient to show state of mind without having to show actual intent to cause harm.

On-the-Ice Violence

The typical hockey fistfight involving players dropping their gloves and punching one another while the referees stand back and watch is a time-honored acceptable aspect of the game of professional hockey. On the ice, referees impose penalties for prohibited activities. Off the ice, the league can impose fines, suspensions, or even expel players. In 1927, the NHL banned a player for attacking a referee in a Stanley Cup finals game. No criminal charges were brought.

There have been more than a dozen on-the-ice incidents of player violence in professional hockey that have resulted in criminal charges. In the vast majority of player-on-player altercations, the accused hockey players were acquitted. In one of these deliberations, Lord Judge Bramwell aptly summed up the prevailing legal rationale. He remarked that, as a Canadian judge, "he was unwilling to decry the manly sports of this country."

Three egregious NHL cases stand out in opposition to the majority view. In 1988, Dino Ciccarelli of the Minnesota North Stars struck Toronto Maple Leafs defenseman Luke Richardson repeatedly in the head and neck with his hockey stick. Ciccarelli became the first NHL player ever sentenced to jail, a day, for assault. The Canadian court held that striking a player in the head area with a hockey stick was *not a reasonable part of the game* and *beyond the ambit of implied consent* (*Regina v. Ciccarelli*, 54 CCC, 3rd, 121, 1989).

Twelve years later, Boston Bruins player Marty McSorley slashed Donald Brashear of the Vancouver Canucks in the head with his stick. McSorley's hit came near the end of the game, after Brashear had gotten the better of

McSorley in an earlier fight. Upon being attacked from behind, Brashear fell backward. His head hit the ice hard, causing loss of consciousness.

The league suspended McSorley for the remainder of the season with loss of pay. Concurrently, McSorley was criminally charged with assaulting Brashear. The court ruled that the blow to the head was outside the customary norms and rules of the game. The slash was deemed too dangerous of an act for a player to give consent. In finding McSorley guilty of assault with a weapon, to wit, a hockey stick, the court determined he *deliberately intended* to hit Brashear in the head. McSorley never played another minute of NHL hockey after being sentenced to an eighteen-month conditional discharge (*Regina v. McSorley*, 2000 British Columbia Provincial Ct. 0116, Criminal Div. 2000).

In 2004, Vancouver Canucks player Todd Bertuzzi sucker-punched Steve Moore of the Colorado Avalanche to the back of his head from behind after Moore refused to fight him. The blow's impact knocked Moore onto the ice. Bertuzzi then fell on Moore pushing his face into the ice while continuing to punch him unconscious. In the melee that followed, several other players from both teams fell onto Bertuzzi and Moore.

Moore's injuries were so substantial that his professional playing days ended: three fractured vertebrae, grade 3 concussion, facial injuries, and damage to the brachial plexus nerves. Civil and criminal assault charges were filed. To avoid trial, Bertuzzi pled guilty and was sentenced to eighty hours of community service and placed on probation. The NHL fined him $250,000, along with a lengthy suspension. Ten years after the incident, Bertuzzi reached an undisclosed out-of-court monetary settlement with Moore. For additional information on this case, see *Moore v. Bertuzzi*, 2012 Ontario Superior Court 597 (2012).

These three NHL incidents are all available on YouTube for viewing. The use of the term *assault* by the Canadian provincial criminal courts is consistent with how the US criminal courts refer to battery.

The NHL players' union has taken the position that criminal liability attaches only when the actions are intentional and blatant and inflict permanent mental and physical harm where there was no player consent. The NHL league must better address the growing concern that concussions can lead to significant brain injury. Already, scores of former NHL players have filed civil, not criminal, class-action suits against the league, seeking compensation for injuries related to chronic brain injuries, medical costs, and financial losses resulting from claims that the league failed to protect players from concussions.

Spectator and Fan Violence

According to experts, incidents of spectator and fan violence are more common in Europe than North America. A perusal of the hundreds of documented reports of fights in the stands or spectators tossing objects onto the playing field regardless of geography or sport generally have one common ingredient: intoxicated fans.

More than forty years ago, in a baseball game between the Cleveland Indians and the Texas Rangers, fans could buy all the beer they wanted for a dime a cup. Fans became more rowdy as the game progressed into the ninth inning, when a fan jumped over a fence and onto the field. After the drunken fan grabbed the hat of a Rangers outfielder, other players ran to the outfield to protect the player. Meanwhile, hundreds of fans tumbled onto the field to join the pandemonium. Chairs were thrown from the stands. Lit firecrackers were tossed into the Rangers' dugout. Players grabbed baseball bats to protect themselves. Fans, players, and an umpire were injured. Assault and battery charges were lodged against scores of fans.

The night that beer and violence bubbled over in Cleveland has rarely been surpassed as an example of an ill-fated marketing promotion. Yet, the most famous brawl in the annals of American sports took place decades later in an NBA contest between the Detroit Pistons and the Indiana Pacers.

In 2004, near the end of the game, a tussle broke out between players after Ron Artest of the Pacers delivered a hard foul on Ben Wallace of the Pistons. Wallace retaliated by pushing Artest. Players from both teams jumped into the action. Backpedaling, Artest worked his way over to the scorers' table. There a fan threw a cup of some liquid at him. Artest leaped into the stands and began pummeling spectators. More players joined the scuffle in the stands. Punches were thrown. Fans sprawled onto the court.

Nine players received suspensions and fines from the league. Five players pled guilty to misdemeanor criminal assault and battery charges and were sentenced to probation and/or fined. Numerous fans were barred from attending any event at the arena. Five fans were charged with misdemeanor assault and battery for fighting, along with two fans charged with the offense of illegally trespassing onto the court.

To circumvent a similar incident, the league banned the sale of beer after the third quarter of every game, reduced the size of the beer cups, and limited beer sales to a maximum of two purchases per spectator. Enhanced security presence is visible at every NBA game.

Even the beautiful game of soccer has a violent side. While the English are noted for inventing *hooliganism*, fan thuggery has spread across the world, especially where soccer enjoys strong national support. Not infrequently, fan violence fueled by alcohol is combined with long-standing *intolerance* for fans from other nations, *racism*, and *anti-Semitism*. Disturbing the peace, inciting a riot, illegally possessing weapons, trespassing, and assault and battery lead the list of the most shared successful criminal prosecutions brought against unruly, defiant fans who commit acts of violence.

Fifty spectators were injured when fights broke out between rival fans at a game between French and Turkish soccer clubs in France. Those arrested were charged with assault, deliberately entering the stadium to attack Turkish fans, throwing items, and racism. A few years later, police killed a French fan, and others were injured when French fans fought police after the host club lost a match to a visiting club from Israel. The fan who was shot was linked to an "ultra" group that purportedly modeled itself after a British hooligan group. Racial insults by white fans hurled against nonwhite players has led to countries enacting legislation to ban fans who are known to instigate violent conduct.

Sexual Assaults by Coaches

In 2011, after a lengthy grand jury investigation, former Penn State football coach Jerry Sandusky was indicted on fifty-two counts of *child sexual abuse*. A year later, Sandusky was convicted on forty-five of the sexual abuse charges and sentenced to a minimum thirty years and maximum sixty years of imprisonment. Particularly troubling was the findings of an independent investigation commissioned by Penn State. It determined that the university knew about allegations of child abuse and failed to properly disclose them to authorities. According to the report, for fourteen years, Sandusky was "empowered" to continue his abuse on and off the school's campus.

After Sandusky's trial, three Penn State administrators were criminally charged with failing to report his crimes. A similar failing-to-report charge occurred when two preteenage sisters notified a counselor that their swim coach was inappropriately touching them. The coach, who admitted to sexually assaulting the young swimmers in exchange for food and sleepover privileges, was sentenced to eight years of jail. The counselor awaits trial for failing to properly notify authorities.

A 2010 shocking *20/20* ABC investigation of swimming coaches revealed dozens of cases of adult swim coaches sexually molesting young swimmers. The television report revealed that thirty-six certified swim coaches had been banned for sexual conduct ranging from videotaping female swimmers in the nude in the locker room to raping teenage victims. The official governing body for swimming, USA Swimming, is facing charges of failing to protect swimmers from predatory coaches and allegations of cover-ups.

In the aftermath of these revelations, USA Swimming implemented centralized background checks for swim coaches, volunteers, and staff. An example of the prior laxity occurred when San Jose, California, swim coach Andy King consistently received clean background checks from USA Swimming. King received a forty-year sentence for abusing a dozen girls over decades. Additional protections enacted to protect swimmers include a prohibition against rubdowns or massages by coaches and a ban on shared hotel rooms between athletes and coaches.

HAZING AND BULLYING

For weeks in 2013, the number-one sports story in America was the alleged *bullying and hazing* by Miami Dolphin offensive tackle Richie Incognito against African American teammate Jonathan Martin, who unexpectedly bolted from the team during the season. The facts of who said what to whom, when, and why are still unclear. It is clear that both players engaged in vulgar conversations and veiled threats of physical attacks that are difficult for those outside the professional locker-room setting to comprehend.

Incognito's use of the *N* word and physical intimidation fears may constitute bullying and *harassment* on the basis of race and sex, offenses under Title VII of the Civil Rights Act of 1964. In the event the Dolphins were aware of or encouraged these acts, they may be liable for failing to prevent a *hostile work environment.*

A working definition of ***bullying*** is an act by an individual or group with the specific *intent of harming another person psychologically or physically.* Common bullying tactics are name calling, spreading rumors over social media, taunting, threatening, intimidating, or hitting. **Hazing** is any act by a group that intends to *embarrass, harass, ridicule or cause mental or physical discomfort. Hazing* is *a ritual* imposed on those who want to *join* or be a part of a team or group. Acts of *bullying* seek to *exclude* someone from a team or group.

Some states, such as Massachusetts, define *hazing* as any conduct or method of initiation into any student organization that *recklessly or willfully endangers the physical or mental health* of any student or person. The statute identifies common examples that were once considered innocent rites of passage; for instance, forced athletic activity, extensive exposure to extreme weather, forced consumption of alcohol or food or drugs, whipping, beating, branding, extended isolation, and deprivation of sleep, which is likely to adversely affect the physical or mental health of a student or person. High school and college officials must inform student teams, clubs, and organizations annually of these rules. Violations are misdemeanor offenses that can lead to up to a year in jail and fines of $3,000. A witness to hazing who fails to report an offense may be fined up to $1,000.

Depending on the severity of the acts, bullying and hazing may be classified as misdemeanor or felony offenses. Depending on the age of the perpetrators, incidents may fall within the purview of the juvenile court system, so the results of these cases are not publicly reported. About half of all high school students indicate they have been hazed before entering college. The vast majority of all hazing occurs on sports teams. In nearly a quarter of all hazing cases, adults were aware of the incident or participated. Increasingly, coaches who fail to stop or report hazing and bullying events are punished administratively and subject to criminal penalties under state law.

A review of the case law suggests school suspensions for so-called minor bullying or hazing offenses are the norm at the high school level. In the 1990s, reflecting the times, even more serious charges, such as varsity athletes sodomizing a junior varsity athlete, only resulted in the imposition of community service and a small fine after guilty pleas to misdemeanor charges. Today hazing is viewed as a serious offense. In California, for instance, forcible acts of sexual penetration accompanied by threats of retaliation against a minor who fails to go along with the offense may result in twelve years of incarceration. Hazing that involves willful touching of someone against his or her will, such as paddling or spanking, may lead to criminal battery charges.

SPORTS BETTING AND MATCH FIXING IN SPORTS

In a startling 2007 revelation, NBA referee Tim Donaghy pled guilty to conspiracy to commit wire fraud and transmit wagering tips on basketball games he officiated. In a *60 Minutes* television interview, Donaghy admitted to betting on around one hundred NBA games and winning about 75 percent of his bets, although he claims he didn't let his betting influence his officiating. Donaghy was sentenced to fifteen months in prison.

That same year, a handful of basketball and football players from the University of Toledo received jail terms for conspiring to fix games on behalf of Detroit gamblers. Once the Army–Navy football game at Yankee Stadium was canceled because of all the gamblers who were spotted in team hotels after more than a million dollars in bets had been placed.

Internationally, the sport of cricket has been plagued by ongoing admissions by leading players of accepting money in exchange for fixing outcomes. Soccer's governing body, FIFA, has banned several players for life for fixing matches in Eastern Europe. The international police agency Interpol has determined that sixty to eighty countries have reported allegations of soccer-match fixing by players, team officials, or referees for each of the past three years. Organized crime groups from Russia, Italy, the Balkans, China, and the United States are raking in millions of dollars based on the Interpol report.

After examining news reports in dozen of countries, universally, the soccer players who are caught for accepting cash for altering game outcomes were either suspended or banned but not indicted for criminal *fraud*. In Europe, sports fraud is deemed a crime in only five countries, according to Interpol. The absence of a global agreement on sports bribery regulation and lack of extradition treaties makes catching and prosecuting those who orchestrate the fixing of sports matches difficult.

Sports betting is not limited to fixing matches to leverage an illegal financial gain. Fantasy sports leagues DraftKings and FanDuel are under investigation by federal and state regulators regarding the legality of their business models. In what originally began decades ago as fun "rotisserie-league baseball" has grown into a $2 billion a year Internet business played by millions of fans daily. To play, fantasy team operators charge a fee to players. They, in turn, build an online team in sports ranging from professional soccer to professional football, with real-life athletes, hoping to cash out a winner based on selecting athletes and teams that perform the best.

The Unlawful Internet bling Enforcement Act of 2006 exempts financial payouts in Internet games of skill from unlawful gambling charges. The legal issue facing these fantasy leagues is whether regulators, and the courts, will view online games as ones of chance or skill.

For many observers, there is irony in the relationship between professional sports teams and fantasy sports leagues. For decades the owners and commissioners of all the major professional sports leagues in North America have publicly complained about the evils of allowing gambling on the outcomes of games. Yet many of the major professional sports leagues and media companies that broadcast games have financially invested in these fantasy sports league businesses. Additionally, DraftKings and FanDuel have executed sponsorship agreements with many of these same professional sports teams, including fifteen NFL clubs.

ATHLETES GONE WRONG

A snapshot of topical sporting news events reveals a host of prominent professional athletes charged with crimes, including drunk driving (Michael Phelps), child abuse (Adrian Peterson), murder (Aaron Hernandez), domestic abuse (Ray Rice), and weapons possession (Raymond Felton). Although it is documented that elite athletes score lower on moral reasoning, what is not conclusive is whether on-the-field aggressive behavior, especially in contact sports, leads to off-the-field violence.

The number-one criminal offense committed by athletes is domestic abuse. In nearly every reported case, the fact pattern is as follows: A male athlete who plays a violent sport physically abuses or harms his wife or girlfriend. TMZ has become a leader in sharing accounts like that of running back Stephen Jackson beating up his nine-month-pregnant girlfriend and then telling her to lie and say she fell in the shower. This was followed up by TMZ sharing the graphic video of running back Ray Rice knocking out his girlfriend in a hotel elevator.

According to Ronald B. Woods in his book *Social Issues in Sport*, there is insufficient research to determine whether athletes commit domestic violence at a higher rate than the general population. Compounding the complexity of examining the issue is the reluctance of women to report such incidents until they become frequent or debilitating. Even after contacting the police, many women refuse to testify at trial. The role of alcohol and drugs as a contributing factor to domestic abuse cannot be ignored, in addition to elite athletes' unique sense of entitlement.

Professor Richard Lapchick, founder of the Institute for Diversity and Ethics in Sports (TIDES), University of Central Florida, and author of numerous studies on race and gender in sports, cites statistical reports that indicate most white Americans believe that African Americans are more violent than Caucasians. African American men dominate the rosters of the NFL and NBA. Therefore, when they are involved in violent conduct off the field, it is likely to receive extensive publicity on chat rooms, social media, online news services, print newspapers, and broadcast reports. It all adds to the perception that African American male athletes are major perpetrators of domestic violence, when the reality is that most abusers are men who try to control women, regardless of their status or profession.

SUMMARY

The application of criminal law principles is adjusted to meet the customs and rules of sport. The implicit notion that athletes participating in a sporting event assume all risks of injury is slowly fading. The most frequent on-the-ice criminal charge leveled by a government prosecutor is assault and battery. Determining whether a player's actions go beyond the acceptable threshold of violence requires a simultaneous finding of a requisite state of mind to perform harm or acting in a willful or reckless manner likely to cause harm and performance of the actual act that causes harm. Spectators who behave in an unacceptable manner that inflicts harm on other fans, referees, or players also may be subject to criminal charges ranging from public intoxication to racism. The Sandusky case brought national attention to the problem of some coaches using their perceived power to assault vulnerable children.

The notoriety of prominent athletes engaging in unacceptable off-the-field acts of violence toward women is raising awareness about domestic violence. The causal connection between aggressive athletic behavior rewarded on the playing field and violent behavior by athletes off the court is unclear. Hazing and bullying are now viewed as serious criminal offenses that can lead to jail sentences or juvenile detention.

KEY WORDS

Actus Reus. The actual carrying out of the intent to knowingly place another person in imminent fear is called actus reus.

Aggravated Assault or Battery. Committing an assault or battery when using a weapon, to wit, a hockey stick, tennis racket, or baseball bat, constitutes aggravated assault or battery.

Assault. Purposefully or willfully placing another player, coach, referee, or spectator in fear of imminent bodily injury is an assault.

Battery. Actually physically harming a player, coach, referee, or spectator by force is a battery.

Bullying. A working definition of *bullying* is an act by an individual or group with the specific intent of harming another person psychologically or physically. Common bullying tactics are name calling, spreading rumors over social media, taunting, threatening, intimidating, or hitting. Acts of bullying seek to exclude someone from a team or group.

Crime. A crime is an offense against the government that is prosecuted by the government.

Felonies. In general, crimes that carry the possibility of incarceration of a year or more and involve serious offenses, such as embezzlement, theft by force, child abuse, assault and battery, kidnapping, illegal gambling, bribery, statutory rape, and murder, are identified as felonies.

Hazing. Hazing is any act by a group that intends to embarrass, harass, ridicule, or cause mental or physical discomfort. Hazing is a ritual imposed on those who want to join or be a part of a team or group. Acts of bullying seek to exclude someone from a team or group.

Mens Rea. The mental intent of a violent action is referred to as mens rea.

Misdemeanors. Less serious crimes, such as first-time driving while impaired, shoplifting, public intoxication, hazing, bullying, and selling alcohol to a minor, that carry a maximum sentence of a year or less in jail along with a fine and/or community service are called misdemeanors.

Requisite State of Mind. A successful prosecution of the crime of assault requires the government to prove beyond a reasonable doubt that the player had the requisite state of mind to commit the threatening offense and then carried out that intent.

Violations. In many jurisdictions, even less serious offenses, such as operating without a driver's license, speeding, underage possession of alcohol, or loitering, are not classified as a crime. Instead, they are deemed violations and cannot result in incarceration.

DISCUSSION QUESTIONS

1. Q: How is crime different from civil tort law?

A: Tort law allows an individual to seek compensation for a loss suffered within the scope of a legally recognized interest. A crime is an offense against the government that is prosecuted by the government.

2. Q: What is the measure of proving guilt in a criminal case compared to a tort?

A: Another important distinction between a crime prosecuted in criminal court by the government and a private tort filed in civil court by a harmed person is the standard of proof. In criminal cases, the government must prove each and every element of an alleged offense beyond a reasonable doubt. In contrast, the level of proof in most private tort lawsuit jurisdictions is a preponderance of the evidence. Crimes, unlike torts, carry the possibility of incarceration as punishment.

3. Q: What is required for the crime of battery to have occurred?

A: The crime of battery requires the additional elements of a physical contact or touch that cause the bodily injury. A successful criminal battery conviction obligates the government to demonstrate the requisite mens rea and actus reus. Proving the player had a reckless disregard for the safety of the victim is sufficient to show state of mind without having to show actual intent to cause harm.

4. Q: How does the state of Massachusetts define *hazing*?

A: Some states, such as Massachusetts, define *hazing* as any conduct or method of initiation into any student organization that recklessly or willfully endangers the physical or mental health of any student or person.

5. Q: What are common examples of hazing?

A: The statute against hazing identifies common examples that were once considered innocent rites of passage; for instance, forced athletic activity, extensive exposure to extreme weather, forced consumption of alcohol or food or drugs, whipping, beating, branding, extended isolation, and deprivation of sleep, which is likely to adversely affect the physical or mental health of a student or person.

6. Q: What is the penalty for hazing violations?

A: Violations are misdemeanor offenses that can lead to up to a year in jail and fines of $3,000. A witness to hazing who fails to report an offense may be fined up to $1,000.

7. Q: Can coaches be punished for failing to prevent hazing or bullying?

A: Coaches who fail to stop or report hazing and bullying events are punished administratively and subject to criminal penalties under state law.

8. Q: How many high school students claim to have been hazed?

A: About half of all high school students indicate that they have been hazed before entering college.

9. Q: Where do most acts of hazing take place?

A: The vast majority of all hazing occurs on sports teams.

10. Q: In how many European countries is sports fraud a crime?

A: In Europe, sports fraud is deemed a crime in only five countries, according to Interpol.

11. Q: What is the number-one criminal offense committed by athletes?

A: The number-one criminal offense committed by athletes is domestic abuse. In nearly every reported case, the fact pattern is as follows: A male athlete who plays a violent sport physically abuses or harms his wife or girlfriend.

Appendix A

Drug Testing Consent Form (NCAA)

Form 15-3b   **Academic Year: 2015-16**

Drug-Testing Consent – NCAA Division I

For:	Student-athletes.
Action:	Sign and return to your director of athletics.
Due date:	At the time your intercollegiate squad first reports for practice or the Monday of the institution's fourth week of classes, whichever date occurs first.
Required by:	NCAA Constitution 3.2.4.7 and NCAA Bylaw 12.7.3.
Effective date:	This consent form shall be in effect from the date this document is signed and shall remain in effect until a subsequent Drug-Testing Consent Form is executed.

Requirement to Sign Drug-Testing Consent Form.

Name of your institution: _____

Name of student-athlete: _____ Sport(s): _____

You must sign this form to participate (i.e., practice or compete) in intercollegiate athletics per NCAA Constitution 3.2.4.7 and NCAA Bylaw 12.7.3. If you have any questions, you should discuss them with your director of athletics.

Consent to Testing.

You agree to allow the NCAA to test you on a year-round basis and in relation to any participation by you in any NCAA championship and in any postseason football game for drugs in the banned drug classes listed in Bylaw 31.2.3 (see attached). Examples of drugs in each class can be found at www.ncaa.org/drugtesting. Note: There is no complete list of banned substances. Check the Resource Exchange Center (see attached) for questions about supplements, medications and banned drugs. [Attachment]

Consequences for a Positive Drug Test.

By signing this form, you affirm that you are aware of the NCAA drug-testing program, which provides:

1. A student-athlete who tests positive for an NCAA banned drug must be immediately declared ineligible;

2. A student-athlete who tests positive for a banned drug other than a "street drug" shall be withheld from competition in all sports for 365 days from the drug-test collection date and shall lose a year of eligibility. A student-athlete who tests positive for a "street drug" shall be withheld from competition for 50 percent of a season in all sports (50 percent of regular-season contests or dates of competition);

3.   A student-athlete who tests positive has an opportunity to appeal the sanction;

4.   A student-athlete who tests positive a second time for the use of any drug other than a "street drug" shall lose all remaining regular-season and postseason eligibility in all sports. A student-athlete who tests positive a second time for a street drug shall be withheld from competition for 365 days from the date of the test and shall lose a year of eligibility;

5.   The penalty for missing a scheduled drug test is the same as the penalty for testing positive for the use of a banned drug other than a street drug;

6.   A student-athlete who is found to have tampered with an NCAA drug test sample shall be charged with the loss of a minimum of two seasons of competition in all sports and shall remain ineligible for all regular-season and postseason competition during the time period ending two-calendar years (730 days) from the date of the test; and

7.   If a student-athlete transfers to a non-NCAA institution while ineligible because of a positive NCAA drug test, and competes in collegiate competition within the prescribed penalty at a non-NCAA institution, the student-athlete will be ineligible for all NCAA regular-season and postseason competition until the student-athlete does not compete in collegiate competition for the entirety of the prescribed penalty.

Signatures.

By signing below, I consent:

1.   To be tested by the NCAA in accordance with NCAA drug-testing policy, which provides among other things that:

   a.   I will be notified of selection to be tested;

   b.   I must appear for NCAA testing or be sanctioned for a positive drug test; and

   c.   My urine sample collection will be observed by a person of my same gender.

2.   To accept the consequences of a positive drug test or a breach of drug testing protocol;

3.   To allow my drug-test sample to be used by the NCAA drug-testing laboratories for research purposes to improve drug-testing detection; and

4.   To allow disclosure of my drug-testing results only for purposes related to eligibility for participation in NCAA competition.

Drug-Testing Consent – NCAA Division I
Form 15-3b
Page No. 3

_____

I understand that if I sign this statement falsely or erroneously, I violate NCAA legislation on ethical conduct and will jeopardize my eligibility.

_____	_____
Date	Signature of student-athlete
_____	_____
Date	Signature of parent or legal guardian (if student-athlete is a minor)

_____   _____   _____
Name (please print)   Date of birth   Age

_____
Home address (street, city, state and zip code)

_____
Sport(s)

What to do with this form: Sign and return it to your director of athletics at the time your intercollegiate squad first reports for practice or the Monday of the institution's fourth week of classes (whichever date occurs first).   This form is to be kept on file at the institution for **six years**.

2015-16 NCAA Banned Drugs

It is your responsibility to check with the appropriate or designated athletics staff before using any substance.

The NCAA bans the following classes of drugs:

1. Stimulants;
2. Anabolic Agents;
3. Alcohol and Beta Blockers (banned for rifle only);
4. Diuretics and Other Masking Agents;
5. Street Drugs;
6. Peptide Hormones and Analogues;
7. Anti-estrogens; and
8. Beta-2 Agonists.

Note: Any substance chemically related to these classes is also banned.

The institution and the student-athlete shall be held accountable for all drugs within the banned drug class regardless of whether they have been specifically identified.

Drugs and Procedures Subject to Restrictions:

1. Blood doping;
2. Gene doping;
3. Local anesthetics (under some conditions);
4. Manipulation of urine samples; and
5. Beta-2 Agonists permitted only by prescription and inhalation.

NCAA Nutritional/Dietary Supplements Warning:

Before consuming any nutritional/dietary supplement product, review the product with the appropriate or designated athletics department staff. There are no NCAA approved supplement products.

1. Dietary supplements, including vitamins and minerals, are not well regulated and may cause a positive drug test result.
2. Student-athletes have tested positive and lost their eligibility from using dietary supplements.
3. Many dietary supplements are contaminated with banned drugs not listed on the label.
4. **Any product containing a dietary supplement ingredient is taken at your own risk.**

Check with your athletics department staff prior to using a supplement.

Attachment
Page No. 2
_____

Examples of NCAA Banned Substances in Each Drug Class

**Note to Student-Athletes: There is NO complete list of banned substances.
Do not rely on this list to rule out any label ingredient.**

1. **Stimulants**: Amphetamine (Adderall); caffeine (guarana); cocaine; ephedrine; fenfluramine (Fen); methamphetamine; methylphenidate (Ritalin); phentermine (Phen); synephrine (bitter orange); methylhexaneamine, "bath salts" (mephedrone); octopamne; DMBA; etc. *Exceptions*: phenylephrine and pseudoephedrine are not banned.

2. **Anabolic Agents** (sometimes listed as a chemical formula, such as 3,6,17-androstenetrione): Androstenedione; boldenone; clenbuterol; DHEA (7-Keto); epi-trenbolone; etiocholanolone; methasterone; methandienone; nandrolone; norandrostenedione; ostarine, stanozolol; stenbolone; testosterone; trenbolone; SARMS (ostarine); etc.

3. **Alcohol and Beta Blockers** (banned for rifle only): Alcohol; atenolol; metoprolol; nadolol; pindolol; propranolol; timolol; etc.

4. **Diuretics** (water pills) **and Other Masking Agents**: Bumetanide; chlorothiazide; furosemide; hydrochlorothiazide; probenecid; spironolactone (canrenone); triameterene; trichlormethiazide; etc.

5. **Street Drugs**: Heroin; marijuana; tetrahydrocannabinol (THC); synthetic cannabinoids (e.g., spice, K2, JWH-018, JWH-073).

6. **Peptide Hormones and Analogues**: Growth hormone (hGH); human chorionic gonadotropin (hCG); erythropoietin (EPO); IGF-1; etc.

7. **Anti-Estrogens**: Anastrozole; tamoxifen; formestane; ATD; clomiphene; SERMS (nolvadex); etc.

8. **Beta-2 Agonists**: Bambuterol; formoterol; salbutamol; salmeterol; higenamine; norcoclaurine; etc.

Additional examples of banned drugs can be found at www.ncaa.org/drugtesting.

**Any substance that is chemically related to the class,
even if it is not listed as an example, is also banned!**

Information about ingredients in medications and nutritional/dietary supplements can be obtained by contacting the **Resource Exchange Center 877/202-0769 or www.drugfreesport.com/rec
password: ncaa1, ncaa2 or ncaa3.**

**It is your responsibility to check with the appropriate or designated
athletics staff before using any substance.**

Appendix B

Standard Player Contract (NFL)

THIS   CONTRACT   is   between
_____, hereinafter "Player,"
and _____, a _____ corporation
(limited partnership) (partnership), hereinafter "Club," operating under the
name   of   the
_____ as a
member of the National Football League, hereinafter "League." In consideration of the promises made by each to the other, Player and Club agree as
follows:

1. TERM. This contract covers _____ football season(s), and will begin on the date of execution or March 1, _____, whichever is later, and
end on February 28 or 29, _____, unless extended, terminated, or
renewed as specified elsewhere in this contract.

2. EMPLOYMENT AND SERVICES. Club employs Player as a skilled
football player. Player accepts such employment. He agrees to give his best
efforts and loyalty to the Club, and to conduct himself on and off the field
with appropriate recognition of the fact that the success of professional football depends largely on public respect for and approval of those associated
with the game. Player will report promptly for and participate fully in Club's
official mandatory minicamp(s), official preseason training camp, all Club
meetings and practice sessions, and all preseason, regular season, and postseason football games scheduled for or by Club. If invited, Player will practice for and play in any all-star football game sponsored by the League.

Player will not participate in any football game not sponsored by the League unless the game is first approved by the League.

3. OTHER ACTIVITIES. Without prior written consent of Club, Player will not play football or engage in activities related to football otherwise than for Club or engage in any activity other than football which may involve a significant risk of personal injury. Player represents that he has special, exceptional, and unique knowledge, skill, ability, and experience as a football player, the loss of which cannot be estimated with any certainty and cannot be fairly or adequately compensated by damages. Player therefore agrees that Club will have the right, in addition to any other right which Club may possess, to enjoin Player by appropriate proceedings from playing football or engaging in football-related activities other than for Club or from engaging in any activity other than football which may involve a significant risk of personal injury.

4. PUBLICITY AND NFLPA GROUP LICENSING PROGRAM.

(a) Player hereby grants to Club and the League, separately and together, the right and authority to use, and to authorize others to use solely as described below, his name, nickname, initials, likeness, image, picture, photograph, animation, persona, autograph/signature (including facsimiles thereof), voice, biographical information, and/or any and all other identifying characteristics (collectively, "Publicity Rights"), for any and all uses or purposes that publicize and promote NFL Football, the League, or any of its member clubs in any way in any and all media or formats, whether analog, digital, or other, now known or hereafter developed, including, but not limited to, print, tape, disc, computer file, radio, television, motion pictures, other audio-visual and audio works, Internet, broadband platforms, mobile platforms, applications, and other distribution platforms. Without limiting the foregoing, this grant includes the right to use Player's Publicity Rights for the purpose of publicizing and promoting the following aspects of NFL Football, the League, and/or any of its member clubs: brands, games, ticket sales, game broadcasts and telecasts, programming focused on the NFL, one or more NFL clubs, and/or their games and events (e.g., coaches shows, highlight-based shows, such as *Inside the NFL*, behind-the-scenes programming, such as *Hard Knocks*), other NFL-related media offerings (e.g., branded content segments featuring NFL game footage and other programming enhancements), media distribution platforms (e.g., NFL.com, NFL Mobile, NFL Network), official events (e.g., NFL Kickoff, NFL Draft), officially sanctioned awards programs (e.g., Rookie of the Year), and public service or community-oriented initiatives (e.g., Play60). For purposes of clarity, the foregoing grant of rights includes the right and authority to use, and to authorize affiliates or business partners to use, after the term of this Agreement any Publicity Rights fixed in a tangible medium (e.g., filmed, photographed, recorded, or otherwise captured) during the term of this Agreement solely for the purposes described herein. Notwithstanding anything to the contrary, the foregoing grant does not confer, during or after the term of this Agreement, any right or authority to use Player's Publicity Rights in a manner that constitutes any endorsement by Player of a third-party brand, product, or service ("Endorsement"). For purposes of clarity, and without limitation, it shall not be an Endorsement for Club or the League to use, or authorize others to use, including, without limitation, in third-party advertising and promotional materials, footage, and photographs of Player's participation in NFL games or other NFL events that does not unduly focus on, feature, or highlight Player in a manner that leads the reasonable consumer to believe that Player is a spokesperson for, or promoter of, a third-party commercial product or service.

Player will cooperate with the news media, and will participate upon request in reasonable activities to promote the Club and the League.

Player and National Football League Players Association, including any of its affiliates ("NFLPA"), do not and will not contest during or after the term of this agreement, and this hereby confirms their acknowledgment of the exclusive rights of the League, Club, and any NFL member club (i) to telecast, broadcast, or otherwise distribute, transmit, or perform, on a live, delayed, or archived basis, in any and all media now known or hereafter developed, any NFL games or any excerpts thereof and (ii) to produce, license, offer for sale, sell, market, or otherwise distribute or perform (or authorize a third party to do any of the foregoing), on a live, delayed, or archived basis, any NFL games or any excerpts thereof, in any and all media now known or hereafter developed, including, but not limited to, packaged or other electronic or digital media.

Nothing herein shall be construed to grant any Publicity Rights for use in licensed consumer products, whether traditional or digital (e.g., video games, trading cards, apparel), other than such products that constitute programming (as described herein) or news and information offerings regardless of medium (e.g., DVDs, digital highlight offerings).

(b) Player hereby assigns the NFLPA and its licensing affiliates, if any, the exclusive and unlimited right to use, license, and sublicense the right to use his name, nickname, initials, autograph/signature (including facsimiles), voice, picture, photograph, animation, image, likeness, persona, jersey number, statistics, data, copyrights, biographical information, and/or other personal indicia (individually and collectively, "Rights") for use in connection with any product, brand, service, appearance, product line, or other commercial use and any sponsorship, endorsement, or promotion thereof, when more than five (5) NFL player Rights are involved, regardless of team affiliation and whether that number is reached using player Rights simultaneously or individually, in any form, media, or medium (now known or hereafter developed) during a consecutive 12-month period (a "group licensing program"). For sponsorships, endorsements, and promotions, group licensing programs are further defined as those: (a) in any one product category, as defined by industry standards; or (b) in different categories if the products all use similar or derivative design or artwork, or one player product is used to promote another player product.

The Rights may also be used for the promotion of the NFLPA, its affiliated entities, and/or its designees (the "NFLPA Entities"), provided such promotion does not constitute an endorsement by Player of a commercial product not a part of a group licensing program. Player agrees to participate, upon request of the NFLPA and without additional compensation, in reasonable activities to promote the NFLPA Entities, which shall include (i) up to three (3) personal appearances per year or (ii) up to fifteen (15) minutes per week dedicated to promoting the NFLPA Entities. Player retains the right to grant permission to others to utilize his Rights if that individual or entity is not concurrently utilizing the Rights of five (5) or more other NFL players for any commercial purpose whatsoever. If Player's inclusion in an NFLPA program is precluded by an individual exclusive endorsement agreement, and Player provides the NFLPA with immediate written notice of that preclusion, the NFLPA agrees to exclude Player from that particular program. Should Player fail to perform any of his obligations hereunder, the NFLPA may withhold payments owed to Player, if any, in connection with this Group Licensing Assignment.

In consideration for this assignment of rights, the NFLPA agrees to use the revenues it receives from group licensing programs to support the objectives as set forth in the Bylaws of the NFLPA and as otherwise determined by the NFLPA Board. The NFLPA further agrees to use reasonable efforts to promote the use of NFL player Rights in group licensing programs, to provide group licensing opportunities to all NFL players, and to monitor and police unauthorized third-party use of the Rights. The NFLPA makes no representations regarding group licensing other than those expressed herein. This agreement shall be construed under [state] law.

The assignment in this paragraph shall expire on December 31 of the latter of (i) the third year following the execution of this contract, or (ii) the year after this contract expires, and may not be revoked, terminated, or otherwise assigned in any manner by Player until such date. Neither Club nor the League is a party to the terms of this paragraph, which is included herein solely for the administrative convenience and benefit of Player and the NFLPA.

Nothing in Paragraph 4b shall be construed or deemed to modify in any way the rights set forth in Paragraph 4a, and the fact that Paragraph 4b (or any of the terms thereof) appears in the Player Contract shall not be referred to, relied upon, or otherwise cited by Player and/or the NFLPA or any of its affiliates in any dispute or legal proceeding as evidence that the NFL, any NFL entity, any Club or Club Affiliate, or any licensee of any of the foregoing has consented, agreed, acknowledged, or does not contest the applicability or interpretation of Paragraph 4b.

5. COMPENSATION. For performance of Player's services and all other promises of Player, Club will pay Player a yearly salary as follows:

$ _____   * _____   for the 20____ season;

$ _____   * _____   for the 20____ season;

$ _____   * _____   for the 20 ____season;

$ _____   * _____   for the 20 ____season;

$ _____   * _____   for the 20____ season.

(* designates the compensation Club will pay player if the player is not on Club's Active/Inactive List)

In addition, Club will pay Player such earned performance bonuses as may be called for in this contract; Player's necessary traveling expenses from his residence to training camp; Player's reasonable board and lodging expenses during preseason training and in connection with playing preseason, regular season, and postseason football games outside Club's home city; Player's necessary traveling expenses to and from preseason, regular season, and postseason football games outside Club's home city; Player's necessary traveling expenses to his residence if this contract is terminated by Club; and such additional compensation, benefits, and reimbursement of expenses as may be called for in any collective bargaining agreement in existence during the term of this contract. (For purposes of this contract, a collective bargaining agreement will be deemed to be "in existence" during its stated term or during any period for which the parties to that agreement agree to extend it.)

6. PAYMENT. Unless this contract or any collective bargaining agreement in existence during the term of this contract specifically provides otherwise, Player will be paid 100% of his yearly salary under this contract in equal weekly or biweekly installments over the course of the applicable regular season period, commencing with the first regular season game played by Club in each season. Unless this contract specifically provides otherwise, if this contract is executed or Player is activated after the beginning of the regular season, the yearly salary payable to Player will be reduced proportionately and Player will be paid the weekly or biweekly portions of his

yearly salary becoming due and payable after he is activated. Unless this contract specifically provides otherwise, if this contract is terminated after the beginning of the regular season, the yearly salary payable to Player will be reduced proportionately and Player will be paid the weekly or biweekly portions of his yearly salary having become due and payable up to the time of termination.

7. DEDUCTIONS. Any advance made to Player will be repaid to Club, and any properly levied Club fine or Commissioner fine against Player will be paid, in cash on demand or by means of deductions from payments coming due to the Player under this contract, the amount of such deductions to be determined by Club unless this contract or any collective bargaining agreement in existence during the term of this contract specifically provides otherwise.

8. PHYSICAL CONDITION. Player represents to Club that he is and will maintain himself in excellent physical condition. Player will undergo a complete physical examination by the Club physician upon Club request, during which physical examination Player agrees to make full and complete disclosure of any physical or mental condition known to him which might impair his performance under this contract and to respond fully and in good faith when questioned by the Club physician about such condition. If Player fails to establish or maintain his excellent physical condition to the satisfaction of the Club physician, or make the required full and complete disclosure and good faith responses to the Club physician, then Club may terminate this contract.

9. INJURY. Unless this contract specifically provides otherwise, if Player is injured in the performance of his services under this contract and promptly reports such injury to the Club physician or trainer, then Player will receive such medical and hospital care during the term of this contract as the Club physician may deem necessary, and will continue to receive his yearly salary for so long, during the season of injury only and for no subsequent period covered by this contract, as Player is physically unable to perform the services required of him by this contract because of such injury. If Player's injury in the performance of his services under this contract results in his death, the unpaid balance of his yearly salary for the season of injury will be paid to his stated beneficiary, or in the absence of a stated beneficiary, to his estate.

10. WORKERS' COMPENSATION. Any compensation paid to Player under this contract or under any collective bargaining agreement in existence during the term of this contract for a period during which he is entitled to

workers' compensation benefits by reason of temporary total, permanent total, temporary partial, or permanent partial disability will be deemed an advance payment of workers' compensation benefits due Player, and Club will be entitled to be reimbursed the amount of such payment out of any award of workers' compensation.

11. SKILL, PERFORMANCE, AND CONDUCT. Player understands that he is competing with other players for a position on Club's roster within the applicable player limits. If at any time, in the sole judgment of Club, Player's skill or performance has been unsatisfactory as compared with that of other players competing for positions on Club's roster, or if Player has engaged in personal conduct reasonably judged by Club to adversely affect or reflect on Club, then Club may terminate this contract. In addition, during the period any salary cap is legally in effect, this contract may be terminated if, in Club's opinion, Player is anticipated to make less of a contribution to Club's ability to compete on the playing field than another player or players whom Club intends to sign or attempts to sign, or another player or players who is or are already on Club's roster, and for whom Club needs room.

12. TERMINATION. The rights of termination set forth in this contract will be in addition to any other rights of termination allowed either party by law. Termination will be effective upon the giving of written notice, except that Player's death, other than as a result of injury incurred in the performance of his services under this contract, will automatically terminate this contract. If this contract is terminated by Club and either Player or Club so requests, Player will promptly undergo a complete physical examination by the Club physician.

13. INJURY GRIEVANCE. Unless a collective bargaining agreement in existence at the time of termination of this contract by Club provides otherwise, the following Injury Grievance procedure will apply: If Player believes that at the time of termination of this contract by Club he was physically unable to perform the services required of him by this contract because of an injury incurred in the performance of his services under this contract, Player may, within 60 days after examination by the Club physician, submit at his own expense to examination by a physician of his choice. If the opinion of Player's physician with respect to his physical ability to perform the services required of him by this contract is contrary to that of the Club's physician, the dispute will be submitted within a reasonable time to final and binding arbitration by an arbitrator selected by Club and Player or, if they are unable to agree, one selected in accordance with the procedures of the American Arbitration Association on application by either party.

14. RULES. Player will comply with and be bound by all reasonable Club rules and regulations in effect during the term of this contract which are not inconsistent with the provisions of this contract or of any collective bargaining agreement in existence during the term of this contract. Player's attention is also called to the fact that the League functions with certain rules and procedures expressive of its operation as a joint venture among its member clubs and that these rules and practices may affect Player's relationship to the League and its member clubs independently of the provisions of this contract.

15. INTEGRITY OF GAME. Player recognizes the detriment to the League and professional football that would result from impairment of public confidence in the honest and orderly conduct of NFL games or the integrity and good character of NFL players. Player therefore acknowledges his awareness that if he accepts a bribe or agrees to throw or fix an NFL game; fails to promptly report a bribe offer or an attempt to throw or fix an NFL game; bets on an NFL game; knowingly associates with gamblers or gambling activity; uses or provides other players with stimulants or other drugs for the purpose of attempting to enhance on-field performance; or is guilty of any other form of conduct reasonably judged by the League Commissioner to be detrimental to the League or professional football, the Commissioner will have the right, but only after giving Player the opportunity for a hearing at which he may be represented by counsel of his choice, to fine Player in a reasonable amount; to suspend Player for a period certain or indefinitely; and/or to terminate this contract.

16. EXTENSION. Unless this contract specifically provides otherwise, if Player becomes a member of the Armed Forces of the United States or any other country, or retires from professional football as an active player, or otherwise fails or refuses to perform his services under this contract, then this contract will be tolled between the date of Player's induction into the Armed Forces, or his retirement, or his failure or refusal to perform, and the later date of his return to professional football. During the period this contract is tolled, Player will not be entitled to any compensation or benefits. On Player's return to professional football, the term of this contract will be extended for a period of time equal to the number of seasons (to the nearest multiple of one) remaining at the time the contract was tolled. The right of renewal, if any, contained in this contract will remain in effect until the end of any such extended term.

17. ASSIGNMENT. Unless this contract specifically provides otherwise, Club may assign this contract and Player's services under this contract to any successor to Club's franchise or to any other Club in the League. Player will

report to the assignee Club promptly upon being informed of the assignment of his contract and will faithfully perform his services under this contract. The assignee club will pay Player's necessary traveling expenses in reporting to it and will faithfully perform this contract with Player.

18. FILING. This contract will be valid and binding upon Player and Club immediately upon execution. A copy of this contract, including any attachment to it, will be filed by Club with the League Commissioner within 10 days after execution. The Commissioner will have the right to disapprove this contract on reasonable grounds, including but not limited to an attempt by the parties to abridge or impair the rights of any other club, uncertainty or incompleteness in expression of the parties' respective rights and obligations, or conflict between the terms of this contract and any collective bargaining agreement then in existence. Approval will be automatic unless, within 10 days after receipt of this contract in his office, the Commissioner notifies the parties either of disapproval or of extension of this 10-day period for purposes of investigation or clarification pending his decision. On the receipt of notice of disapproval and termination, both parties will be relieved of their respective rights and obligations under this contract.

19. DISPUTES. During the term of any collective bargaining agreement, any dispute between Player and Club involving the interpretation or application of any provision of the NFL collective bargaining agreement or this contract will be submitted to final and binding arbitration in accordance with the procedure called for in any collective bargaining agreement in existence at the time the event giving rise to any such dispute occurs.

20. NOTICE. Any notice, request, approval, or consent under this contract will be sufficiently given if in writing and delivered in person or mailed (certified or first class) by one party to the other at the address set forth in this contract or to such other address as the recipient may subsequently have furnished in writing to the sender.

21. OTHER AGREEMENTS. This contract, including any attachment to it, sets forth the entire agreement between Player and Club and cannot be modified or supplemented orally. Player and Club represent that no other agreement, oral or written, except as attached to or specifically incorporated in this contract, exists between them. The provisions of this contract will govern the relationship between Player and Club unless there are conflicting provisions in any collective bargaining agreement in existence during the term of this contract, in which case the provisions of the collective bargaining agreement will take precedence over conflicting provisions of this contract relating to the rights or obligations of either party.

22. LAW. This contract is made under and shall be governed by the laws of the State of _____ .

23. WAIVER AND RELEASE. Player waives and releases: (i) any claims relating to the 2011 lockout; (ii) any antitrust claims relating to the Draft, restrictions on free agency, franchise player designations, transition player designations, the Entering Player Pool, the Rookie Compensation Pool, or any other term or condition of employment relating to conduct engaged in prior to the date of this Agreement; and (iii) any claims relating to conduct engaged in pursuant to the express terms of any collective bargaining agreement during the term of any such agreement. This waiver and release also extends to any conduct engaged in pursuant to the express terms of the Stipulation and Settlement Agreement in White. This waiver and release does not waive any rights player may have to commence a grievance under the 2006 CBA or to commence a grievance or other arbitration under the 2011 CBA.

24. OTHER PROVISIONS.

(a) Each of the undersigned hereby confirms that (i) this contract, renegotiation, extension, or amendment sets forth all components of the player's remuneration for playing professional football (whether such compensation is being furnished directly by the Club or by a related or affiliated entity); and (ii) there are not undisclosed agreements of any kind, whether express or implied, oral or written, and there are no promises, undertakings, representations, commitments, inducements, assurances of intent, or understandings of any kind that have not been disclosed to the NFL involving consideration of any kind to be paid, furnished, or made available to Player or any entity or person owned or controlled by, affiliated with, or related to Player, either during the term of this contract or thereafter.

(b) Each of the undersigned further confirms that, except insofar as any of the undersigned may describe in an addendum to this contract, to the best of their knowledge, no conduct in violation of the Anti-Collusion rules took place with respect to this contract. Each of the undersigned further confirms that nothing in this contract is designed or intended to defeat or circumvent any provisions of the collective bargaining agreement dated [date], including but not limited to the Rookie Compensation Pool and Salary Cap provisions; however, any conduct permitted by that Agreement shall not be considered a violation of this confirmation.

(c) PERFORMANCE-BASED PAY. Player's attention is called to the fact that he may be entitled to Performance-Based Pay in accordance with the procedures outlined in Article 28, and that his eligibility for such pay is based on a formula that takes into account his playtime percentage and compensation.

25. SPECIAL PROVISIONS. THIS CONTRACT is executed in six (6) copies. Player acknowledges that before signing this contract he was given the opportunity to seek advice from or be represented by persons of his own selection.

_____   _____

PLAYER   CLUB

_____   _____

Home Address   By

_____   _____

Telephone Number   Club Address

_____   _____

Date   Date

_____

PLAYER'S AGENT

_____

Address

_____

Telephone Number

_____

Date

Copy Distribution:

White—League Office   Yellow—Player

Green—Member Club   Blue—Management Council

Gold—NFLPA   Pink—Player Agent

Appendix C

Required NFLPA Representation Contract

This AGREEMENT made this _____ day of _____, 20___, by and between _____ (hereinafter "Player") and _____ (hereinafter "Contract Advisor")

WITNESSETH:
In consideration of the mutual promises hereinafter made by each to the other, Player and Contract Advisor agree as follows:

1. General Principles
This Agreement is entered into pursuant to and in accordance with the National Football League Players Association (hereinafter "NFLPA") Regulations Governing Contract Advisors (hereinafter the "Regulations") effective December 1, 1994, and as amended thereafter from time to time.

2. Representations
Contract Advisor represents that in advance of executing this Agreement, he/she has been duly certified as a Contract Advisor by the NFLPA. Player acknowledges that the NFLPA Certification of the Contract Advisor is neither a recommendation of the Contract Advisor, nor a warranty by NFLPA of the Contract Advisor's competence, honesty, skills, or qualifications.

Contract Advisor hereby discloses that he/she (check one): [ ] represents or has represented; [ ] does not represent and has not represented NFL management personnel, any NFL coaches, other professional football league coaches, or college football coaches in matters pertaining to their employment by or association with any NFL Club, other professional football league club, or college. If Contract Advisor responds in the affirmative, Contract Advisor must attach a properly completed and signed SRA Coaches and NFL Personnel Disclosure Form (Appendix G of the Regulations).

3. Contract Services

Player hereby retains Contract Advisor to represent, advise, counsel, and assist Player in the negotiation, execution, and enforcement of his playing contract(s) in the National Football League. In performing these services, Contract Advisor acknowledges that he/she is acting in a fiduciary capacity on behalf of Player and agrees to act in such manner as to protect the best interests of Player and assure effective representation of Player in individual contract negotiations with NFL Clubs. Contract Advisor shall be the exclusive representative for the purpose of negotiating player contracts for Player. However, Contract Advisor shall not have the authority to bind or commit Player to enter into any contract without actual execution thereof by Player. Once Player agrees to and executes his player contract, Contract Advisor agrees to also sign the player contract and send a copy (by facsimile or overnight mail) to the NFLPA and the NFL Club within 48 hours of execution by Player. Player and Contract Advisor (check one): [ ] have [ ] have not entered into any agreements or contracts relating to services other than the individual negotiating services described in this Paragraph (e.g., financial advice, tax preparation). If the parties have, complete 3(A) and 3(B) below.

A. Describe the nature of the other services covered by the separate agreements:

B. Contract Advisor and Player hereby acknowledge that Player was given the opportunity to enter into any of the agreements described in Paragraph 3(A) above and this Standard Representation Agreement, without the signing of one agreement being conditioned upon the signing of any of the other agreements in violation of Section 3(B)(22) of the NFLPA Regulations Governing Contract Advisors.

Contract Advisor: Player:

4. Compensation for Services

A. If a Contract Advisor succeeds in negotiating an NFL Player Contract acceptable to Player and signed by Player during the term hereof, Contract Advisor shall receive a fee as set forth in subparagraph B below. CONTRACT ADVISOR AND PLAYER AGREE AND ACKNOWLEDGE THAT THE AMOUNT OF SUCH FEE IS FREELY NEGOTIABLE BE-TWEEN THEM, EXCEPT THAT NO AGREED-UPON FEE MAY BE GREATER THAN:

(1) Three percent (3%) of the compensation received by Player for each playing season covered by a Player Contract which is the result of negotiations between Contract Advisor and an NFL Club; or

(2) The lesser percentage specified in Section 4(B)(1)(a) of the Regulations in a case where Player signs a one-year tender as a Franchise, Transition, or Restricted Free Agent player.

B. The fee for Contract Advisor's services shall be as follows (Both Contract Advisor and Player must initial the appropriate line below):

	Contract Advisor	Player
Three Percent (3%)		
Two-and-one-half Percent (2½%)		
Two Percent (2%)		
One-and-one-half Percent (1½%)		
One Percent (1%)		

Other (specify below):

In computing the allowable fee pursuant to this Paragraph 4 the term "compensation" shall include only base salaries, signing bonuses, reporting bonuses, roster bonuses, Practice Squad salary in excess of the minimum Practice Squad salary specified in Article XXXIV of the Collective Bargaining Agreement, and any performance incentives actually received by Player. The term "compensation" shall not include any "honor" incentive bonuses (i.e., ALL PRO, PRO BOWL, Rookie of the Year), or any collectively bargained benefits.

5. Payment of Contract Advisor's Fee

Contract Advisor shall not be entitled to receive any fee for the performance of his/her services pursuant to this Agreement until Player receives the compensation upon which the fee is based. However, Player may enter into an agreement with Contract Advisor to pay any fee attributable to deferred compensation due and payable to Player in advance of when the deferred compensation is paid to Player, provided that Player has performed the services necessary under his contract to entitle him to the deferred compensation. Such fee shall be reduced to its present value as specified in the NFLPA Regulations (see Section 4(B)). Such an agreement must also be in writing, with a copy sent to the NFLPA.

In no case shall Contract Advisor accept, directly or indirectly, payment of any fees hereunder from Player's club. Further, Contract Advisor is prohibited from discussing any aspect of his/her fee arrangement hereunder with any club.

6. Expenses

A. Player shall reimburse Contract Advisor for all reasonable and necessary communication expenses (i.e., telephone and postage) actually incurred by Contract Advisor in connection with the negotiation of Player's NFL contract. Player also shall reimburse Contract Advisor for all reasonable and necessary travel expenses actually incurred by Contract Advisor during the term hereof in the negotiation of Player's NFL contract, but only if such expenses and approximate amounts thereof are approved in advance by Player. Player shall promptly pay all such expenses upon receipt of an itemized, written statement from Contract Advisor.

B. After each NFL season and prior to the first day of May following each season for which Contract Advisor has received fees and expenses, Contract Advisor must send to Player (with a copy of the NFLPA) an itemized statement covering the period beginning March 1 of the prior year through February 28 or 29 of that year. Such statement shall set forth both the fees charged to Player for, and any expenses incurred in connection with, the performance of the following services: (a) individual player salary negotiations, (b) management of player's assets, (c) financial, investment, legal, tax, and/or other advice, and (d) any other miscellaneous services.

7. Disclaimer of Liability
Player and Contract Advisor agree that they are not subject to the control or direction of any other person with respect to the timing, place, manner, or fashion in which individual negotiations are to be conducted pursuant to this Agreement (except to the extent that Contract Advisor shall comply with NFLPA Regulations) and that they will save and hold harmless the NFLPA,

its officers, employees, and representatives from any liability whatsoever with respect to their conduct or activities relating to or in connection with this Agreement or such individual negotiations.

8. Disputes

Any and all disputes between Player and Contract Advisor involving the meaning, interpretation, application, or enforcement of this Agreement or the obligations of the parties under this Agreement shall be resolved exclusively through the arbitration procedures set forth in Section 5 of the NFLPA Regulations Governing Contract Advisors.

9. Notices

All notices hereunder shall be effective if sent by certified mail, postage prepaid, to the following addresses.

If to the Contract Advisor:

If to the Player:

10. Entire Agreement

This Agreement, along with the NFLPA Regulations, sets forth the entire agreement between the parties hereto and cannot be amended, modified, or changed orally. Any written amendments or changes shall be effective only to the extent that they are consistent with the Standard Representation Agreement as approved by the NFLPA.

11. Filing

This contract is signed in quadruplicate. Contract Advisor agrees to deliver two (2) copies to the NFLPA within five (5) days of its execution; one (1) copy to the Player; and retain one (1) copy for his/her files. Contract Advisor further agrees to submit any other executed agreements between Player and Contract Advisor to NFLPA.

12. Term

The term of this Agreement shall begin on the date hereof and shall remain in effect until such time that it is terminated by either party in which case termination of this Agreement shall be effective five (5) days after written notice of termination is given to the other party. Notice shall be effective for purposes of this paragraph if sent by confirmed facsimile or overnight delivery to the appropriate address contained in this Agreement. Notwithstanding the above, if this Standard Representation Agreement is being signed by a prospective rookie player (a "rookie" shall be defined as a person who has never signed an NFL Player Contract) prior to the date which is thirty (30) days before the NFL Draft, then this Agreement shall not be terminable by Player until at least 30 days after it has been signed by Player.

If termination pursuant to the above provision occurs prior to the completion of negotiations for an NFL player contract(s) acceptable to Player and signed by Player, Contract Advisor shall be entitled to compensation for the reasonable value of the services performed in the attempted negotiation of such contract(s) provided such services and time spent thereon are adequately documented by Contract Advisor. If termination pursuant to the above provision occurs after Player has signed an NFL player contract negotiated by Contract Advisor, Contract Advisor shall be entitled to the fee prescribed in Paragraph 4 above for negotiation of such contract(s).

In the event that Player is able to renegotiate any contract(s) previously negotiated by Contract Advisor prior to expiration thereof, and such renegotiated contract(s) for a given year equals or exceeds the compensation in the original contract, the Contract Advisor who negotiated the original contract shall still be entitled to the fee he/she would have been paid pursuant to Paragraph 4 above as if such original contract(s) had not been renegotiated. If Contract Advisor represents Player in the renegotiation of the original contract(s), and such renegotiated contract(s) for a given year equals or exceeds the compensation in the original contract, the fee for such renegotiation shall be based solely upon the amount by which the new compensation in the renegotiated contract(s) exceeds the compensation in the original contract(s), whether or not Contract Advisor negotiated the original contract(s).

In the event that the Player renegotiates any contract(s) and the renegotiated compensation for a given year is less than the compensation in the original contract, the fee to the Contract Advisor who negotiated the original contract shall be his/her fee percentage applied to the new compensation, but only after the new compensation is reduced by the percentage which the compensation was reduced from the original contract. The fee to the Contract Advisor who negotiated the new contract shall be his/her fee percentage applied to the new compensation, but only after the new compensation is reduced by the compensation applicable to the original Contract Advisor's fee as calculated pursuant to the immediately preceding sentence.

If the Contract Advisor's Certification is suspended or revoked by the NFLPA or the Contract Advisor is otherwise prohibited by the NFLPA from performing the services he/she has agreed to perform herein, this Agreement shall automatically terminate, effective as of the date of such suspension or termination.

13. Governing Law

This Agreement shall be construed, interpreted, and enforced according to the laws of the State of _____.

Contract Advisor and Player recognize that certain state statutes regulating sports agents require specified language in the player/agent contract. The parties therefore agree to the following additional language as required by state statute:

EXAMINE THIS CONTRACT CAREFULLY BEFORE SIGNING IT

IN WITNESS WHEREOF, the parties hereto have hereunder signed their names hereinafter set forth.

(Contract Advisor)	(Player)
(Street Address)	(Street or P.O. Box)
(City, State, Zip Code)	(City, State, Zip Code)
(Telephone)	(In-Season Telephone)
(Fax Number)	(Off-Season Telephone)
(Player's Birthdate)	(College/University)

Print name and signature of PARENT or GUARDIAN (if player is under 21 Years of Age):

_____

(Street Address)

_____

(City, State, Zip Code)

_____

(Telephone)

References

Chapter 1

Bonesteel, Matt, "Former North Carolina Basketball Player Rashad McCants Recounts Academic Fraud at the School," *Washington Post*, June 6, 2014.

Champion, Walter T., *Sports Law: Cases, Documents and Materials*, Aspen Publishing, New York, 2005.

Farrey, Tom, "Judge Rules against NCAA," *ESPN.com: OTL*, August 9, 2014.

Farrey, Tom, "Players, Game Makers Settle for $40m," *ESPN.com: OTL*, May 30, 2014.

Ganim, Sara, "'Amateurism Is a Myth': Athletes File Class-Action against NCAA," *CNN Justice*, April 5, 2014.

Hawes, Kay, "Debate on Amateurism Has Evolved over Time," *NCAA News Archive—2000*, January 3, 2000.

Jones, Michael E., *Sports Law*, Prentice-Hall, Saddle River, NJ, 1999.

Masteralexis, Lisa Pike, Barr, Carol A., and Hums, Mary A., comps. and eds., *Principles and Practices of Sport Management*, Aspen Publications, Gaithersburg, MD, 1998.

Mitten, Matthew J., Davis, Timothy, Shropshire, Kenneth L., Osborne, Barbara, and Smith, Rodney K., *Sports Law: Governance and Regulation*, Wolters Kluwer, Frederick, MD, 2013.

Munson, Lester, "O'Bannon Ruling Could Haunt NCAA," *ESPN.com*, August 8, 2014.

"NCAA Health and Safety Policy: Drugs," *NCAA.org*, 2015.

"NCAA Hits UNC with 5 Violations in Wake of Academic Scandal," *Chicago Tribune*, June 4, 2015.

Nocerra, Joe, "This Is Reform? The N.C.A.A.'s Feeble Reform Impulse," *New York Times*, August 8, 2014.

Rittenberg, Adam, "College CEOs' Pushing NCAA Change," *ESPN.com: College Football*, June 6, 2014.

Smith, Rodney K., "A Brief History of the National Collegiate Athletic Association's Role in Regulating Intercollegiate Athletics," *Marquette Sports Law Review* 11, no. 9, 2000.

Strauss, Ben, "N.R.L.B. Rejects Northwestern Football Players' Union Bid," *New York Times*, August 17, 2015.

Strauss, Ben, and Eder, Steve, "N.C.A.A. Settles One Video Game Suit for $20 Million as a Second Begins," *New York Times*, June 9, 2014.

Tracy, Mark, and Strauss, Ben, "Court Strikes Down Payments to College Athletes," *New York Times*, September 30, 2015.

Yasser, Ray, McCurdy, James R., Goplerud, C. Peter, and Weston, Maureen A., *Sports Law: Cases and Materials*, 7th ed., Anderson, Cincinnati, OH, 2011.

Chapter 2

"Beyond Title IX: Gender Equity Issues for Schools," *Mid-Atlantic Equity Center*, 1993.

Edelman, Marc, "The Truth about Gender Equity in College Sports and the College Athletes' Rights Movement," *SPORTSMONEY*, April 8, 2014.

Epstein, Adam, *Sports Law*, South-Western, Mason, OH, 2013.

"Gender Equity in Athletics and Sports," *Feminist Majority Foundation*, 2014.

Horrow, Ellen J., "The Evolution of Women's College Sports," *USA Today*, September 26, 2001.

Jones, Michael E., *Sports Law*, Prentice-Hall, Saddle River, NJ, 1999.

Mitten, Matthew J., Davis, Timothy, Shropshire, Kenneth L., Osborne, Barbara, and Smith, Rodney K., *Sports Law: Governance and Regulation*, Wolters Kluwer, Frederick, MD, 2013.

Ryan, Molly M. "Title IX and the Drive for Gender Equity in Sports," *Litigation Minority Trial Lawyer*, January 15, 2013.

Sander, Libby, "U. of Colorado at Boulder Settles Lawsuit over Alleged Rapes at Football Recruiting Party for $2.8 Million," *Chronicle of Higher Education*, 2014.

Schaffer, Amanda, "Gender Games: The Olympics Has a New Way to Test Whether Athletes Are Men or Women. Is It Fair?" *Slate*, July 25, 2012.

Spengler, John O., Anderson, Paul M., Connaughton, Daniel P., Baker III, Thomas A., *Introduction to Sport Law*, Human Kinetics, Champaign, IL, 2009.

"Standard Language of Title IX," *Women's Sports Foundation*, March 8, 2013.

Thomas, Katie, "Long Fights for Sports Equity, Even with a Law," *New York Times*, July 28, 2011.

US Department of Education, Office for Civil Rights, *Sexual Harassment: It's Not Academic*, Washington, DC, 2008.

Yasser, Ray, McCurdy, James R., Goplerud, C. Peter, and Weston, Maureen A., *Sports Law: Cases and Materials*, 7th ed., Anderson, Cincinnati, OH, 2011.

Chapter 3

"About the USOC," *United States Olympic Committee*, 2014.

"Ancient Olympic Games," *History.com*, June 19, 2014.

"Broadcasting & Media Rights in Sport," *World Intellectual Property Organization*, 2014.

Epstein, Adam, *Sports Law*, South-Western, Mason, OH, 2013.

Greenfeld, Karl Taro, "ESPN: Everywhere Sports Profit Network," *Bloomberg Businessweek*, August 30, 2012.

"International Sports Issues," *USLegal*, 2014.

Jones, Michael E., *Sports Law*, Prentice-Hall, Saddle River, NJ, 1999.

Joseph, Kaitlyn, "The Governing Structure of International Olympic Committee (IOC)," *YahooSports*, April 12, 2010.

Kohli, Shan, "London 2012: IOC's New Rules for Transgender Athletes Are Sexist," *Sports Lawyer*, May 20, 2011.

"Match-Fixing Update: Global Efforts to Ensure World Cup Safety," *LawInSport*, June 15, 2014.

Mitten, Matthew J., Davis, Timothy, Shropshire, Kenneth L., Osborne, Barbara, and Smith, Rodney K., *Sports Law: Governance and Regulation*, Wolters Kluwer, Frederick, MD, 2013.

"Olympics and International Sports Law Research Guide," *Georgetown Law Library*, February 2014.

"Paralympics—History of the Movement," www.paralympic.org, June 3, 2015.

Pells, Eddie, "USOC Sets Up Agency to Investigate Sex Abuse," *Miami Herald*, June 10, 2014.

"Questions and Answers about the FIFA Case, One Day After," *New York Times*, May 28, 2015.

Reeb, Matthieu, "Court of Arbitration for Sport," *WHO'SWHOLEGAL*, March 2013.

Vranica, Suzanne, Mickle, Tripp, and Robinson, Joshua, "Scandal Pressures Soccer's Sponsors," *Wall Street Journal*, May 29, 2015.

Chapter 4

"Anti-Doping Rules," *International Olympic Committee*, 2012.
"Blood Doping: Lance Armstrong and the USPS Pro Cycling Team," *Drugs.com*, 2012.
"Drugs and Testing," *US Legal*, 2014.
"Drugs in Sport: WADA Doubles Doping Ban in New Code," *BBC*, November 15, 2013.
"Drug Testing Program," *NCAA.org*, 2013.
Epstein, Adam, *Sports Law*, South-Western, Mason, OH, 2013.
Halt, James, "Where Is the Privacy in WADA's 'Whereabouts' Rule?" *Marquette Sports Law Review* 20, no. 1, 2009.
Jones, Michael E., *Sports Law*, Prentice-Hall, Saddle River, NJ, 1999.
"Lance Armstrong Verdict Upheld," *ESPN.com*, October 22, 2012.
"The World Anti-Doping Code," *World Anti-Doping Agency*, 2014.
Mitten, Matthew J., Davis, Timothy, Shropshire, Kenneth L., Osborne, Barbara, and Smith, Rodney K., *Sports Law: Governance and Regulation*, Wolters Kluwer, Frederick, MD, 2013.
Yasalis, Charles E., and Bahrke, Michael S., "History of Doping in Sport," *International Sport Studies* 24, no. 1, 2002.
Yasser, Ray, McCurdy, James R., Goplerud, C. Peter, and Weston, Maureen A., *Sports Law: Cases and Materials*, 7th ed., Anderson, Cincinnati, OH, 2011.

Chapter 5

"Antitrust Labor Issues in Sports," *USLegal*, 2014.
Bartee, Howard, "The Role of Antitrust Laws in the Professional Sports Industry from a Financial Perspective," *Sports Journal*, 2008.
Champion, Walter T., *Sports Law: Cases, Documents and Materials*, Aspen Publishing, New York, 2005.
Edelman, Marc, "Single-Entity Status Must Pass Legal Test," *Sports Business Journal*, April 28, 2008.
Epstein, Adam, *Sports Law*, South-Western, Mason, OH, 2013.
Foster, George, Greyser, Stephen, and Walsh, Bill, *The Business of Sports*, Thomson, Mason, OH, 2006.
Jones, Michael E., *Sports Law*, Prentice-Hall, Saddle River, NJ, 1999.
Miller, Stephen, "Head of Baseball Union Transformed Pro Sports," *Wall Street Journal*, November 27, 2012.
Mitten, Matthew J., Davis, Timothy, Shropshire, Kenneth L., Osborne, Barbara, and Smith, Rodney K., *Sports Law: Governance and Regulation*, Wolters Kluwer, Frederick, MD, 2013.
Spengler, John O., Anderson, Paul M., Connaughton, Daniel P., Baker III, Thomas A., *Introduction to Sport Law*, Human Kinetics, Champaign, IL, 2009.
Surowiecki, James, "Scrimmage," *New Yorker*, March 21, 2011.
Washburn, Gary, "NBA Delivers Historic Ban to Donald Sterling," *Boston Globe*, April 29, 2014.
Yasser, Ray, McCurdy, James R., Goplerud, C. Peter, and Weston, Maureen A., *Sports Law: Cases and Materials*, 7th ed., Anderson, Cincinnati, OH, 2011.
Zimbalist, Andrew, and Noll, Roger G., "Sports, Jobs, & Taxes: Are New Stadiums Worth the Cost?" *Brookings*, Summer 1997.

Chapter 6

"Agent Regulations," *NFL Players Association*, 2012.

Belson, Ken, "With New Move, Jay-Z Enters a Sports Agent State of Mind," *New York Times*, April 2, 2013.

Belzer, Jason, "The World's Most Valuable Sports Agencies," *SPORTSMONEY*, June 24, 2013.

Epstein, Adam, *Sports Law*, South-Western, Mason, OH, 2013.

Fike, Gregory, "Memorandum: Persons Wishing to Apply for U.S. Soccer International Players' Agents Licenses," *U.S. Soccer*, June 2013.

Foster, George, Greyser, Stephen, and Walsh, Bill, *The Business of Sports*, Thomson, Mason, OH, 2006.

Heitner, Darren, "Duties of Sports Agents to Athletes and Statutory Regulation Thereof," *Dartmouth Law Journal* 7, no. 3, Fall 2009.

Jones, Michael E., *Sports Law*, Prentice-Hall, Saddle River, NJ, 1999.

Mitten, Matthew J., Davis, Timothy, Shropshire, Kenneth L., Osborne, Barbara, and Smith, Rodney K., *Sports Law: Governance and Regulation*, Wolters Kluwer, Frederick, MD, 2013.

"MLBPA Regulations Governing Player Agents," *MLBPlayers.com*, 2015.

O'Keefe, Michael, "Agent of Change," Daily News, September 12, 2009.

"Sports Agents—History and Law," *USLegal*, 2014.

Steinberg, Leigh, "How to Be a Great Sports Agent," *SPORTSMONEY*, August. 15, 2012.

Yasser, Ray, McCurdy, James R., Goplerud, C. Peter, Weston, Maureen A., *Sports Law: Cases and Materials*, 7th ed., Anderson, Cincinnati, OH, 2011.

Chapter 7

Chisu, Donald, Ochoa, Tyler, Ghosh, Shubha, and LaFrance, Mary, *Understanding Intellectual Property Law*, 2nd ed., LexisNexis, New Providence, NJ, 2011.

Cornish, W., Llewelyn, D., and Aplin, T., *Intellectual Property: Patents, Copyright, Trade Marks and Allied Rights*, 7 ed., Sweet & Maxwell, London, 2010.

Decker, Susan, "Nike LeBrons to NFL Helmets Protecting Edges in Patent Lawsuits," *Bloomberg Businessweek*, May 13, 2013.

Elder, Josh, "Jawbone Hits Fitbit with Second Lawsuit in Two Weeks," *Wall Street Journal*, June 19, 2015.

"Ex-Illinois Soccer Player Joins Those Alleging Poor Medical Treatment," *ESPN.com*, June 8, 2015.

Hanna, Joseph, "Washington Redskins Claim Trademark Cancellation Unconstitutional," *Sports and Entertainment Law Insider*, August 16, 2014.

Jacob, Robin, Alexander, Daniel, and Lane, Lindsay, *A Guidebook to Intellectual Property*, 5th ed., Sweet & Maxwell, London, 2004.

Jones, Michael, Toomey, Walter, Aiken, M. Nancy, and Bazin, Michelle, *Intellectual Property Law Fundamentals*, Carolina Academic Press, Durham, NC, 2014.

Liptak, Adam, and Steel, Emily, "Aereo Loses at Supreme Court, in Victory for TV Broadcasters," *New York Times*, June 25, 2014.

Masnick, Mike, "Is It Infringement to Get Your Favorite Sports Team Logo Tattooed on Your Body?" *techdirt*, April 14, 2011.

"Premier League Drops Copyright Infringement Case against YouTube," *Guardian*, November 11, 2013.

Rovell, Darren, "Jordan Ruling Could Set Precedent," *ESPN.com*, February 20, 2014.

Rovell, Darren, "Patent Office: Redskins 'Disparaging,'" *ESPN.com*, June 18, 2014.

"Sports and Branding," *World Intellectual Property Organization*, 2014.

"What Is Intellectual Property," *World Intellectual Property Organization*, 2014.

Wilmot, Alan, "We Must Protect This Trademark," *Sport Law*, February 9, 2014.

Chapter 8

"'Ambush Marketing' and the 2012 London Olympics," *worldsportslawreport*, February 13, 2012.

Ben-Atar, Assaf, "Sports and the Right of Publicity," *Intellectual Property, Media and Entertainment Law Journal*, April 2, 2009.

Ederer, Jason L., "Advantage, William Sisters," *Sports and Entertainment Law Insider*, August 30, 2013.

Epstein, Adam, *Entertainment Law*, Pearson, Upper Saddle River, NJ, 2006.

"Game Over in College Sports Rights Dispute," *Licensing Law Blog*, July 4, 2014.

Hanna, Joseph H., "Michael Jordan Wins in 7th Circuit Case over Supermarket Ad," *Sports and Entertainment Law Insider*, February 27, 2014.

Hudson, David, "Defamation and the First Amendment," *First Amendment Center*, September 13, 2002.

Jones, Michael E., *Sports Law*, Prentice-Hall, Saddle River, NJ, 1999.

Mitten, Matthew J., Davis, Timothy, Shropshire, Kenneth L., Osborne, Barbara, and Smith, Rodney K., *Sports Law: Governance and Regulation*, Wolters Kluwer, Frederick, MD, 2013.

"Privacy and Publicity Rights," *Library of Congress*, 2003.

Rovell, Darren, "Jordan Ruling Could Set Precedent," *ESPN.com*, February 20, 2014.

"US Supreme Court Rejects Pippen's Defamation Case vs. Media Outlets," *Foxsports.com*, June 16, 2014.

Chapter 9

"2014 Youth Safety Summit," *Youth Sports Safety Alliance*, www.youthsports safetyalliance.org.

Belson, Ken, "Judge Approves Deal in N.F.L. Concussion Suit," *New York Times*, April 22, 2015.

Chimienti, Matthew, and Casmere, Edward, "Heads-Up Play: AMA Adopts Concussion Policy for Youth Sports," *National Law Review*, June 13, 2015.

Foster, George, Greyser, Stephen, and Walsh, Bill, *The Business of Sports*, Thomson, Mason, OH, 2006.

Jones, Michael E., *Sports Law*, Prentice-Hall, Saddle River, NJ, 1999.

Mitten, Matthew J., Davis, Timothy, Shropshire, Kenneth L., Osborne, Barbara, and Smith, Rodney K., *Sports Law: Governance and Regulation*, Wolters Kluwer, Frederick, MD, 2013.

Moura, Pedro, "Stafon Johnson Files Suit against USC," *ESPN.com*, January 25, 2011.

"NCAA Settles Head-Injury Lawsuit," *ESPN.com*, July 29, 2014.

Popke, Michael, "High School Sports Injury Lawsuits Often Dismissed," *athleticbusiness.com*, June 2010.

Sanders, Casey, "Somebody May Beat Me, but They Are Going to Have to Bleed to Do It: Injury Liability in Sports," *The Legality*, April 23, 2009.

"Tort Law," *USLegal*, 2014.

Yasser, Ray, McCurdy, James R., Goplerud, C. Peter, and Weston, Maureen A., *Sports Law: Cases and Materials*, 7th ed., Anderson, Cincinnati, OH, 2011.

Chapter 10

Belson, Ken, "Ray Rice Cut by Ravens and Suspended by N.F.L.," *New York Times*, September 8, 2014.

Drape, Joe, and Williams, Jacqueline, "Scandal Erupts in Unregulated World of Fantasy Sports," *New York Times*, October 5, 2015.

Epstein, Adam, "Incorporating the Criminal Law in Sport Studies," *Sports Journal*, July 10, 2009.

Foster, George, Greyser, Stephen, and Walsh, Bill, *The Business of Sports*, Thomson, Mason, OH, 2006.

Gardiner, Simon, "Sports Participation and Criminal Law," *Sports and the Law Journal* 15, no. 1, 2007.

Hanna, Joseph M., "Moore & Bertuzzi Officially Reach an Agreement: NFL Violence Avoids Spotlight for Now," *LawinSport*, September 11, 2014.

Heitner, Darren, "Gambling Laws in the UK and US," *Sport in Law*, November 4, 2013.

Heitner, Darren, "The NBA vs. Donald (and Shelly) Sterling," *Sport in Law*, May 13, 2014.

Jones, Michael E., *Sports Law*, Prentice-Hall, Saddle River, NJ, 1999.

"Lack of Moral Reasoning = Bad Behavior by Jocks," *ESPN.com*, September 25, 2005.

Macramalia, Eric, "From Cross-Checking to a Crime: When Is Violence in Hockey Criminal," *Offside Sports Law*, June 30, 2010.

McCarthy, Michael, "Sports, Crime and Money: Athletes Gone Wrong," *Sports Business*, August 9, 2013.

Mitten, Matthew J., Davis, Timothy, Shropshire, Kenneth L., Osborne, Barbara, and Smith, Rodney K., *Sports Law: Governance and Regulation*, Wolters Kluwer, Frederick, MD, 2013.

"Sports Violence," *USLegal*, 2014.

Yasser, Ray, McCurdy, James R., Goplerud, C. Peter, Weston, Maureen A., *Sports Law: Cases and Materials*, 7th ed., Anderson, Cincinnati, OH, 2011.

Index

About the Author

Michael E. Jones has experienced an illustrious career in the world of amateur and professional sports. On the academic side, he developed and taught the first undergraduate sports law class ever offered. His original *Sports Law* text published in 1979 was the leading book in the field for more than twenty years. Professor Jones has lectured throughout the world on various sports law issues. He served as the inaugural chair of the International Division of the American Bar Association's Forum Committee on Sports and Entertainment Law. He and his esteemed colleague Professor William Weston of the University of Baltimore Law School established the first professional organization to assist sports agents in the process of negotiating contracts, the Association of Representatives of Professional Athletes (ARPA). In his capacity as a sports agent in the 1970s and 1980s, he helped draft the first collective-bargaining agreement for professional soccer in America. His more than twenty years' experience as a trial court judge made him a natural choice to assist a number of different national governing bodies resolve complex legal issues. He continues to preside as a hearing officer adjudicating non-drug-related legal disputes for the sport of triathlon. For three separate Olympic triathlon trials, he performed as the chief judge during the competitions. Jones excelled in his own athletic career, winning numerous national and world championships while competing at the highest level as a sponsored elite athlete. For the last four summer Olympic Games, including the Rio 2016 Olympics, he has crafted the official USOC poster for the sport of triathlon. Jones's sports-related paintings (an example is in chapter 4) can be found in leading sports museums throughout the world.